PRESIDENTS OF THE UNITED STATES

By the Authors

PRESIDENTS OF THE UNITED STATES

OUR FIRST LADIES

By Jane McConnell

FAMOUS BALLET DANCERS

CORNELIA:

THE STORY OF A CIVIL WAR NURSE

PRESIDENTS OF
THE UNITED STATES

*The story of their lives, closely inter-
woven with the vast political and
economic changes of the nation*

JANE AND BURT McCONNELL

Portraits by Constance Joan Naar

NEW YORK

THOMAS Y. CROWELL COMPANY

328

PREFACE

Much of the romance of American history lies in the lives of the men chosen by the people to become President of the United States. These men have come from every walk of life; every condition of society. Some, from earliest childhood, had to struggle against poverty to get an education; others, with little formal education at all, got their training in the school of experience. But they all had one thing in common: They rose from obscurity to the leadership of this nation, and their lives are closely interwoven with the vast political and economic changes that have marked the growth of our country since the first administration of George Washington.

Through the years, many Presidents of the United States have become almost legendary characters in the pageant of history. Sometimes we forget to regard them as human beings who made mistakes; suffered shortcomings, doubts, and perplexities; and faced sorrows, uncertainties, and even defeat. But it is important to remember these things. It is equally important not to magnify the mistakes of these men to such an extent that their achievements are overshadowed or forgotten.

We find in their accomplishments a true picture of their contributions to the establishment and growth of the United States. In the following chapters, it has been our aim to give the reader the facts; to present an intimate picture of the early years of the Presidents, as well as the part they later played in history. In their lives we find proof that almost any American boy can become President of the United States. Democracy favors no class or creed and chooses as its leaders those who, by their ability and integrity, can convince the majority of all the voters that they are capable of leadership.

Some of our Presidents have been greater statesmen than others. Some were born in an era that offered a serious challenge to their ability. But all have worked toward an ideal and have been aware of their responsibilities in taking this solemn oath:

> I do solemnly swear that I will faithfully execute the Office of President of the United States, and will to the best of my ability preserve, protect, and defend the Constitution of the United States.

In this book is the story of the lives of the men who took that oath and occupied that high office. Their records show clearly what they accomplished in building and guiding this nation.

In the years since the election of our first President, the United States has become great, powerful, and respected among the nations of the world; and we, with our leaders, share the responsibilities as well as the privileges of freedom and democracy. It is a precious heritage; and it was endowed and held secure for us by the effort, perseverance, and faith of all Americans, under the guidance of the statesmen they chose to lead them—the Presidents of the United States.

JANE AND BURT McCONNELL

CONTENTS

CONTENTS

CONTENTS

GEORGE WASHINGTON

First in the Hearts of His Countrymen

IN 1775 the destiny of the original thirteen colonies lay in the hands of one man: George Washington. Yet if young George, at the age of fourteen, had carried out his intention of joining the British Navy, his name might have been lost forever to American history. Once having pledged himself, he would have remained loyal to his Majesty's Navy, for loyalty was a part of his nature. Then there would have been no General Washington to lead the colonists through the Revolutionary War to victory; and he would not have become the first, and best-loved, President of the United States. Without him, indeed, there might have been no United States.

Going to sea was not just an idea with the boy. It was a dream very close to his heart. As he struggled with his lessons, his thoughts turned again and again to the sea and adventures in faraway places. Finally he told his elder half-brother, Lawrence, of his desire to join the Navy. Lawrence, who was always fond of George, secured for him a midshipman's warrant in the Royal Navy. Young Washington was filled with excitement. His kit was actually on board a ship, and he was about to follow, when a message arrived from his mother. She implored him to give up the idea of becoming a naval officer and to return home and finish his schooling. With a heavy heart, he turned back.

In her next letter to London, Mary Ball Washington ordered a fine, white-handled penknife for her disappointed, but obedient, son. He carried it all through his life. It is now in a museum in Alexandria, District of Columbia.

George Washington was born in a plain, substantial farmhouse on the west bank of the Potomac River, on February 22, 1732. Much of our country was then a wilderness.

John Washington, great-grandfather of the new-born baby, had emigrated to Westmoreland County, Virginia, seventy-five years before. In England, the Washingtons had been respectable landowners of Northamptonshire; they remained respectable landowners in Virginia. They knew something of wars, something of books, and something of the sea. And, most important in the new land, they knew farming, by which they made their living.

Augustine Washington, George's father, owned a large plantation. When George was three, the family moved into a new house farther up the Potomac. Fire destroyed this house four years later, and again the Washingtons moved into a new home, this time on the east bank of the Rappahannock, nearly opposite Fredericksburg. Here young George spent his active boyhood.

So far as we know, he did not throw any silver dollars across the river, and he did not chop down any cherry trees. But like most boys, he probably spent many happy hours wandering through the woods and along the riverbank. At the age of six he started off to a little school known as a "dame school." He wore buckles on his shoes, a three-cornered hat, a little plum-colored coat, and knee breeches. He was a poor speller, often getting his *i*'s and *e*'s in the wrong places.

Even when he became President, Washington was a poor speller. But he had one advantage over the children of today; he didn't have to *study* American history. He *made* it. He did, however, have to study Latin, and arithmetic, and deportment. Still, during his early years in the dame school,

3

and later, as he progressed to other instructors, George found time for play. He fished and hunted; he rode horses, and enjoyed many hours in the open.

In 1743, when George was eleven, he was saddened by the sudden death of his father. The boy felt an increase of responsibility, and began to wonder what he would do to earn his living. He applied himself more seriously to his studies, and was sent to a school where he became proficient enough in mathematics to set himself up as a surveyor.

His brother, Lawrence, as the eldest son of Augustine Washington's first marriage, inherited the estate. When Lawrence and Anne Fairfax were married, George was introduced into the family of one of the great landed proprietors of Virginia. Lord Thomas Fairfax, of the English branch of Anne's family, had come to Virginia to look over his huge land holdings. He noticed what a fine, tall, straight, hard-riding surveyor young George was and engaged him to survey those holdings. A life-long friendship began between the stern old Englishman and the lad. They had much in common. Both loved horses, fox hunting, and agriculture. And Lord Fairfax admired Washington's modesty, frankness, intelligence, and gracious manners. He saw, though the boy was only sixteen, that he was already a man in maturity of judgment and character.

George was then more than six feet tall, and he was strong and healthy. His hair was brown; his eyes a steady blue-gray; his nose quite large. He had a firm and friendly way about him, but he was shy with the girls, and they often teased him about that.

His father had left him little property. But he earned good wages as a surveyor. The surveys which he made stand unquestioned to this day, and the months he spent in this work must have been among the happiest of his life. At an age when most boys of today are in high school, young Washington started out to cut his way through the uncharted forest. The country west of the Blue Ridge Mountains was largely wilderness. Often the youthful surveyor slept in the open, with his feet toward the camp fire. Sometimes he was invited into an Indian wigwam, or spent the night with a settler beyond the frontier. This was his chance to earn a living, and he was eager to show his employer that he was worthy of the assignment.

Lord Fairfax must have been well pleased, for at his suggestion, the colony of Virginia employed George Washington as a public surveyor. He became a woodsman, a pathfinder, a good judge of wild country and wild natures.

Lawrence, his brother, who had built the house of his dreams, did not live long to enjoy it. At the age of thirty-four he died, and shortly afterward his young daughter passed away, leaving George heir to the estates. Thus, Washington became a wealthy landowner and lord of Mount Vernon when he was in his early twenties. No doubt he was tempted to settle down to a life of comfort and ease. Then, and all through his later life, he loved the beautiful house and the broad acres on the banks of the Potomac. But wider adventures called him. Two old soldiers had provided him with a military education, teaching him tactics, the manual of arms, and fencing. He had been appointed adjutant general of his district, with the rank of major. Now he was given a dangerous mission.

The royal governor of Virginia received word that the French had left Canada in force and were about to build forts on the Ohio. Washington was sent to inquire by what right they presumed to invade the dominions of the king of England, and to learn the number, strength, and position of the French garrisons. This involved a journey of some five hundred miles, through wild country, inhabited, in part, by unfriendly Indians; but the young major returned safely to Williamsburg with his report. The royal governor organized a force to drive out the French, and with four hundred men, Washington, promoted now to colonel, started back again through the wilderness. Thus began a war which was to last for seven years.

One of England's first offensive moves was to send General Braddock to Virginia with two regiments of regular troops. The General, unfamiliar with American territory and scoffing at the fighting abilities of the French and the Indians, marched straight into an ambush laid by the enemy. Washington had warned him and offered to have his own Virginia rangers act as scouts, an offer which was haughtily refused. Braddock paid for his conceit with his life; his men were mowed down by the hundreds. The remaining regulars fled, leaving Washington and the provincials to cover their retreat. In November, 1758, after a long and bitter struggle, the young colonel from Virginia marched with his advance guard into the French fort that had been Braddock's objective, and raised the English flag. This brought to a close the war for the Ohio country.

During Washington's absence he had been chosen a member of the Virginia House of Burgesses. Now he was hailed everywhere as a hero and placed in command of all of the colony's military forces, though he was only twenty-seven.

He now began to think about taking a wife, and on January 6 of the following year he was married to Martha Custis. Martha was the young widow of Daniel Parke Custis, with two little children. Washington, who never had any children of his own, came to love them dearly. In his account books are to be found such items as: "10 shillings worth of toys," "6 little books for children beginning to read," "a box of gingerbread toys and sugar images or comfits."

George Washington found much happiness in his married life, and Mount Vernon was always gay with the laughter and talk of friends and relatives. His nickname for his wife was "Patsy," and in private she called him her "old man." Whenever she asked him for some special favor, she would hold onto his coat buttons and look up at him and smile. Because of false teeth which fitted badly, Washington himself seldom smiled. When he did, he usually laughed with such heartiness that tears came to his eyes. Sometimes, in later years, he really cried when he saw his soldiers shot down on Revolutionary War battlefields.

For the sixteen years following his marriage, Washington lived at Mount Vernon, developing new crops, improving the breed of his livestock, attending the winter sessions of the Assembly, and leading a life typical of the wealthy Virginia planter. He had no ability as a public speaker and took little interest in politics. He would have liked nothing better than to spend his remaining years in the home he loved. But that was not to be; storm clouds were gathering across the Atlantic.

From his quiet acres in Virginia, Washington watched with a sad heart the rising resentment of the colonists against the high taxes and other restrictions that England was imposing upon them. Great Britain had always regarded her colonies as a source of raw materials and a market for finished goods. But when she tried to raise money by imposing a stamp tax, there was indignation everywhere. Settlers were also forbidden to cross the Appalachian Mountains, and in addition, the British Parliament permitted the East India Tea Company to carry its surplus tea to the colonies in its own ships, avoiding the English tax. Since it was required to pay only a small duty at American ports, it could undersell colonial merchants who had bought their own stocks in London and paid the regular tax. This discrimination resulted in a revolt by the colonists, who staged the historic Boston Tea Party and tossed the objectionable tea into the harbor.

Washington was a member of the Williamsburg convention which adopted some bold resolutions against taxation without representation; and he was among the deputies to the general Congress which met in Philadelphia in September, 1774. He and other patriots refused to buy British goods, and indignation was high among the colonists against the mother country.

The man from Mount Vernon had no illusions about the relative military strength of England and the colonies. England was the mistress of the seas, and the strongest military power on earth. The little handful of colonists had neither fleet, army, powder, trained soldiers, military resources, nor supplies. Though Washington was a patriot from the beginning, his heart was sore at the thought of breaking with the mother country; he wished devoutly that Great Britain and the colonies could get along peaceably together.

Less than a year later, something happened which left no doubt as to the trouble that lay ahead. Shots were fired in

Lexington and Concord! That was in April, 1775. In May, Washington journeyed to Philadelphia to attend the meeting of the Second Continental Congress. Six long years were to pass before he would see his beloved Mount Vernon again— years of war in which he would suffer hardship and criticism, despondency, and defeat. Only his faith in the cause and his wonderful zeal as commander-in-chief of the Continental Army gave his soldiers the strength and courage to continue the struggle. Through hunger, cold, and bloodshed they fought desperately, often for long months without pay. Washington himself received only his expenses throughout the Revolutionary War. In the end, liberty—and Washington —triumphed.

At that time there were less than four million people in this country. Their great problem was the consolidation of the newly formed states into a central government. In the spring of 1787 a Constitutional Convention was called in Philadelphia, to which twelve states sent delegates. General Washington was a delegate from Virginia, and presided over the convention. The present Constitution of the United States resulted from this convention. The delegates unanimously elected Washington the first President of the United States, to serve four years, beginning March 4, 1789.

Washington was reluctant to take on the responsibilities of the Chief Executive; many of the Indian tribes were on the verge of an outbreak. America and Great Britain still had important issues to settle. Our relations with European nations in general were critical. Pirates were ravaging our shipping. Our credit was practically nonexistent.

In his two terms of four years each, Washington, with the help of his Cabinet, overcame many of these difficulties. During his presidency he recommended to Congress measures which he believed were essential to our independence, honor, security, and prosperity. The first among these was the creation of a navy. He also advocated a department of agriculture, a military academy, and a national university. Though Washington lacked a college education, it does not seem to have been a handicap. He had no working model; the whole machinery of government had to be evolved. He had no experience in civil administration. Yet the machinery was created, and under his two administrations he saw a national government firmly established.

He saw the United States rise to a position of strength and respectability, controversies with foreign nations settled, war debts funded and national credit restored, our agriculture and commerce flourish, and the nation's capital doubled. He saw the Indian uprisings put down, the Bank of the United States established; and he himself marked the site of the federal government on the banks of the Potomac, in the city which is now Washington.

At the close of his second administration, in 1797, he retired to Mount Vernon. Three years later he died there, in his sixty-eighth year. In his will there was this clause: "Upon the death of my wife, it is my desire that all the slaves which I hold in my own right shall receive their freedom." Martha Washington, when the will was read, at once relinquished her rights and had the slaves released from bondage. Some, who were too young or too old to earn a living, were provided for in the will.

The life of George Washington was woven so closely into the fabric of America's beginning that he has become the center of a composite tapestry—of Paul Revere's Ride, of the

Minute Men and the Spirit of '76, of the Liberty Bell, the Declaration of Independence, and the Constitution. He had his enemies, as all public men have had before and since. Yet even the most critical acknowledge his achievements and recognize the quality of his greatness—his integrity, his faith in his country and in its future, and his ability to put the same faith into the hearts of his countrymen.

That faith and that spirit still live. They linger in the very air that surrounds to this day the home he loved so well. There at Mount Vernon, in the quiet shade among the trees he planted, is his simple red-brick tomb. In the big house nearby are his books, his swords, and, among other treasured mementoes, the key to the Bastille sent to him by his friend, Lafayette. Beyond the windows is the garden he laid out so carefully, with the neat box hedges, the winding paths, and the green terraces reaching toward the river.

It was December 14, 1799, when he died in that upper room where his bed still stands. The years between have brought new men, new customs to our land. Yet the ideal remains unchanged. For George Washington left part of his heart in the hearts of all freedom-loving people, part of the faith and determination that have built and preserved the United States of America.

JOHN ADAMS

The Massachusetts Patriot

WHEN George Washington, down in Virginia, was a wide-eyed little boy of three, John Adams, who was to become our second President, first saw the light of day at Braintree, Massachusetts. He was born on October 30, 1735.

One of our greatest historians, James Truslow Adams, has written of Washington: "Had it not been for his singleness of purpose and the strength and nobility of his character, the country would never have emerged successfully from the Revolutionary War." This might be said, too, of John Adams. For it was he who rose in Congress and urged that Washington be made commander-in-chief of the Continental forces. It was Adams who commissioned more than a hundred fighting ships during the war for freedom. He also recommended, twelve years before it was finally brought up in Congress, the republican form of government which we have today. It was John Adams who provided the foundation for the Constitution of the United States, and who, almost singlehanded, kept us out of war with France.

But let us go back now, and meet the small boy who was to take such a prominent part in America's beginnings. His father was a hard-working farmer. The Adams family were devoutly religious. They enjoyed few luxuries, but they loved their home and were happy and contented. As a youngster, John knew the fragrant smell of the pine woods, of new-mown hay, of freshly plowed earth in the spring, and the good salty breath of the sea. He learned how to split wood, milk the cows, curry the horses, shovel the deep drifting snows of the long New England winter, and hoe corn in the hot summer sun.

John's mother said he was just about the busiest boy she ever saw. When he wasn't doing farm chores, he was making and flying kites, swimming at Wollaston Beach, or whittling out little boats and rushing to the brook to launch them. He tramped over every inch of his father's acres, and hunted and trapped in the woods and on the tide flats. In winter there were coasting and skating. Each season brought its own excitements to the Braintree boy, and he enjoyed them all.

From a hill near the farm he could see the blue waters of Boston harbor and, when the day was bright and clear, the city itself. There were large numbers of Indians nearby and they were friendly. Often, they visited his father's house, and now and then young John would return their visits, his blue eyes filled with wonder as he sat in a wigwam, eating wild strawberries or venison.

He learned to read when he was six; and later, a chubby, tanned, barefoot boy, he trudged off to school down the dusty road about a mile from home.

At the age of sixteen, filled with awe and excitement, John Adams rode the ten miles to Cambridge, tied his horse to the hitching post, and entered Harvard College. In those days students were ranked according to their social position; on being graduated, John was fourteenth in his class of twenty-four. Graded according to scholarship, he stood among the first three. At the commencement exercises of 1755, a clergyman from Worcester was so impressed by the Braintree boy's Latin oration that he offered him the position of Latin master at a Worcester school.

So off went the young graduate on horseback to the one-room log-cabin school, with its big fireplace and rows of battered desks and benches.

There was great excitement in the colonies during this period. France and England were at war for the possession of the Ohio country. Braddock had landed with his regiments of British regulars. Young George Washington was becoming a military authority. And John Adams knew he must speedily decide about his own future. He was torn between his duty to his parents, who hoped he would be a clergyman, and his own desire to equip himself for an active part in a revolution against England. Then something happened which fired his mind with decision.

Court Week arrived in Worcester. The schools were closed for the occasion, and the whole town turned out to enjoy the festivities. Lawyers arrived by carriage and on horseback, bringing along their briefs and books. Refreshment booths were set up under the trees. A ring was roped off where village youths wrestled and boxed while the girls cheered from the sidelines. The music of fiddles filled the spring evening air, and couples danced gaily on the village green.

Court sat all day, and there, too, sat young John Adams, watching and listening to the proceedings. He knew definitely then that he wanted to be a lawyer. He knew, too, that he could expect no further help from his father, and a lawyer willing to teach him would charge a fee. There was also the question of board, room, and clothing for two years. The schoolmaster's spirits must have sunk very low at that time. "I have no books, no time, no friends," he wrote in his diary. "I must therefore be contented to live and die an ignorant fellow."

That gloomy prophecy faded when he met Colonel Rufus Putnam, a practicing lawyer of Worcester. Putnam owned fourteen or fifteen law books, which was considered quite a library in those days. Harvard College had only twenty! The attorney not only agreed to take John Adams into his office; he invited him to live at the Putnam home. John continued to teach his class of lively little boys, but in his spare time he pored over the law books. In the summer of 1758, having been sworn in as a member of the Boston bar, he put out his shingle at Braintree, and received clients in the neat front parlor of the farmhouse.

In pretty young Abigail Smith, daughter of the minister at nearby Weymouth, he found a most sympathetic listener to his plans for the future. And it was not long before John realized that he was deeply in love. He and Abigail were married one clear, cold day in October, 1764. Since Abby was related to some of the leading families of the province, she no doubt brought her husband additional clients. John Adams was well on the road to wealth when England passed the Stamp Act, and he was among the first to denounce the oppressive taxes.

He was then thirty years old. It was clear to him that the colonies could not expect adequate representation in a British Parliament three thousand miles across the sea. There could be no government without taxation—and taxation without representation was unjust. The colonies, he reasoned, must therefore be free to govern themselves.

He was asked to prepare a draft of instructions for Braintree's representatives in the Assembly. These instructions found their way into the Boston newspapers, and later were reprinted in many newspapers in the province. Forty other towns adopted the Braintree instructions. The young lawyer's influence was widening.

Abigail and John moved to Boston when their first-born son, John Quincy, was one year old. The city was a hotbed of unrest. Some two thousand British soldiers were quartered there, and frequent quarrels occurred between the hated Redcoats and the citizens. Early in the spring of 1770, a crowd of men and boys stoned a British sentry. Captain Preston with six British soldiers came to his aid. One of them was knocked down, and he fired a shot into the crowd. The others fired a volley at their tormentors, killing three and mortally wounding two more.

Captain Preston and his men were arrested on a charge of murder. Early the following morning, a friend of Preston's pleaded with John Adams to undertake the defense. No other lawyer in Boston, he said, would risk his personal safety and his good name by defending the British officer.

Adams had much to lose—and nothing to gain. He had plenty of clients. Yet his sense of justice was strong, even when it concerned an enemy. The British officer had only done his duty. John Adams took the case. Despite all the odds against him, his clear reasoning obtained a complete exoneration of Preston. Nor did the courage of his convictions cost John Adams the confidence of his fellow-citizens. Before the case came to trial, he was elected to the Massachusetts House of Representatives.

He served only one term, however. He and his Abigail were finding it impossible to make ends meet. He returned to his law practice.

Then came the Boston Tea Party. British tea was dumped into the harbor by angry patriots, and marked the beaches as far south as Nantasket. This daring maneuver delighted John Adams. "It is a bold and intrepid stroke," he wrote. And Abigail, in a letter to her friend, Mercy Warren, wrote (with charming disregard for spelling and punctuation): "The tea that bainful weed is arrived. Great and I hope effectual opposition has been made to the landing of it. The proceedings of our Citizens have been united spirited and firm. The flame is kindled and like lightning it catches from Soul to Soul. . . ."

John Adams realized that the British Parliament would take steps to retaliate. It did. In May, 1774, the port of Boston was blockaded by warships of the Royal Navy. No food or fuel could be brought into the city except by a narrow neck of land.

On June 17, the Assembly met behind locked doors—while the Secretary stood outside, armed with an order from the royal governor, dissolving the gathering! It appointed John Adams and four other patriots to attend a Continental Congress at Philadelphia. On September 5, Adams was among the delegates, handsome in powdered wigs, knee breeches, silk stockings, silver-buckled shoes, and three-cornered hats, who filed into Carpenters' Hall for the first meeting. The men gathered together on that historic occasion were not thinking about their clothes, however. They were met for a grave purpose; their whole way of life was being threatened by the mother country.

The battle of Lexington in 1775 brought matters to a climax. A few weeks later, in the Second Continental Congress at Philadelphia, John Adams delivered a speech eulogizing George Washington, and proposed that he be appointed commander-in-chief of all the Continental forces. Adams realized that if he could get Virginia excited over the troops gathered about Boston, the colonies would then be united in a war against England. Until then, it had been only a local conflict in New England. His strategy succeeded. North and South were now bound together through the personality and military reputation of the only man who could possibly have been accepted by all sections. Late in the summer Congress adjourned. John Adams returned to Philadelphia in the fall; and again in May, 1776—a short, plump, determined figure with puckered face, bald head, and twinkling eyes. And, as he had done ever since the beginning of the trouble, he demanded a quick, sharp, and definite break with England.

On June 7, 1776, Richard Henry Lee, of the Virginia delegation, offered his famous resolution "that these United colonies are, and of right ought to be, free and independent states." Adams quickly seconded the resolution. A committee, including Adams and Thomas Jefferson, was appointed to prepare a declaration based on the Lee resolution. Though the members probably regarded this document as important, certainly they never dreamed then that it would become immortal.

Virginia would be more likely to support the declaration if it were written by Thomas Jefferson, John Adams thought shrewdly. So he presented a convincing list of arguments, and Thomas Jefferson went to work. The Declaration which he prepared, embodying the fundamental principles of all human rights, was adopted on July 4, 1776.

The following year, Congress sent John Adams to France, to be ready to negotiate the treaty of peace which would soon be needed, it was hoped, to end the American Revolution. Meanwhile, the man from Braintree, who always disliked inaction, decided to visit Holland. He had the permission of the government to try to get a loan there, and he not only succeeded in persuading Holland to lend the colonies five million guilders, but also to recognize the United States of America as an independent nation!

After considerable maneuvering, following the surrender of Cornwallis and the end of the Revolutionary War, the English and American commissioners signed papers setting forth the conditions of a peace treaty to become final when England and France came to terms.

In February, 1785, John Adams was appointed minister to England. There he came face-to-face with the King who had for many years regarded him as a traitor. The mission in Great Britain was a trying and unhappy one. At the end of three years Adams resigned and returned to the United States.

Meanwhile, important events were taking place at home. It had become necessary to organize the federal government; to draw up a Constitution; and to elect the first President. Washington, of course, was the first choice for President, and Adams was elected Vice President. Under the system then prevailing, the electors did not vote for President and Vice President. The man who received the highest number of votes became President, and the man receiving the next highest was declared Vice President.

When Washington retired at the end of eight years, there was a hotly contested election in which John Adams, by a slender majority, was chosen President; and Thomas Jefferson, Vice President.

The new President was handicapped from the start. In the first place, he succeeded a man whom the people loved as a great general even before they made him their Chief Executive. Also, John Adams lacked Washington's charm and tact. Most disastrous of all, he made the mistake of retaining Washington's cabinet. Three of the members turned out to be disloyal. Adams was also continually at odds with Alexander Hamilton, Washington's chief financial adviser.

Dissension marked the first part of the Adams administration. The French monarchy had been overthrown and there was trouble with the new regime. Hostilities commenced upon the sea. Feeling ran high in the United States, but the President was determined to keep his new and struggling country out of war, if possible. He succeeded in averting war, but he failed to get re-elected. He was widely disliked and continually criticized. Yet, in almost every conflict in which he was engaged, it is now generally admitted that he was right.

As John Adams was the first independent American to stand before the throne of England, so he was the first President to live in Washington. Almost at the end of his term, on November 1, 1800, he and his family moved into the unfinished White House. Abigail Adams had a hard time to get wood enough to keep them warm in the big, drafty house, and her letters tell of how she hung her washing to dry in the East Room.

At the age of sixty-five, Adams retired from the world of affairs and settled down on his farm in Braintree. He lived to see his political principles established; and when he was an old man, he had the satisfaction and pride of seeing his first-born son, John Quincy Adams, made President of the United States.

John Adams was ninety when he died on July 4, 1826—exactly half a century after that memorable July 4, 1776, which marked the birth of the Declaration of Independence.

THOMAS JEFFERSON

Author of the Declaration of Independence

MUCH of the romance of American history lies in the fact that our Presidents were reared among the common people. They came from every section of the country and every walk of life. Probably they never once thought, as small boys, that they would some day occupy the highest office in the land. Yet they learned early that it is possible for any boy born in the United States to become President, no matter how humble his station. Many, like Abraham Lincoln, Andrew Jackson, and James Garfield knew extreme poverty during their childhood.

Thomas Jefferson, who became our third President, certainly never dreamed as a young lad that he would ever become our Chief Executive. For at that time there was no United States, and the American colonists were subjects of Great Britain. Thomas was the first-born son of Peter Jefferson. He was born in April, 1743, at Shadwell, the family homestead, not far from the present city of Charlottesville, Virginia.

His ancestors are said to have come from Wales. They were among the earliest settlers. Peter Jefferson himself was a giant of a man and a lusty pioneer. He loved outdoor life, was a fine rider and huntsman, and was chosen early by his neighbors as county surveyor and county sheriff. He treated his slaves well and trained them to work in the shops on his large plantation. He must have possessed great personal charm, for when he was thirty-two, Jane Randolph, whose family ranked among the first in the colony, became his bride.

The Virginia into which their son, Thomas, was born was the largest and most important of the American colonies. In those early days it included what are now West Virginia, Kentucky, Ohio, Illinois, Indiana, Michigan, and Wisconsin. Much of this vast territory was wilderness, inhabited by Indians and a scattering of hardy pioneers.

In the foothills of the Blue Ridge Mountains where the house at Shadwell stood, young Tom Jefferson found plenty to occupy his early years. There were no near neighbors, but there were fields to explore, hills to climb, and forest paths to follow. Often he sat on the bank of a silvery stream, with a fishing rod in his hand, watching the birds and listening to their song. His father's land covered more than a thousand acres, and the carrot-haired boy with the hazel-blue eyes and lean freckled face came to know every inch of that land, and to hold it dear.

Tom's father was determined that his son should have a good education. The boy was put in an English school at the age of five; four years later he was studying Latin, French, Greek and mathematics. He was only fourteen when his father died, leaving him the responsible head of the family of eight children and the Shadwell farm. He continued with his studies, spending two years at the private school of the Reverend Dr. James Maury.

At seventeen, young Jefferson left the plantation to enter William and Mary College at Williamsburg, capital of the Virginia colony. He was anything but handsome at this time. He was six feet two inches tall, thin, loose-jointed, and awkward. His hair was a sandy red, his freckles were still prominent, and his features were angular. Yet the girls liked to dance with the keen-eyed youth from Albemarle County. He did his share of flirting, strolling through the lanes, and riding his horse about the countryside, often escorting the

25

pretty daughters of the planters who attended the winter sessions of the legislature. The gay social life of the capital was centered in the palace of the royal governor. Here young Jefferson danced the quadrille, the minuet, and the Virginia reel, and was often a dinner guest. The backwoods boy was growing up, not only in the social graces, but as a student and a thinker.

It was about this time that he met and became a close friend of Patrick Henry, then unknown to fame. It was natural that they should be attracted to each other. Both were extremely fond of music and played the fiddle. Both were ardent patriots and had long discussions concerning the rights of citizens. They were living in an era of brilliant minds and strong convictions.

While at college Jefferson also met two other men who influenced the shaping of his character and career. Dr. Small, a thinker and philosopher, was deeply interested in the eager young student, and introduced him to George Wythe (pronounced *With*), a distinguished lawyer. As soon as Jefferson finished college, he entered Wythe's law office, and studied there for five years. Wythe was a member of the House of Burgesses, and during its sessions his young protégé saw the political institutions of the Virginia colony in actual operation. It was in the Capitol, too, that he first saw George Washington, a tall, quiet, soldierly figure, impressive in his uniform. Later, at old St. John's Church, near Richmond, Jefferson was among the brilliant gathering addressed by Patrick Henry, a member of the House of Burgesses, when he spoke those inspired words:

"Is life so dear or peace so sweet as to be purchased at the price of chains and slavery? *No! We must fight!* I know not what course others may take, but as for me, *give me liberty or give me death!"*

Young Jefferson listened, entranced, to his friend's outburst. But much was to happen in the life of Thomas Jefferson before the exciting period when Patrick Henry made his ringing speech.

Sponsored by Wythe, Jefferson set up his own office in Williamsburg and soon was earning a good income at the bar. He felt that he could afford to marry. But one day Shadwell, which held so many happy memories, burned to the ground. Jefferson's papers and his large collection of books went up in flames. He could never replace the papers, and it took him some time to get more books; but he began planning at once a new home, high on a hilltop overlooking the spot where his birthplace had stood. He not only designed the new house and laid out the grounds, but had his workmen make the bricks and cut the timber used in building it. Monticello, however, was constructed a little at a time. The first building, for his immediate use, contained parlor, kitchen, hall, bedroom, and study, all in one. In later years Monticello was to become the most beautiful home in all Virginia.

At this period in colonial history, a man of Jefferson's station in life was expected to share the burden of government. In 1768, the freeholders of Albemarle County elected him as one of their two Burgesses; and in May of the following year he took his seat for the first time as a member of a legislative body. Also, he became justice of the peace, a member of the county court, and, at the age of twenty-seven, colonel in charge of the county militia.

There was an attractive young widow living between Williamsburg and Monticello who was literally besieged by suitors. Gradually they faded from the scene as Jefferson's visits became more frequent. This was his first real romance, and his marriage to Martha Wayles Skelton on New Year's Day, 1772, ushered in the happiest period of his life.

In the years directly following, the colonists became more and more angered by British proposals to impose a stamp tax, using the revenue to maintain British troops on American soil. Another proposed law decreed that Americans charged with political offenses must be sent three thousand miles to England for trial. Resolutions were passed in the Virginia legislature denouncing these unfair practices. Washington, Patrick Henry, Jefferson, and others pledged themselves to buy no more British goods. Jefferson wrote a powerful indictment against the mother country, called "A Summary View of the Rights of British America," which was published in Philadelphia and later in London. His eloquence delighted the patriots; suddenly he became a well-known colonial figure.

Though only thirty-three years of age, he had great vision. He saw clearly the opportunity to create a new American system which would better protect the rights and liberties of the people. In the spring of 1775 he was sent as a delegate to the Richmond Convention. Two months later he was on his way to Philadelphia and the Second Continental Congress.

In the meantime, British troops had gone into action against the colonists at Lexington and Concord, and soon after he reached Philadelphia, Jefferson was called upon to draft the great document which has remained his outstanding achievement. Jefferson labored mightily over his task in those seventeen days between June 11 and June 28. He weighed each phrase carefully, earnestly, to give the Declaration the proper tone and spirit. Finally his work was done. After a few minor changes were made, Congress adopted the Declaration of Independence on July 4, 1776.

Strictly speaking, what actually happened was this: The great decision for secession and independence was made on July 2, when Lee's Resolution of Independence was adopted. Two days later, *twelve states* agreed to the written Declaration; New York did not vote. Acceptance became unanimous on July 15 when the resolutions of the New York convention were laid before Congress. Meanwhile, the presiding officer and the secretary had authenticated the document, which was then printed and sent to the various provincial assemblies. Not until July 19 did Congress order that the Declaration be engrossed on parchment and signed by the members.

Jefferson then returned to the Virginia legislature, where he outlined several changes in state laws. Among his proposals was one prohibiting further importation of slaves. He also advocated complete freedom of religion and a system of general education. All these suggestions were adopted. Long years afterward, the public-school system of our nation would be built on the Jefferson pattern.

On June 1, 1779, when Virginia elected him governor, Jefferson's first task was to find men, arms, rations, and money for Washington's army. Often he put Washington's needs ahead of those of his own state. He remained in the governor's chair for two one-year terms. Soon after that, when Lord Cornwallis surrendered his sword to General Washington, Jefferson was called upon to write and report the ratification of the peace treaty.

But the man from Monticello, elated as he was over victory,

was worried and sick at heart. His wife was seriously ill. For four months he stayed close beside her, doing his writing in a small alcove off her bedroom, and refusing to consider all requests to return to public life. To his great and lasting sorrow, she died in September, 1782.

The following year the lonely man returned to public life as a member of Congress. One of his first accomplishments was the working out of a new coinage system, based on the Spanish dollar as a unit and the penny as the smallest coin. That system, adopted more than a century and a half ago, is the one in use today.

Jefferson had written the instructions for diplomatic agents who were sent to Europe. Now he was sent to France to lay the framework of the future commercial policy of the United States; later he was to succeed the aging Benjamin Franklin as minister. While abroad, in letters to Madison and Monroe, Jefferson strongly urged the inclusion of a Bill of Rights in the draft of the new Constitution. He also declared that without a government strong enough to impose federal taxes, all that had been achieved by the Revolution would be lost.

When he returned to America in 1789, Jefferson was induced to become Secretary of State in Washington's Cabinet. Four years later he went back to Monticello and began building up, mostly by correspondence, what was then known as the Republican party. It was a party of protest, in which farmers and landowners were arrayed against the banking and manufacturing class—the Federalists. When Jefferson returned to public life in 1797, as Vice President under John Adams, he was the head of an established party. It was during this period that he prepared a manual for the Senate which has since been the guide of Congress for the transaction of business.

In the presidential election of 1800, Jefferson and Aaron Burr received the same number of electoral votes. The election therefore had to be decided by the House of Representatives. On the thirty-sixth ballot, Jefferson received a majority and became President. Four years later, he was re-elected almost without opposition.

During those eight eventful years in the White House, President Jefferson's outstanding achievement was the purchase of all the land lying between the Mexican border and Canada and between the Mississippi River and the Rocky Mountains. This huge territory, then called Louisiana, belonged to France. Napoleon feared it would be captured by the British, and Jefferson bought it for fifteen million dollars.

But the brilliant statesman who was so talented in handling the affairs of our country, never saved a great deal of money for himself. When he retired from the presidency at the age of sixty-six, he was twenty thousand dollars in debt.

In his sunset years, still following his dream of education for his countrymen, Jefferson founded the University of Virginia, and persuaded the state legislature to support it. He was the architect of the magnificent buildings, laid out the grounds, and acted as rector until his death at the age of eighty-three.

Thomas Jefferson died at Monticello on the Fourth of July, 1826. On that same day, John Adams, in Braintree, passed away. Thus America lost, on the fiftieth anniversary of the Declaration of Independence, the great statesman who wrote it and the New England patriot who was its most ardent champion.

JAMES MADISON

Father of the Constitution

JAMES MADISON, who became our fourth President, had a genius for politics. He richly deserves the title of "Father of the Constitution," although in a letter written in 1834, he said: "You give me a credit to which I have no claim, in calling me 'The writer of the Constitution of the United States.' This was not . . . . the offspring of a single brain. It ought to be regarded as the work of many heads and many hands."

"Jimmy," as he was called all through his boyhood, was born on March 16, 1751, at the Port Conway, Virginia, home of his grandparents. Soon afterward his mother took her infant son home to the plantation, Montpelier, in Orange County. Young Madison was a frail child. He was often ill, and grew up shy, studious, and not at all fond of outdoor sports. He was first sent to school, then later tutored at home by the parish clergyman, and prepared to enter what is now Princeton University.

Madison was an eager student, with marked ability in debate. His long hours of study nearly wrecked his health, and he was a very discouraged young man indeed when, upon graduating from Princeton, he was called upon to take over the schooling of his young brothers and sisters at home. Surely, he thought, after his learning, life should hold something better for him than that.

In his spare time, he studied law under Thomas Jefferson, whose home was only about twenty-five miles from Montpelier, and a friendship grew up between the frail, shy youth and his brilliant neighbor which lasted until Jefferson's death.

Madison was physically unfit for military duty when the

Revolutionary War came. Besides, he seemed to lack the qualities which make a good soldier. He was quiet and precise, his personality was anything but forceful; it was hard for him to make decisions. Yet his placid nature was a good balance for the impulsiveness and vigor of Jefferson. Madison never swerved in his loyalty to the older man, and as President he carried out the policies his predecessor had established.

In 1774, when he was twenty-three years old, James Madison was appointed a member of the Orange County Committee of Safety; in 1776 he was sent to the convention which was substituted for the usual legislature. There he received his first training as a statesman and began the study of all forms of government, ancient and modern. He invented a kind of shorthand of his own, making many notes and spending long hours at night in his room laboriously transcribing them.

Even though he was young and diffident, the members of the Virginia convention recognized his ability and asked him to help draft a constitution for the Colony. The following year he was placed on the Executive Council.

The year 1780 was the darkest of the Revolutionary War. In that year Madison was a delegate to the Congress of the confederation, and had a chance to meet and talk with the most illustrious men in our land. He labored diligently, trying to bring about a settlement of the confederation's financial affairs, but his attempt to raise money by laying an import duty of five per cent failed. In November, 1783, his term of service having expired, he returned to Virginia and was elected a member of the state legislature. He did not, however, forget about the failure of his import-duty bill. He persuaded his friend, Tyler, of the Virginia legislature, to offer a resolution for an inquiry into the commerce of the country. That resolution was adopted and sent to Congress, where it was favorably considered. Madison's import-duty bill did not at that time succeed. But the resolution served to bring up again before Congress the matter of finances, and this fact is important. For the need to raise money and straighten out the chaotic affairs of the new and struggling nation was one of the main reasons for drawing up a Constitution.

In 1786, Madison was again eligible for Congress, and early in the following year he took his seat.

Meanwhile, a convention, proposed by Madison, met at Annapolis in September, 1786. Delegates came from only four other states. The time of these statesmen, however, was well spent. They urgently recommended that all the states be invited to send delegates to a second convention for the purpose of setting up a Constitution. This convention, with George Washington in the chair, met at Philadelphia in that eventful May of 1787 and went about the grave business of revising the federal government and forming a permanent Constitution of the United States.

Madison was largely responsible for the Virginia Plan, on which the Constitution, as finally adopted, was based. He earned his title of "Father of the Constitution" not only by taking the lead in framing the immortal document, but by urging all states, including his own, to adopt it. In Virginia he had to overcome the dazzling eloquence of none other than Patrick Henry, who raised many objections. Henry, like Jefferson (who was then in France, as American minister) feared that the Constitution might deprive the people of their newly won freedom. To meet those objections, which were shared by several of the colonies, Madison proposed

twelve amendments to safeguard the rights of citizens. Ten
of these amendments were ratified by the states. The national charter of government also provided checks and bal-
ances to guard against tyranny and the making of hasty or
ill-considered laws.

In guiding the Constitution to victory, Madison won the
greatest battle of his life. The amendments that were adopted
have stood since 1791 as the major portion of the Bill of
Rights of the American people.

From 1789, when the Constitution became effective, until
1797, Madison was a member of the House of Representatives. There were many stormy sessions. Madison bitterly opposed the financial policies of Alexander Hamilton, Washington's Secretary of the Treasury. Hamilton represented a
strong central government administered in the interests of
the capitalist class, and Madison fought against having his
own Southern section of the country sacrificed to the Northern businessman.

There was also considerable controversy about the site for
the government. The House favored Pennsylvania and specified it in a bill which they passed along to the Senate. The
Senate amended the bill, specifying the banks of the Delaware
River—and the House agreed. This did not suit Madison.
He had labored earnestly for a site on the Potomac. In order
to gain time he had the bill returned to the Senate on the day
before Congress adjourned. By the time the next session
opened, Madison had lined up enough votes for the Potomac
site!

While he was a member of Congress he fell in love with
the pretty, young Quakeress, Dolly Payne Todd. At the time
of their marriage, Madison was forty-three and Dolly was

twenty-six, a widow with a young son. Dolly (spelled "Dolley" on her tombstone and in the Payne family Bible) became almost as famous in history as James Madison himself. Her beauty, charm, and high spirits won her instant popularity with everybody she met, and there is no doubt that she added also to her middle-aged husband's popularity as a statesman.

Three years after the marriage of Dolly and James in 1794, they retired to private life at Montpelier. Their retirement, however, did not last long. About this time the country was seething over the Alien and Sedition Laws, which President John Adams considered necessary to the safety and welfare of the nation. Adams favored the laws as a means of removing from the United States dangerous and suspicious aliens and punishing libels against high government officials, including himself. Jefferson, though he was Vice President in the Adams administration, bitterly opposed the measures; and Madison probably was urged by him to prepare a resolution, which Congress adopted, denouncing the laws as being contrary to the Constitution.

Madison had drifted gradually over to the Democratic party of Jefferson. This party believed in reserving to the states all rights except those which must be surrendered to the federal government. The other party (the Federalist) was in favor of a strong central government which could undertake public improvements and make a closely united nation, while still giving the state governments full authority in all local matters.

When Jefferson was elected President in 1801, and the Democrats came into power, Madison became his closest confidential adviser. As Secretary of State for Jefferson's two terms, he discharged the duties of this responsible office with great ability. He also became familiar with foreign problems which had existed as far back as the Washington and Adams administrations. Most of these concerned England and France. Year by year these problems grew more involved; more perplexing. The smaller nations had little choice between England and France as allies, or encountering them as foes.

When Madison took his seat as President on March 4, 1809, he was determined to keep clear of entanglement with foreign politics; to maintain neutrality, keep relations friendly, and leave England and France to fight their own battles. This was a difficult task indeed. England had not removed her forts and armed forces from the Ohio country as she had agreed by treaty to do. She was disturbed by the rapid growth of our foreign trade and jealous of us as a commercial rival. We were also loading goods of the French colonies on American vessels, bringing them to the United States, and shipping them to France as American property.

England, at war with France, seized American ships, not only on the high seas but within the coastal waters of the United States, and removed American seamen from the vessels, charging them with being British deserters. Enterprising Yankees loaded their ships with English goods in English ports, and landed them in France under the pretext that the ships came directly from the United States or some other neutral country. France, in turn, authorized the seizure and confiscation of *all* American vessels! This decree is said to have cost American merchants and shipowners some forty million dollars.

For years, Madison had opposed a war with England. He

believed the ends he sought could be gained at less cost by peaceful measures. But on June 18, 1812, he approved an Act of Congress declaring war against Great Britain. Madison thereupon was re-elected for a second term.

The War of 1812 came very near to being disastrous for America. The following year a British fleet entered Chesapeake Bay, and a large landing party marched upon Washington and burned the Presidential Mansion, the Capitol, and all the public buildings. The British are said to have consumed the food and wine that had been set on the table for President Madison and a party of friends. Following close upon Jackson's victory at New Orleans, however, came news of a treaty of peace. The battle of New Orleans was fought, actually, *after* the treaty was signed, six weeks being required in those days to bring news from across the Atlantic. This was somewhat embarrassing to all concerned; but the joy was so great over peace that even the Federalists and Democrats forgot, for a time, their differences and their hates.

On the fourth of March, 1817, Madison's second term of office expired, and he retired with his Dolly to Montpelier.

In addition to his work on the Constitution, Madison was the author of the first protective tariff measure in the United States; of the law creating the State, Treasury, and War Departments; and of the first ten amendments to the Constitution. Navigation laws were revised during his two terms, and an act was passed authorizing the territories to be represented in Congress by a single delegate each. During his presidency, Indiana and Louisiana were admitted to the Union. Upon the subject of slavery he wrote and thought much. From the time he was a young lad he hated slavery.

It was one subject which stirred him out of his usual placid good temper.

For many years he opposed the idea of the federal government assuming state debts; but he never tired of urging the government to discharge our indebtedness to France.

He supported Jefferson in founding the University of Virginia and, at the older man's death, took his place as rector.

James Madison, who was frail, thin, and under average height, and who had many illnesses during his lifetime, lived, strangely enough, to the ripe old age of eighty-five. He died on June 28, 1836, after enjoying many peaceful years at his Montpelier home.

JAMES MONROE

Sponsor of the Monroe Doctrine

ALTHOUGH the Monroe family made no claim to special distinction in colonial days, James Monroe was included among that favored group known as the Tidewater aristocracy. Of our first five Presidents, he was the fourth to be born in Virginia. His earliest colonial ancestor, Major Andrew Monroe, is said to have landed on the western bank of the Potomac River in 1660. James himself was born on his father's plantation in Westmoreland County, April 28, 1758.

Like Madison and Jefferson, the young Virginian received a good education. When he was sixteen he entered the College of William and Mary. That was in 1774, and the feeling against Great Britain was rising higher and higher among the colonists. Two years later, when the inspiring words of the Declaration of Independence rang out across the land, James Monroe and many of his classmates and teachers put away their books to join the fight for freedom in the Revolutionary War. James was a husky, broad-shouldered lad. He knew how to handle a rifle, a pistol, and a sword, and was eager to get into action. He saddled his horse, stuffed a few changes of clothing into his saddlebags, and started off for New York to offer his services to General Washington. That was the beginning of more than forty-eight years in public service, in one capacity or another.

The colonies were not prepared for war. Our feeble militia, with very little training and not much equipment, were fighting a delaying action. Some of them, it must be admitted, were deserting. They had their farms and their homes to look after, and it seemed to some of them that it was hopeless to fight against the powerful mother country. The Tories, who favored the cause of England, became more arrogant and defiant every day. British troops were sweeping all before them.

The fighting blood of James Monroe was thoroughly aroused. He entered the ranks of Washington's volunteers, and was active in the disastrous battles of Harlem Heights and White Plains. He must have been a very brave soldier, for Washington soon made him a lieutenant. At the battle of Trenton, the young officer received a bullet wound in the shoulder. Distinguished service brought him another promotion—to captain. Later, as a general's aide, he took part in the battles of Brandywine, Germantown, and Monmouth, and with the army spent a freezing, starving winter at Valley Forge.

Washington was proud of this modest and courageous young man. He figured that, with a regiment of his own, Monroe would give a good account of himself. The General sent him back to Virginia to recruit men for such a regiment. Only a handful of soldiers responded. Having failed because of the exhausted condition of the colony, and having sacrificed his rank in the process, Monroe decided to withdraw from the army and study law.

James Monroe was only twenty-two. Jefferson, who was then serving his second term as governor of Virginia, had a fine collection of law books and he liked to start ambitious young men on the road to success. He mapped out a course of study, and this was to become a stepping stone in Monroe's career.

In 1782, when Monroe was twenty-four, he was elected to the Assembly and was made a member of the Governor's

Council. A year later he was chosen a member of the Congress of the United States. These were high honors for a young man of twenty-five. Often he sat with the grave and brilliant statesmen, deliberating on ways of getting money into the empty Treasury, how to deal with the rising national debt, how to satisfy pressing creditors, and what recommendations to make to the various state legislatures. Congress realized, too, that some states would adopt the recommendations, others would accept them only conditionally, and still others would postpone action or flatly refuse the suggestions offered.

James Monroe discovered, during his three-year term in Congress, that the compact for the preservation and welfare of the Union was not working as smoothly as it should. He might have felt that his time spent in New York was wasted, had he not met there a beautiful and accomplished girl with whom he fell in love. He and Elizabeth Kortwright were married and went to Virginia at the end of Monroe's term. There he persuaded his old friend, Thomas Jefferson, to draw the plans for their new home.

For four years after that, Monroe practiced law, with an office at Fredericksburg. In December, 1789, Senator Grayson having died, he was sent to the United States Senate to fill the vacancy and served there during Washington's first administration. The Senator was not outstandingly brilliant like Jefferson; and he lacked the intellectual powers which Madison possessed. But he developed into a dependable and industrious public servant, for he had firmness, integrity, great patriotism, and was untiring in his zeal to serve our country. The good-looking young man, with the large mouth, honest blue eyes, fair hair, and erect figure, was a supporter of Jefferson, and was thus opposed to the new Constitution and to the Bank of the United States.

Since Monroe was in sympathy with France, Washington decided to send him as minister to the new republic. England and Spain were presenting a united front against France, while Washington had issued a proclamation of neutrality. The French people welcomed the young American warmly, but he showed so openly where his sympathies lay that England complained to the United States, and he was recalled.

Monroe's recall did not weaken the confidence of his fellow-Virginians, however, and he was elected to the state legislature, and soon afterward to the office of governor. He served for the three years allowable under the state constitution.

Jefferson had now succeeded John Adams as President; and the sprawling territory of Louisiana had been transferred by Spain to France, and Napoleon was planning to set up a military colony in the territory. This, to the United States, presented staggering possibilities. In the crisis, Jefferson at once thought of his former pupil, James Monroe. He would send Monroe to France and Spain to negotiate, with the help of our ministers, for the purchase of the island of New Orleans and the Spanish territory east of the Mississippi River.

Fortunately for the United States, Napoleon needed money in that January of 1803. Also he feared the powerful English navy might rob him of the lands beyond the Mississippi. It would be better to sell them at a low price than to lose them altogether. Minister Livingston and Monroe were amazed when Napoleon offered to sell the entire Louisiana tract for fifteen million dollars. The instructions did not permit any such large-scale negotiations. It would take many weeks to send a message to President Jefferson and to get a reply across the ocean on a sailing vessel. By that time Napoleon might have changed his mind, and the great opportunity would be lost. They decided to accept the French offer at once on their own responsibility, and thus obtain for the United States an area almost equal to that of the entire country as it then existed. The negotiations were concluded in two weeks and later ratified in Washington. The United States now stretched from the Atlantic Ocean to the Rocky Mountains!

Monroe then went to Madrid to try to buy the remnant of Spain's title to Florida, but without immediate success. He proceeded to England, where he relieved the American minister, negotiated a treaty with the British that was unacceptable to Jefferson, and returned home. Again he served in the Virginia legislature, and again became governor. In 1811 he resigned to become Madison's Secretary of State. It was a time of crisis, with England seizing our merchant ships bound for Spain or France.

The War of 1812 followed. England sent ten thousand picked soldiers to take the port of New Orleans, and they probably would have succeeded had not Monroe, who was then also Secretary of War, sent General Andrew Jackson to defend the city. At that time our Treasury was almost empty, and our national credit at a low ebb. Monroe could not raise the funds to carry out his bold plans. Without hesitation, he pledged his own individual credit, as subsidiary to that of the nation—and the battle of New Orleans became history. It was also largely due to Monroe's quick and decisive action that Baltimore was saved from the enemy, and The Star-Spangled Banner continued to wave over Fort

McHenry. The story of that historic engagement was immortalized by Francis Scott Key in our national anthem.

James Monroe was elected to succeed Madison as President in 1816; and in 1820 was re-elected with practically no opposition. During his two terms he secured Florida from Spain, took a strong stand for protective tariffs, and proclaimed to the world in plain language that "an attempt by any nation of Europe to reduce an independent nation of North or South America to the condition of a colony" would never be tolerated by the United States. This proclamation became known as the Monroe Doctrine. Monroe also arranged to set aside each year money for reducing the national debt; he began a system of roads, canals, and other improvements; started the building of coast and frontier fortifications; re-established the Bank of the United States; held out the hand of friendship to the Indians; and encouraged settlement of the West by selling the public lands to settlers at a fair price.

During Monroe's two administrations, Maine, Mississippi, Missouri, Illinois, and Alabama were granted admittance to the Union as states. British and American naval forces on the Great Lakes were reduced by agreement. A boundary line was established between Canada and the United States; and by a mere exchange of notes the two nations put into effect the world's outstanding example of disarmament—the unfortified border. Americans were also permitted to fish off the coast of Newfoundland. The well-known Missouri Compromise, forever prohibiting slavery in any part of the United States lying north of 36° 30′ north latitude, was passed by Congress and signed by the President.

During his second administration, Monroe sent a special message to Congress, which that body approved, recommending the spending of $100,000 to establish commercial relations with the Spanish colonies in South America which had recently won their freedom. A treaty of navigation and commerce with France was signed.

All these constructive acts of statesmanship brought a new era of international peace and growing trade to our nation.

James Monroe lived for six years after retiring from the White House. He had little money, and was feeble and lonely after the death of his wife. In 1830 he sold his Virginia farm and went to live with his married daughter in New York city. There, on July 4 of the following year, he passed away, at the age of seventy-three—the third ex-President to die on the anniversary of America's independence.

James Monroe was the last President to cling to the outmoded knee breeches, cockade, and sword. But nobody ever laughed at the dignified old gentleman who had devoted so many years to the service of his country, as soldier and statesman. His patriotism and integrity never swerved. Thomas Jefferson once said of him: "Monroe is so honest that if you turned his soul inside out, there would be no spot upon it."

JOHN QUINCY ADAMS

Draftsman of the Monroe Doctrine

THE story of the life of John Quincy Adams shows clearly that he was the true son of his father. Like John Adams, second President of the United States, John Quincy was fearless, stubborn, and outspoken. Like his father, he served his country well, especially in dealing with foreign nations.

John Quincy was born at the Adams farm, just outside of Braintree, in Massachusetts. The date was July 11, 1767. At this time his mother's grandfather lay dying, and when the new baby was baptized they called him John Quincy to carry on the old man's name.

As a small boy, young John was grave and studious. When he was nearly eight years old, he and his mother watched from a distance the first battle for American independence— the famous battle of Bunker Hill. The two gazed, fascinated at the smoke and flames billowing up from the fire at Charlestown, and the boy's diary was soon filled with crude drawings of soldiers and sailing ships. The following year, though he was only a little fellow, he often started out alone and rode his horse to Boston, to bring back mail and news of the war— a round trip of twenty miles. Two years later, when he was eleven, he said a sorrowful good-by to his mother and was rowed to a ship anchored in the bay. On that ship he sailed with his father to France, by way of Spain, running the British blockade and being shipwrecked on the Spanish coast.

He was a bright, patriotic youngster, and a great favorite with Benjamin Franklin, who was then our minister to France. He liked foreign travel; he even enjoyed studying

Latin and Greek! Before he was twelve he had crossed the Atlantic four times; and at fourteen he was taken to Russia as Minister Dana's secretary. He remained at St. Petersburg for about a year. Later he went with his father to Holland, where he went to school in Amsterdam and then to the University of Leyden. By the time he was seventeen, young John Quincy Adams had traveled over much of Europe, and had decided definitely on a career in public life.

John Adams was then our minister to the Court of St. James's. His son liked living abroad and he was tempted to remain in London. But he felt that, as a good American, he should complete his education in the United States. So he returned home and entered Harvard as a junior. Two years later he was graduated—almost at the top of his class. Again following in his father's footsteps, he studied law, was admitted to the Massachusetts bar, and in 1790 opened his own law office in Boston.

For the first year or two, clients were scarce, and the young lawyer spent much of his time studying and writing. In 1793, when England tried to stop the French Revolution by force, he wrote a series of articles for a Boston newspaper, signing the pieces with a pen name. Washington, then President, read the articles with deep satisfaction. Here was a man who thought as he did, and was not afraid to take the unpopular view of the question. President Washington took the trouble to find out who had written the articles, and much to John Quincy's surprise appointed him minister to The Netherlands. His father, Vice President Adams, feared that, at twenty-seven, John was too young for such an important assignment. Washington had no such fears. In a letter to the elder Adams he wrote, "There remains no doubt in my

53

mind that he will prove himself to be the ablest of all our diplomatic corps."

The affairs of The Netherlands were in confusion. French armies were marching through the country. The other European ministers fled, but John Quincy Adams stuck to his post. He had a difficult time, dealing with the French on the one side, and the Hollanders on the other. But neither side in the conflict succeeded in making a tool of him.

Diplomatic business had taken him to London on several occasions. There he met Miss Louisa Johnson, daughter of the United States consul. They were married in the summer of 1797; and young Adams was transferred to Berlin as minister. This was rather embarrassing for both father and son, now that John Adams had succeeded Washington as President. John Quincy accordingly asked that he be recalled. His father obliged, and a year later the young man was elected to the state Senate from the Boston district. In 1803, he was sent to Washington as United States Senator.

By this time we were a nation of more than five million people. There were two political parties: the Jefferson Republicans (we would call them Democrats today); and the Federalists, which included many people of wealth and social position.

John Quincy aligned himself with the Federalists—the party of his father. But he had shown himself independent of party in the state Senate; and now, in Washington, he displayed the family trait of independence by supporting many of the measures of the Jefferson Republicans. Never in his long political career could John Quincy Adams be persuaded to sacrifice his convictions for party politics. He cared nothing for public opinion. He was blunt and outspoken, saying exactly what he thought and doing his duty as he saw it for the good of our country. For these reasons he, like his father, made many enemies, and both were generally unpopular. In Massachusetts, the legislature instructed John Quincy to vote in a certain way—and he refused. The infuriated Federalists of Massachusetts thereupon made his situation in Washington so difficult that he resigned his Senate seat.

Stung by this shabby treatment, but still firmly declining to sacrifice his integrity "for the good of the party," he became more and more in sympathy with the policies of Madison, Jefferson, and Monroe. President Madison was now in the White House. He had high regard for the ability of John Quincy Adams, and appointed him minister to Russia. Later Madison sent him to Ghent to preside over the American peace commission. The President also offered him an appointment to the Supreme Court of the United States, but Adams declined this honor.

He had spent half his life in the capitals of Europe. He had made good use of his opportunities, and was now a man of culture and learning, with a thoughtful, mature mind and an unselfish conception of public service. At the conclusion of the peace negotiations, President Madison appointed him minister to the Court of St. James's, our most important diplomatic post. He was still following in the footsteps of his famous father!

In 1817, when James Monroe succeeded Madison as President, he remembered that as Secretary of State he had greatly admired the diplomatic talents of young Adams. Monroe appointed him Secretary of State. With his wide knowledge of foreign affairs, he was well suited to the office which he occupied during Monroe's two terms.

Up to 1815, the currents of American life had been swayed this way and that by the Napoleonic wars and other events abroad. Now the United States turned resolutely away from the Old World and we concentrated our thoughts and energies upon ourselves. The tide of immigration was rising rapidly, as the downtrodden people of Europe began to realize that across the Atlantic a wonderful new land, brimful of opportunities, awaited them. Our own people were drifting westward, where good farm land could be bought for a dollar an acre. New states were being admitted to the Union. Manufacturing had developed enormously, and America began to dream of a nation which could produce its own raw materials, make its own products, sell them in its own expanding market—and in other countries less fortunately endowed.

Of course there were many problems to solve; and John Quincy Adams inherited his share of them. There was the pressing question of Florida. One difficulty was that the Spanish minister had to ask his government for instructions on every question that came up. In that period of sailing ships, it took a long time to get mail from Europe. Sometimes negotiations were halted for months at a time. But Secretary of State Adams finally solved the Florida problem by acquiring the Spanish holdings for $5,000,000, payable—not to Spain, but to citizens of the United States to satisfy claims against that country. In February, 1819, Florida was ceded to the United States.

During the second Monroe administration it became necessary for the United States to do something to protect America from interference by European Powers. The colonies of Spain in South America had been carrying on a long revolt against the mother country. Russia, Austria, and Prussia were eager to aid Spain. England wanted to join the United States in recognizing the independent colonies. As Secretary of State Adams watched developments, a general policy formed in his mind. In the main, this policy was adopted by the Monroe administration, and worked over, no doubt, by the President and his Cabinet. When it was proclaimed in December, 1823, naturally it took the name of the President and became known as the Monroe Doctrine. In effect, it declared that the United States was against colonization by European countries in the Western Hemisphere.

In those days, the office of Secretary of State was considered a steppingstone to the presidency. Yet John Quincy Adams refused to lift a finger to get the nomination. "I have neither talent nor inclination for intrigue," he said to a friend. Nevertheless, he was chosen when the election devolved upon the House of Representatives, and he was inaugurated on March 4, 1825.

It soon became clear that his administration was bound to be a failure. It is true he kept the western lands and natural resources under control of the government, and spent for public improvements the money which came from the sale of government land. But his beliefs ran counter to the changing political ideas of his time. He had only a small following, and he did absolutely nothing to make himself more popular. He refused to use any office to pay political debts. He had no interest in building up a political machine.

The object of government, he declared, was to improve the

57

condition of the American people. Yet he could accomplish nothing, for in the mid-term Congressional elections the opposition (the Jefferson Democrats) won an overwhelming victory in both Senate and House of Representatives.

In the next presidential campaign, Adams was soundly beaten by Andrew Jackson, and he retired to the old homestead at Braintree. But he was soon sent to the House of Representatives by the citizens of his district—and remained for seventeen years. There, under the dome of the Capitol, his hands shaking, his voice cracking with age, he stood his ground like the fighter he was. For eight stormy years he battled for the abolition of slavery. He lifted his voice also again and again for the Smithsonian Institution, and it was he more than anyone else, except the original donor of the money, who was responsible for the fact that we have it today. He held himself accountable to no party and to no section; he took orders from no one—and the voters of Massachusetts were proud to re-elect him on those terms.

On February 21, 1848, Congressman Adams was in his usual place in the House. He started to rise, then pitched forward to the floor. He was carried to the Speaker's room and the doctors were called, but they could do nothing. They decided not to move him, for the end was near. Two days later he died there, in his eighty-first year, saying: "This is the last of earth. I am content."

ANDREW JACKSON
Our First Log-Cabin President

THE story of Andrew Jackson is truly a success story in the American tradition. For it is the tale of a boy who made good against fearful odds. His father, a Scotch-Irish linen draper, died before the boy was born. The widow had no money; no home. She scarcely knew what to do or where to turn. But a married sister had a log cabin in the vicinity, and there, in the North Carolina wilderness, near the boundary line, Andrew Jackson was born. The date was March 15, 1767.

Two years before, Andrew Jackson, the father, had emigrated with his wife and their two small sons to the Waxhaw settlement. He had dreams of making a good living. But the rough frontiers of the new land brought him only struggle and hardship.

Mrs. Jackson had nothing but courage, but she had plenty of that. When Andy was only three weeks old, she took him and the younger boy to the home of Mrs. Crawford, her other sister; the oldest boy Mrs. Jackson left behind. For the next ten years, in exchange for a home, she cooked, scrubbed, washed, and mended for the family of her invalid sister and her own children. There, in dire poverty and in wild surroundings, where backwoods conditions were at their worst, Andrew Jackson spent his childhood.

He learned to read and became familiar with simple arithmetic, but he never did learn to spell. He grew into a rowdy youngster, tall, lanky, and ungainly, with coarse reddish hair and a lean freckled face.

Andy, as his mother called him, was only eight years old when the Revolutionary War began. And that war left him with a string of sad and bitter memories. For it took from him all those who were near and dear.

His older brother died, after a local battle, from fatigue and exposure; he and his brother Robert, mere children, were captured by the British. It is said that young Andy received a saber cut from a British officer when, as a prisoner, he refused to clean the officer's boots. Whether or not this has any basis in fact, he hated the English for the hardship and sorrow he suffered at their hands. He and Robert, along with other prisoners, were marched off to Camden, South Carolina, forty miles through the wilderness. Conditions in that British prison camp were unspeakable. There were no doctors, no nurses, no medicines, no bedding, and little food or clothing; and soon an epidemic of smallpox broke out.

Mrs. Jackson was frantic with worry for her boys. She had remained behind as a volunteer nurse in the Waxhaw settlement. Gathering together several English prisoners of war, she took them to Camden, and arranged to exchange them for her young sons and five other American soldiers. Robert, however, was too weak to stand the long journey home, even on horseback. In two days he was dead. Andy was ill and weak, too, but somehow his mother nursed him back to health.

As if this brave, tireless woman had not already done her share of sacrificing and toiling, she placed Andy with a Charlotte family, while she returned to Charleston to nurse the war wounded. There she contracted ship fever and died, leaving Andrew, at fifteen, completely alone in the world without money or kin and with the bitter scars of war, disease, poverty, and grief upon his young heart.

Alone and friendless, the lad became a wild and roving

spirit. He apprenticed himself to a saddle maker, but stayed only six months. He did a bit of drinking, gambling, cock fighting, and following the races at Charleston. Bankrupt and in debt, he still owned a horse, and one day a professional gambler bet two hundred dollars against the fine, spirited animal. Jackson won by a shake of the dice, paid his bills, and never gambled again. For, during this brief period of lawless living, he learned to want something better in life. He rode off to Salisbury, North Carolina, and began seriously to study in the law office of Spruce McKay. When he was twenty he was granted a license to practice law.

The year was now 1787. Jackson was six feet one inch tall, and thin as a rail. His eyes were a deep blue, quick and intelligent. He was highly sensitive, dignified in his bearing, and was less awkward in his actions. He had learned to ride well; he had tried schoolteaching and clerking in a country store. There seemed little opportunity for him to open a law office in North Carolina; but in the unsettled wild land beyond the mountains was the Western District. Later it was to be known as the state of Tennessee. There, the hard-riding, self-reliant young man was appointed prosecuting attorney at Nashville. Frontier life in those days was tough—but Jackson was tougher. Out through the wilderness, where Indians were still attacking wagon trains, rode the 21-year-old guardian of the law, to keep order and to spread the news of the new Constitution that had been ratified by a majority of the thirteen United States.

Jackson enjoyed those rugged days on the frontier. He met men after his own heart. It was an era when men carried a knife and pistol, and were always ready for action. Young Jackson, fearless in combat and strong in purpose, was direct in his dealings with friends as well as enemies. And he had plenty of both. The frontiersmen soon learned to respect and admire the young attorney who made long journeys through the wilderness, sometimes to collect a debt or try a case in a district court.

Andrew Jackson was also a gallant and fascinating man with the ladies, and something happened during this period of his life which left another painful scar upon his heart.

The widow of Colonel Donelson took Jackson into her home as a boarder. There he met Rachel Donelson Robards. Rachel was married to a ne'er-do-well, who became jealous of Jackson. Jackson finally sought lodging elsewhere. Later the Robards separated and the husband applied to the Virginia legislature for a bill of divorce. It was granted, provided the Supreme Court should find sufficient cause for divorce. Robards laid aside the document and did nothing about the case. Some time afterward it was reported in Nashville that he had obtained his freedom.

Implicitly believing this to be true, Jackson and Rachel were married in the autumn of 1791. Two years later they learned that the Virginia divorce had never been made final. Thus Jackson, who adored Rachel and had a deep reverence and respect for all women, learned that he had been living for two years with another man's wife. Robards now sued for divorce, and obtained it in the courts of Kentucky. Jackson and his Rachel were married all over again. But the slander and gossip caused by this honest misunderstanding tortured Andrew Jackson for the rest of his life. He killed one man and fought duels with many others because they made remarks against his wife's character; and he never forgave himself for his failure to search court records concerning the divorce bill.

When Tennessee became a state, Jackson was chosen as her

Representative in Congress. He was then twenty-nine years of age. He rode horseback the eight hundred miles to Philadelphia to attend his first session. There he was regarded as a rough backwoodsman, and was described by one contemporary as "a tall, lank, uncouth-looking personage, with locks of hair hanging over his face, and a cue down his back, tied with an eel-skin . . ."

The following year Jackson was sent north as a member of the Senate. After a year with that body he resigned and was made judge of the Supreme Court of Tennessee. His wild spirit, however, was not tamed. One day, in Knoxville, he met Governor Sevier on the street. The governor taunted him about his rather late marriage to Mrs. Robards. Jackson, furious, opened fire! The governor, in the approved frontier fashion of those times, returned the fire. Luckily neither man was hurt, and friends intervened.

Tiring of the routine of the Supreme Court, Jackson rode home to his cotton plantation. He also owned a store at that time, and thousands of acres of wild land. Then came the financial panic of 1798, in which one merchant who went bankrupt held notes for more than six thousand dollars that bore Jackson's endorsement. Andrew Jackson did not hesitate; he sold enough land, both wild and improved, to pay off the amount.

Without being consulted, he was chosen in 1802 by the field officers of the state's military forces to succeed the late General Conway, with the rank of major general. He held this appointment until he was made a major general in the forces of the United States in 1814.

At the beginning of the War of 1812, twenty-five hundred frontiersmen eagerly answered Jackson's call for volunteers, and in November the War Department ordered him and the Tennessee division to go down the Mississippi and defend the lower country. Two months later the Secretary of War ordered him to dismiss the brave soldiers of his command. The men were five hundred miles from home, they had received no pay, and were without rations or means of transportation. Some 150 of them were on the sick list. But apparently the Secretary did not consider these things!

On receipt of the message, Jackson let loose a string of profanity that amazed even the tough mule-skinners of his command. He wrote letters of protest to the President, to the governor of Tennessee, and to the Army in Washington. Then he issued drafts for transportation, food, and supplies, with assurances that if the government refused to pay the bills he would be responsible for them. His drafts were protested, and General Jackson found himself facing financial ruin because he had disobeyed orders and brought his soldiers home instead of casting them adrift.

But Andrew Jackson was already well known as a hero and a champion of the people. He had become the idol of Tennessee. Somebody pointed out to the Secretary of War that this was a presidential year and that Jackson was highly popular. If the administration allowed the General to pay the expenses of the Army, the President might have difficulty in getting re-elected. Two days later, orders were issued to honor General Jackson's drafts.

It was on that long march back home that General Jackson earned his famous nickname. He loaned his horse to a wounded soldier and made his own way on foot with the others. The toughness and stamina of the General was so great that his men remarked that he was as hard as seasoned hickory, and that started the old Army nickname which clung to him ever after: "Old Hickory."

Jackson's courage and strength were put to many other tests after that. He subdued the Creek and Cherokee Indians; he drove the British forces out of Mobile; he won the historic battle of New Orleans on January 8, 1815, when the British went down in defeat though their forces numbered some eight thousand men against Jackson's four thousand. Had there been in those days any means of quick communication, the battle of New Orleans need never have been fought, Jackson would not have emerged as the great hero, and doubtless would never have been elected to the highest office in the land. But there was no telephone or telegraph then, and a cable had not yet been laid across the Atlantic. So the soldiers on both sides at the battle of New Orleans were not aware until many weeks later that a peace treaty between the United States and Great Britain had been signed late in December!

As it was, "Old Hickory" was wildly acclaimed by the entire nation. He had fought a battle lasting several days, against odds of two to one; had won it with volunteers against seasoned soldiers of the King's armies; and had lost only 13 men against the enemy's 2117.

Three years later, when Jackson and his troops were sent to protect the citizens from Seminole raids, he not only stopped the raids, but also crossed into Spanish Florida and seized two Englishmen accused of urging the Indians to revolt. He gave them a trial by court martial and executed them. This impetuous action was criticized in some circles, but it was applauded in others. It was typical of the temperament of this man Jackson. When he believed he was right, he went ahead, careless of his own safety or reputation.

President Monroe, in 1821, appointed Jackson governor of Florida; but the old General remained there only a few months, then he settled down in The Hermitage, which he had built for his wife near Nashville. Jackson was returned to the U.S. Senate in 1823. A year later he ran for President against John Quincy Adams, and the result was a tie. This campaign was waged against Jackson with complete disregard for decency. Not content with attacking him, opposition newspapers vilified the good name of his wife. Even his mother, dead fifty years, was assailed by the press. The House of Representatives broke the tie in favor of Adams; and in 1825 Jackson resigned from the Senate.

Jackson returned home. The more he thought about the tactics of the politicians, the madder he got. He had received more electoral votes than any other candidate. He had also polled a larger popular vote, and carried more states. Yet the House had voted Adams into office. Something was wrong with our system, and he was going to do something about it!

Ever since the formation of political parties in the United States, presidential candidates had been nominated by a caucus of party representatives in Congress. In the campaign of 1828, this method was abandoned, and nominations were made by state legislators. Jackson won easily. But it was an empty victory; for his Rachel, grieved by the slander against her, died before the inauguration. Jackson entered the White House, a shattered and lonely old man.

In 1832, the present system of nominating candidates was devised, in which delegates from every part of our country gather at a convention. This brought the choice nearer the people; and again Andrew Jackson won!

He had been opposed to the Bank of the United States

as a monopoly which could make or break any enterprise in the country. In 1832, Jackson vetoed a bill providing for a renewal of the charter, took his case before the people, and won a complete victory. He removed the government deposits and left the bank to die a slow death. He failed, however, to provide something to take its place; and the war on the bank was followed by one of the country's worst financial depressions.

Another feature of his administration was his removal from office of great numbers of incumbents, putting his friends in their places. Jackson believed it was right to punish his enemies and reward his loyal supporters. He also took a firm stand toward South Carolina when the governor refused to collect taxes, as required by our tariff laws.

The son of the Scotch-Irish immigrant had come a long way since his log-cabin days. Without friends, money, education, or influence, he had gone into the wilderness of Tennessee and carved out of it an estate and an honorable career. He was the first President who was not a man of culture and experience in foreign affairs; yet he was honest, patriotic, and sincere. When he took office, the national debt amounted to $48,000,000. Jackson paid it off completely, and piled up a surplus in the Treasury. Yet when he retired at the end of his second term, he had to sell his cotton crop to clear up his personal debts in Washington.

He retired in 1837 to The Hermitage, and there he died on June 8, 1845, still loved and revered by the American people as a man of fiery convictions and love of justice. As such, his memory is honored to this day.

MARTIN VAN BUREN

First President from New York

FROM Washington to Jackson, our Presidents were born before the Revolutionary War and played their parts in the struggle for independence. Now, a new generation came forward. Martin Van Buren was our first President to be born under the American flag rather than the flag of the British. He came into this world on December 5, 1782.

His birthplace was Kinderhook, New York, a small village about eighteen miles south of Albany. Both his mother and father were of Dutch ancestry. His earliest American ancestor of whom we have any record reached our shores in 1637, landing with his bride on the island of Manhattan.

Martin's father, Abraham Van Buren, was a thrifty and industrious farmer who also kept the village tavern. The boy, therefore, grew up in an atmosphere of politics. For Albany was the state capital, and stage coaches often brought passengers for an overnight stop at the Van Buren inn. Some of the guests were lawyers, others were state senators. No doubt Martin, acting as bar boy and listening to their talk, decided that when he grew up, he too would be a lawyer and a senator. It is also likely that he confided his hopes and desires to little Hannah Hoes, his childhood sweetheart.

He probably didn't aspire then to the governorship of the great Empire State, or to the presidency, yet both these honors fell to the blond, blue-eyed little Dutch boy from the Rip Van Winkle village of Kinderhook.

Young Martin's brief schooling ended before he was fourteen. There followed an apprenticeship of five years in the law office of Frank Sylvester. The boy's official title was law

70

clerk; but he also swept and dusted the office, ran errands, and kept the logs blazing in the fireplace when the weather was cold. Mr. Sylvester once rewarded him with a complete outfit of new clothes and gave him a lecture on the value of a neat appearance. Young Van Buren never forgot this; all through his later life he was very careful of his grooming and wore his clothes well.

The boy was bright and energetic, but five years seemed a long apprenticeship. By the time he was nineteen, he was drawn to New York city by the glowing tales of his friend, Billy Van Ness, whose older brother was a well-known lawyer and politician. At the end of two years in the Van Ness office, Martin Van Buren was admitted to the bar and returned to his beloved Kinderhook to enter his half-brother's law office. Naturally, he spent much of his spare time in his father's tavern, eagerly listening to the discussions, which were mostly of politics. The conflict between the Federalists and the anti-Federalists was at its height. Both Martin and his father were anti-Federalists. That is, they were followers of Thomas Jefferson, then called Republicans but now known as Democrats. The Federalists believed in granting broad powers to the government, while the Republicans were in favor of states' rights.

At twenty-one Martin Van Buren was under medium height, with deep blue eyes and long, curly flaxen hair. He had a sunny disposition and a ready smile. In those days, a New York state lawyer had to have four years' experience in the lower courts before he could practice before the state supreme court. But lawyer Van Buren was smart and he was politically minded. In four years he had outgrown his native village. He was now a county surrogate and a counsellor of the Supreme Court. He and Hannah Hoes celebrated the promotion by getting married and moving to the busy little city of Hudson, the county seat. Van Buren was twenty-five years old; and his bride was twenty-four.

From the beginning, "Little Van" had shown a flair for politics. Like Jefferson, he was often chosen to draft resolutions and speeches for others, and to write the Democratic party's annual appeal to the electorate. He could explain political questions in plain language which the uneducated voters could understand. In 1812, when he was only thirty, he became a state senator, a member of the highest court of the state, and attorney general. Four years later, as one of the state's leading lawyers, he moved to Albany. There, in 1819, he was saddened and his domestic life broken up by the death of his wife. She had borne him four sons.

Two years later, Van Buren was elected to the United States Senate, and by 1824, he had picked General Jackson as the coming man in the Democratic (Jefferson) party. Undoubtedly there was an understanding between "Old Hickory," who wanted to become President, and Van Buren, the practical politician from Albany. In 1827 Van Buren was re-elected to the Senate.

The governor of New York, who recognized Van Buren's power, sent his brother to try to make a political peace with Van Buren. In reply, Little Van offered the governor an ambassadorship abroad if he would retire from politics! From that day on, it was "war to the knife" between the two men. Clinton was governor; but Van Buren headed a thoroughly organized political machine; he controlled the legislature. The following year, after the death of Governor Clinton, he was elected governor.

72

Van Buren was a clever politician. He had outmaneuvered the governor of the state and elected his own candidate. He saw New York converted to the convention system of nominating state officers. Once he slipped a joker into a bill which held up, for a time, the building of the Erie Canal. But, to his credit, he managed by a backstage move to have Andrew Jackson commissioned a major general in the Army and sent to New Orleans. He also exposed the sham of the national banking system of the period.

It has been said that Van Buren developed the spoils system that was later put into sweeping effect by President Jackson. But that was already in effect at Albany before Van Buren entered politics. Both parties agreed that, with the election of a new governor, or where the least suspicion of disloyalty existed, sheriffs, district attorneys, county clerks, judges, and other state appointees should be removed from their posts and replaced by people loyal to the party of the new governor.

After Jackson's election, in 1828, Van Buren was made Secretary of State in the new Cabinet. There he saw the possibility of building up a political machine with the aid of the Post Office Department. The next step was to transfer the Albany appointment system to the national government. Thus, hundreds of government clerks and old retainers, high and low, were put out of their jobs.

Van Buren, at this time, was very popular socially. His courtly manner, short stature, and flaxen hair were familiar in the drawing rooms of Washington. He was a widower, in his late forties, well-to-do. Also, while the term may not have been in use then, he was President Jackson's "fair-haired boy." Jackson is said to have felt a deep, fatherly affection for Van Buren.

73

As a Senator, Van Buren had voted for the protective tariff and for a bill abolishing imprisonment for debt. He had realized that the nomination of candidates for President and Vice President by a group of national legislators, and the naming of presidential electors by state legislators, were menaces to the nation. As governor of New York, he had, among other reforms, put through a measure setting up a safety fund, guaranteed by the state, for the protection of bank depositors. Now, as Jackson's closest adviser, he was to come to grips with the Bank of the United States.

In April, 1831, Van Buren was appointed minister to the Court of St. James's, at London. But the Senate did not ratify the appointment, and Van Buren was forced to return to the United States. At home, he found the renewal of the bank's charter to be the leading issue in the presidential campaign. Also, he was the vice-presidential nominee on the Jackson ticket.

Soon after Jackson took office for his second term, he vetoed the bill granting a renewal of the bank's charter. The bank was charged with bribing Senators and Congressmen, newspaper editors, and legislators all over the nation. Its opponents accused it of controlling mortgages, loans, paid advertisements; of making men—and breaking them. Senator Daniel Webster received what was called a "loan" of $10,000 from the bank a week after he had made a rousing speech against Jackson's veto message, although Webster already owed some $22,000 to the bank! The bank circulated the Webster speech as a campaign document and altogether spent $80,000 for publicity and pamphlets to keep its campaign alive. A large part of its stock was owned by the aristocracy of England.

During the election campaign, the bank renewed its fight

for a charter. Jackson made the blunt charge that it was trying to create a financial panic. But the election went off well for "Old Hickory" and his protégé, Van Buren. "Little Van" assumed the Vice President's chair—to preside over the same Senate which had refused to confirm his appointment as ambassador. The government's deposits were removed from the Bank of the United States and distributed to other banks; and the nine-million-dollar federal surplus was distributed among the state treasuries.

Four years later, as Jackson himself had planned, Van Buren became President. He kept the Jackson Cabinet, with a single exception. Jackson had made a good beginning in the fight to divorce the bank from the state; but it remained for Van Buren to finish the job. The bank's power had not yet been destroyed; it had simply been transferred to the state banks in which the government had deposited its funds. To oppose this powerful giant took courage. Almost before the new President could get his administration going, there spread over the land one of the worst financial panics the country had ever experienced. Many people blamed the panic on mistakes made in the Jackson administration, but the causes of the panic of 1837 lay deeper than the withdrawal of funds from the Bank of the United States.

Strange as it may seem, it was the Erie Canal that led to the trouble. Investors said to themselves: If the Erie Canal has made its investors wealthy, a similar canal—or a railroad—will make *us* rich! A great wave of speculation swept the country; millions of dollars were borrowed from the banks for the building of towns and villages for which there were neither residents nor demand. In 1834, sales of unimproved public lands amounted to $4,500,000; within the next two years $39,500,000 (most of it borrowed) were invested in lands that had not yet started to produce crops.

The United States Treasury tried to stop this dangerous speculation by ruling that all public lands, except those used by real settlers, must be paid for in silver or gold coin. Then came the day when a New York bank could not make its payments in coin. All New York banks suspended payment in coin; notes were worthless. Within the next ten days, a hundred New York city business firms went bankrupt: the panic was on. No group of men in Washington, no matter how able, could check it. Like a raging forest fire, it had to burn itself out. Van Buren did call an extra session of Congress to urge the enactment of the Sub-Treasury Bill, but without success.

Finally it was England who relieved the situation by shipping gold to America so that the banks could resume payments in coin. Credit was gradually restored. In the end, Congress passed the Sub-Treasury Act, thus striking the chains of the banks from the hands of government. This was the outstanding achievement of the Van Buren administration.

Newspapers under the control of the paper-money bankers carried out a campaign against Van Buren; and he was not re-elected. He was also outspoken against immediate annexation of Texas. Without Mexico's consent, he said, such annexation would mean war.

His son Abraham brought his wife to Kinderhook, and Van Buren, now a grandfather, settled down there. He lived at Kinderhook, a gentleman of leisure—but always with his finger on the political pulse of New York—until his death on July 24, 1862, in his eightieth year.

WILLIAM HENRY HARRISON

First President to Die in Office

WILLIAM HENRY HARRISON was two years old when the Battle of Lexington ushered in the war for independence. He grew up in the turmoil of the Revolution, in which his father, Benjamin Harrison, took an active part. Like most of the planter families in Virginia, the Harrisons came from England. As early as 1641, the first Benjamin Harrison was acting as a delegate in the House of Burgesses, and later his sons and grandsons followed in his footsteps. At the time of the Revolutionary War, the family was one of the wealthiest and most prominent in all Virginia.

Their estate, which they called Berkeley, stood on the banks of the James River. Here, on February 9, 1773, William Henry Harrison was born. His father was a personal friend of George Washington, and served with John Adams in the Continental Congress. Later he was elected governor of Virginia. William Henry, therefore, faced no hardships in childhood, and enjoyed all the advantages which wealth and social position could provide. Like Thomas Jefferson, he spent his spare time as a lad riding, dancing, swimming, and shooting. As a youth he attended Hampden-Sidney College, in Hanover County.

Young Harrison decided that he would become a doctor, and he began the study of medicine at Richmond. Early in 1791 he left Richmond and set out for Philadelphia, which was then the capital of the United States and the center of excitement and gaiety. The news of his father's sudden death reached him on his arrival. William Henry had planned to continue his medical studies, but now he changed his mind. At eighteen he was slender and frail. Maybe he felt that an outdoor life would help him to grow stronger. Anyhow, he did what many young men were doing in those days of Indian uprisings: he joined the Army. His guardian loudly objected to this move, but the young man could not be dissuaded and through one of his father's friends he was given a commission as ensign in the infantry. The young ensign, no doubt, was very proud of his post, for it was his duty to carry the regimental flag in battle.

George Washington was then President of the new and independent nation. Indians were spread over that vast wilderness now occupied by Ohio, Indiana, and Illinois. The settlements on the Ohio River were lonely pioneer towns. There were neither ferries, nor bridges—and very few roads. But, as a protection against the Indians, whom the British had aroused against us, the government had built Fort Washington, on the Ohio. It was a small frontier post of about 130 families, not far from what is now Cincinnati. And to Fort Washington journeyed young Ensign Harrison, still in his teens.

The argument between the government and the Indians was over the land that lay north of the Ohio. General ("Mad Anthony") Wayne was preparing to march against the Indians, and soon William Harrison was promoted to lieutenant and went along as the General's aide. After a highly successful campaign, in which he took part in the great battle of Fallen Timbers in 1794, the young lieutenant was assigned to duty at North Bend. There he met Anna Symmes, the daughter of New Jersey's former chief justice, and the two fell in love.

They were married in 1795; and two years later Harrison was advanced to the rank of captain and placed in command of Fort Washington. He resigned from the army in June, 1798, and a month later was appointed Secretary of the Northwest Territory. At the end of a year, he was elected as the territory's first delegate to Congress; and in May, 1800, President Adams appointed him governor of the newly created territory of Indiana.

So, when he was only twenty-seven years old, William Henry Harrison found himself governor of a wilderness that stretched from the western boundary of Pennsylvania to the Mississippi River. Most of it was still in the hands of the Indians.

Harrison remained governor for twelve years, and great powers lay in his hands. He appointed the territorial officers— even the commanders of the militia and the judges of the county courts. With all these assignments to hand out, it was perhaps natural that he should build up a party, made up of personal friends devoted to his interests. And since it was the custom for almost everybody in the territory to speculate in land, it is likely that Harrison did so, too. He followed many of the customs of his native state of Virginia. He was lavish with hospitality, generous and friendly, and made many flowery speeches.

He was a good administrator. He had a policy and it was governed by his desire to protect the settlers and treat the Indians as generously as the government would permit. One of his accomplishments was preventing a land-grabbing lobby from exploiting the rich and virgin soil of Ohio, Indiana, Illinois, Michigan, and Wisconsin. He also did his best to stop the sale of whiskey to the Indians. By ratifying old treaties and making new ones with the Indians, Harrison secured some sixty million acres of land for the government.

By bold and skillful diplomacy, he postponed a general up-rising of the Indians.

But difficulties with the Indians were increasing. Great Britain fanned the flame by drawing them into an alliance, equipping them with arms and ammunition, and sending them on raids throughout the territory. Seeing the dangers, James Madison, who was then President, appointed Governor Harrison commander-in-chief of the Army of the Northwest and gave orders for him to recapture Detroit. So once again, William Henry Harrison became a soldier. With an army of ten thousand men, and Commodore Perry's help in destroying the British fleet in the Great Lakes, the backbone of the Indians' resistance was broken and the power of the British in the greater part of the Northwest destroyed. Now the settlers of the territory could breathe easier, and they hailed Harrison as a great hero of the War of 1812.

Early in 1814 he went back to his farm at North Bend, near Cincinnati. The care of his wife and their eight children was his first responsibility. He was eager to get back into a government office. Governor Shelby of Kentucky suggested in 1816 that he run for Congress. General Harrison obtained the seat of a Congressman who had resigned, and one of his first attempts at legislation was a bill to establish military training as a branch of education in every school in the United States. Another bill provided for a 160-acre grant of land to certain veterans of the War of 1812. Beginning in 1819, Harrison served for two terms as state senator in Ohio. After that, his political ventures began to meet with defeat on every side. His campaigns for a place in Congress failed, though he tried several times to get elected to office. Embarrassed and angered, he still kept trying. In the 1824 elections he finally won a seat in the United States Senate, where he remained for three years. Again out of office, he persuaded friends to help him, and in 1828 he was appointed minister to Colombia. There he was to act as an observer only, and report developments to Washington. But Harrison failed to obey the instructions that he was not to take sides with any faction or to interfere in Colombia's internal affairs, and he was recalled. The next four years, for him, were filled with money troubles and family misfortunes. He was nominated for President in 1836, only to be defeated by Martin Van Buren.

This defeat, however, did bring Harrison to the attention of the politicians. Whig leaders realized that in the race against Van Buren, Harrison had run a close second. And since they had no better candidate available, he received the nomination at the next Whig Convention, while the nomination for Vice President went to John Tyler, of Virginia.

The campaign of 1840 was anything but dignified. It was run like a carnival. A newspaper opposed to Harrison started the affair, when it suggested that the old General would be out of place in the White House, but no doubt would be quite content with a pension, a barrel of hard cider, and a log cabin. This remark was changed from a slur into a slogan by Harrison's campaign managers. An Ohio parade featured a log-cabin float, with a couple of raccoons on the roof, and a group of men outside the door, drinking from a barrel of cider. From that moment, no Harrison-Tyler parade was complete without its cabin and cider barrel, and many villages set up a log cabin where free cider was handed out to every man old enough to vote. Since Harrison had come from a wealthy and prominent Virginia family, had enjoyed every luxury in childhood, and had been graduated from college, there

82

was little reason to associate him with a backwoods log cabin. The idea, however, captured the imagination of the people, and he won the election.

It was a costly victory. The General, then sixty-eight years old, had been completely exhausted by the strain of the whirlwind campaign. Early in March, 1841, he contracted pneumonia, and died a month after his inauguration.

He was the first President to die in office; and at his death the responsibilities of Chief Executive fell to Vice President Tyler, who was in favor of slavery and states' rights.

Harrison's last concern, as he lay dying, was for his country: "Sir," he said, "I wish you to understand the principles of the government. I wish them carried out. I ask nothing more."

The old soldier's death occurred April 4, 1841, and the nation mourned him sincerely. He was buried on his farm at North Bend, near Fort Washington on the Ohio, where so many years before he had met his bride and set up a home.

JOHN TYLER

Harrison's Vice President—and Successor

JOHN TYLER'S first American an-
cestor acquired in 1653—and his heirs sold to the provincial
government of Virginia—the land on which the Governor's
Palace at Williamsburg was built. Tyler, of course, has not
gone down in history because of that coincidence; nor for
having brought the state of Texas into the Union. He is usually remembered as the first man to become President of the
United States without being elected to that high office. As
Vice President, he succeeded President Harrison, who died
only a month after he was sworn in as Chief Executive.

At the time John Tyler was born, March 29, 1790, Williamsburg was the intellectual and social, as well as the
political, capital of Virginia, as has been pointed out in previous chapters. The boy's father had served as a member of
the House of Delegates, as a judge of the admiralty court; and
as governor for three terms. The family mansion, Greenway,
on the James River, like most plantations of those days, was a
little village in itself. On the grounds were a storehouse,
kitchen, laundry, dairy, meat house, icehouse, barns for the
livestock, storage houses for the grain, carriage houses, a
stable, a pigeon house, living quarters for the house servants,
and other quarters for the slaves who worked in the fields.
Some of those ancient buildings are still standing.

This was the pleasant, comfortable setting in which John
Tyler was born and reared, and where he probably was influenced by some of the convictions and prejudices of his elderly
father. The boy had a slender frame, a mop of golden-brown
hair, and bright blue eyes. He also, apparently, had at an
early age very definite ideas of his own. When he was about

ten years old, he headed a miniature rebellion against tyranny!
He and other boys in the neighborhood attended a school
kept by a Mr. McMurdo, a Scot who was unduly strict with
his young charges and gave them frequent whippings. On
one such whipping occasion, John and his friends overpow-
ered McMurdo, tied his hands and feet, and locked him up
in the schoolhouse. Later, the teacher urged Judge Tyler
to punish his young son for his part in the affair. But the
judge must have had a fine sense of humor, as well as a
sympathetic heart for the boys, for he sent Mr. McMurdo
away with this answer: *"Sic Semper Tyrannis!"* ("Thus ever
to tyrants!"), which was the motto of Virginia. That motto,
incidentally, which was adopted in 1776, still appears on the
State Seal.

But this little story does not mean that John Tyler's father
was over-lenient. In a letter to his son, then in his senior year
at college, Judge Tyler wrote: "I am mortified to find no
improvement in your handwriting, neither do you connect
your lines straight, which makes your letters look so abomina-
ble . . ." That criticism must have spurred the young man
on to greater effort, for in letters which have come down to
us from President Tyler, his writing is quite legible.

In 1802, when he was twelve, John entered the preparatory
school of William and Mary, at Williamsburg; later he entered the college itself, and was graduated at the age of seventeen. Under his father's guidance he studied law, and when
the judge was elected governor, the lad accompanied him
to Richmond, the new capital. There he resumed his studies
under Edmund Randolph, who had been President Washington's attorney general.

Before he was twenty-one, Tyler was issued a license to

practice law. By the time he was twenty-seven he was earning two thousand dollars a year. This was considered a large amount of money then. Daniel Webster, at the same age, was earning less than eight hundred dollars.

Tyler was elected to the Virginia Assembly when he was twenty-one, and remained in office five years. During the first two years he found time to develop a romance with Letitia Christian, a beautiful girl whom he had met at a party in the neighborhood. He addressed many love sonnets to the beloved Letitia, and the two were married on his twenty-third birthday, March 29, 1813. They were ideally suited to each other, and were very happy. The union also had an important bearing on Tyler's career, for the Christians were prominent and influential Virginians; and the legacy received by Letitia from her parents, both of whom died soon after her marriage, must have been a real help to her young lawyer husband.

The couple lived near Greenway for a couple of years, while their new house was being built. Later Tyler bought Greenway.

Tyler was elected a Congressman at the age of twenty-six. In that period of our history this was a great honor, for the membership of the House of Representatives at Washington was of such high caliber that the House then exerted a greater influence on the government than the Senate did. He returned home in 1821, and later served two terms in the Assembly. In 1825 he was elected governor, a position of dignity but of little power. The governor could recommend legislation to the Assembly but had no power of veto. He was even limited in the exercise of his administrative and appointive powers by the advice of the Council of State, a body of eight men chosen by the legislature. During his regime, he did have the honor of delivering the funeral oration over the body of Virginia's famous son, Thomas Jefferson, who had guided both Tyler and his father in their political careers.

Between the years 1827 and 1836 Tyler served in Washington as United States Senator. It was during Jackson's administration that a state convention in South Carolina declared the tariff laws of 1828 and 1832 unconstitutional, and therefore null and void. South Carolina refused to collect the taxes prescribed by these laws and announced that secession would result if force were used by the President to compel obedience. When President Jackson, in his proclamation of December, 1832, made it clear that the tariff laws would be enforced, and was sustained in his stand by Congress, John Tyler came forward and argued for the rights of the South. He also argued for a peaceable settlement of the controversy. The end was a compromise.

Tyler disapproved of Jackson's arbitrary methods. He made a report censuring President Jackson for removing the deposits from the United States Bank and voted for Clay's resolution of censure. When the Virginia legislature adopted a resolution calling on him to vote for having the resolution of censure removed from the record, Tyler refused to obey, resigned his seat in February, 1836, and retired to private life.

His independence in the Senate had attracted the leaders of the Whig Party. Tyler was still what the North would call a Democrat; but when he was approached by the Whigs to run for Vice President, he accepted the invitation. He was defeated in the election, and went back to the Virginia Assembly. His attendance there, in addition to his law practice, required that he move to Williamsburg.

Tyler's second attempt, with General Harrison running for President, was an unqualified success, as we know. This log-cabin, hard-cider campaign caught the imagination of the people, who were reminded also that Harrison and Tyler were born in the same county; and their fathers had stood side by side in the fight for American independence.

When President Harrison died a month after his inauguration, Tyler, as Vice President, moved into the White House. As Harrison was the first President to die in office, and the Constitution was none too specific on whether the Vice President should be considered a substitute or a successor, the Harrison Cabinet, with the exception of Daniel Webster, felt that they owed Tyler no loyalty; Tyler was an "outsider."

Tyler surprised his opponents by adopting an independent attitude. Then and there, he set the precedent that the Vice President is the legitimate successor of the President—and that precedent has been followed to this day. Tyler refused to be browbeaten. When Congress repealed Van Buren's Independent Treasury Act, and passed a bill creating a new Bank of the United States, Tyler declared the bill unconstitutional, and vetoed it. Thereupon the Cabinet, with the exception of Webster, resigned. Tyler brought out a list of Cabinet officers of his own. The Senate approved the list. Two years later, Webster, the last of the old Cabinet, resigned.

Senator Clay, of Kentucky, who had complete control of his party (the Democrats) in both House and Senate, wanted to be the next President of the United States. So he passed the word to his followers that it would not do for Tyler to make too good a showing. Tyler, by vetoing the bank bill, not only had played into Clay's hands; he had acted in opposition to many Whig leaders in Congress. So he could claim the support of neither party. In the midst of this fight for power, Mrs. Tyler died.

Three great diplomatic problems faced the Tyler administration at this time: the settlement of the Oregon boundary dispute with Great Britain, the settlement of the Maine boundary dispute with Great Britain; and the annexation of Texas.

Since 1818, the Oregon Territory had been jointly occupied by England and the United States. President John Quincy Adams had offered to settle the boundary question by accepting latitude 49° (the boundary line east of the Rocky Mountains) westward to the Pacific Ocean. But the British hoped to secure the Columbia River as the southern boundary of their portion. Negotiations were begun between the Secretary of State and the British minister at Washington, but nothing was settled during the Tyler administration. Daniel Webster, Secretary of State, carried on negotiations with Great Britain's representative on the disputed boundary between Maine and Canada; and, when these had been successfully concluded, Webster resigned from the Tyler Cabinet.

The Texas question was also solved before Tyler left office. Texas, having won its independence from Mexico, asked to be admitted to the United States. The people of the North objected because they felt that the huge territory, which might later be divided up into several states, would give too much power to the South. They felt, too, that such states would favor slavery, and they were against anything that would increase the number of slaves.

President Tyler, as a pro-slavery Executive, had been in favor of admitting Texas, but had been restrained by Daniel Webster, his Secretary of State. Now that Webster had resigned, Tyler negotiated a treaty for the annexation of Texas. By this treaty, the public lands of Texas were ceded to the United States; and her debt—amounting to ten million dollars—was assumed. Texas was offered statehood by a joint resolution which was rushed through Congress during the last few days of the Tyler administration and signed by the President. His act was approved by the people of Texas, at a convention called to vote on the question. In December, 1845, Congress voted Texas into the Union.

Tyler came back to the Democratic party in 1844 and sought re-election. Seeing that he had no popular following, he retired from politics, leaving the field to James K. Polk, the regular Democratic candidate. Before he left Washington, Tyler married Miss Julia Gardiner, of Gardiner's Island, New York. He was a widower of fifty-four, and she was thirty years his junior.

There have been many attempts to belittle President Tyler's achievements, without calling attention to his difficulties as a President without a party or a majority in Congress. But these facts remain: He recommended the strengthening of the laws for the suppression of the African slave trade. He fought the Whig newspapers which tried for four years to strip him of every shred of public esteem. He negotiated the first treaty between our country and China, granting Americans the right to live and trade in five ports. He transformed a Post Office Department with a debt of $500,000, into a debt-free organization. He took over the government at the end of a four-year depression, and left it—after paying a considerable portion of the national debt—with $7,000,000 in the Treasury.

When the Great Rebellion came and his state chose the South against the North, Tyler renounced his allegiance to the United States. He was chosen a member of the Confederate Provisional Congress, and was attending a meeting in Richmond when he became seriously ill. He died on January 18, 1862, at the age of seventy-one.

JAMES K. POLK

The First "Dark Horse" President

T WENTY years before James Knox
Polk was born, a small, but determined, group of settlers in
a little country town of the North Carolina frontier held a
meeting. On that nineteenth day of May, in the year 1775,
they firmly declared their freedom, in a document which read
this way:

"We, the citizens of Mecklenburg County, do hereby dis-
solve the political bonds which have connected us to the
mother-country, and hereby absolve ourselves from all allegiance to the British Crown, and we do hereby declare ourselves a free and independent people."

That straightforward statement, written more than a year
before our immortal Declaration of Independence was first
made public at Philadelphia, never became famous. But it
did show the spirit of those North Carolina pioneers. It also
shows the sturdy qualities of the Polk family. For it was the
grandfather and the great-uncle of James K. Polk who
helped to have that little declaration adopted in their Southern colony.

James Knox Polk's life began, not in the extreme poverty
that greeted Andrew Jackson, nor in the wealth and gracious
living enjoyed by Jefferson and Madison. James was born on
November 2, 1795, in Mecklenburg County, North Carolina,
where his ancestors had settled more than a century earlier.
His parents were Scotch-Irish and devout Presbyterians. He
was a thoughtful little boy, with large serious blue eyes, a
firm straight nose, and a wide pleasant mouth. Like other
lads of the frontier, he was well acquainted with the land and

the chores of farming, though he was too frail and slight for heavy labor.

When he was eleven years old, his father and mother, with a group of friends and neighbors, crossed the mountains into Tennessee. There they cleared new land, built their log cabins, and started a settlement.

Thomas Jefferson was President then, and young James was one of his staunch admirers. He listened eagerly to the talk of his elders who held many discussions about the policies and the progress of the infant United States of America.

James was educated in the country schools of the period, and though he was brought up on the frontier, his parents saved money enough to send him east to the University of North Carolina. There, in 1818, he was graduated at the head of his class, excelling in mathematics and the classics. He took up the study of law in the office of Felix Grundy of Nashville, and at the close of the year 1820 he was admitted to the bar. He became chief clerk for the House of Representatives of the Tennessee legislature.

On New Year's Day, 1824, he was married to Sarah Childress, of Rutherford County, Tennessee. A year after their marriage, he was sent to Washington to serve in Congress. He must have been a most satisfactory representative of the people, for he was continued in that office for the next fourteen years. He was made speaker of the House from 1835 to 1839, when he resigned to become governor of Tennessee.

James Polk was a firm believer in states' rights. As governor, and in later years, he used his influence toward strengthening state government, and was alarmed lest the federal government should become so strong as to try to interfere with slavery. He was also against internal improvements by the federal government, against the Bank of the United States, and against high tariffs.

At this time the question of Texas was agitating the United States. Texas had been an independent country since 1835. Organizing a government of their own, the Texans sought admission to the United States, but admission had long been postponed.

James Polk was in favor of the annexation of Texas, as were all the Southern states. They wanted more slave states in order that they might hold the balance of power against the states that were then being formed in the Northwest.

It was Mr. Polk's vigorous stand for annexation, and his reputation in public life for keeping his pledges, that won him the election to the presidency, an election which came as a complete surprise not only to him, but to the entire nation. He had modestly suggested to the Democratic National Convention of 1844 that he would be willing to be a candidate for the vice presidency. When the convention met in Baltimore, Van Buren had 146 votes, which was less than the two-thirds necessary for the nomination. The roll was called seven times without a nomination, and the name of James Knox Polk had not appeared among the eight candidates. On the eighth roll call the New Hampshire delegates voted for Polk, and on the ninth there was a stampede to him. Thus he is known in American history as the first "dark horse" to win a presidential nomination.

He was elected by a narrow margin, and was inaugurated on March 4, 1845, and the first big subject with which he had to deal was Texas. Tyler, just before his term as President expired, had signed the bill for admitting Texas to the union, and Congress in February, 1845, had adopted, by a simple majority vote, a resolution admitting Texas. The controversy now raged as to its southwestern boundary. Texans claimed it was the Rio Grande. Mexico insisted it was the Rio Nueces.

President Polk ordered American troops under General Zachary Taylor to cross the Nueces and hold the disputed territory. Soon they were attacked by Mexican forces and Polk quickly used this as an excuse for starting war. He declared that war had been begun "by an act of Mexico," and Congress supported him in this declaration. While General Taylor drove southward into Mexico, Americans on the Pacific coast, with help from American naval commanders, raised the stars and stripes in California.

The war with Mexico cost the United States twenty thousand lives and more than a hundred million dollars—fifteen millions of which were paid to Mexico. When peace was made, the United States had secured vast new territories, including what are now part of New Mexico, Arizona, part of Colorado, Utah, Nevada, and California.

Other new land came to the United States during President Polk's term of office. Oregon Territory (which then included the area that is now the state of Washington) was occupied jointly with the British. Polk offered to compromise with the British in settling upon a boundary line, and it was finally agreed that the forty-ninth parallel should become the permanent dividing line.

In addition to the acquisition of territories in the South, West, and Northwest, President Polk signed the Walker tariff bill to reduce taxes; and favored the setting up again of the Sub-Treasury system. During his administration there was a wave of prosperity in the country. Gold was discovered in California, and the settlers who flocked there were demanding that the country recently acquired from Mexico be admitted to the Union as a state. The old controversy about slavery was raised once again.

Since Polk was a Southerner and a slaveowner and was felt to be working for the South rather than for the good of the entire nation, he had no chance of being re-elected to a second term. As a matter of fact, he neither wanted nor sought the honor.

On March 4, 1849, he retired to his home in Nashville. Just a few months later, at the age of fifty-three, he died (June 15, 1849) and was buried on the grounds of his estate.

He takes his place in American history, not in the ranks of our greatest statesmen, but as a highly respected Chief Executive who worked hard and earnestly on behalf of his country, and did his best as he saw it.

ZACHARY TAYLOR

"Old Rough and Ready"

FROM the time that Zachary Taylor was old enough to know anything at all, he knew he wanted to be a soldier. His father, Colonel Richard Taylor, was an ardent patriot and a brave soldier in the Revolutionary War. He had many tales of hardship and heroism to tell his little son, and to all of them young Zachary listened eagerly, dreaming of the day when he, too, would march off to the music of the fife and drum.

Zachary Taylor, who became the twelfth President of the United States, was born on November 24, 1784, in Orange County, Virginia. Before he had learned to walk, his father, with his wife, the baby boy, and two older children, journeyed to Kentucky. There, in the pathless wilderness, a few miles from what is now the city of Louisville, the Taylor family settled. And in this rude frontier home, far from civilization, Zachary grew up.

Those childhood years must have been lonely ones for Zachary. There were no books, no social advantages, and very little opportunity to get an education. When Zachary was six he started in a small local school, then called common school. He was a bright, active boy, not especially studious, but quick to learn. Like all boys living on the frontier in those days, he knew at an early age how to handle a rifle. He never hesitated to use it, either, in defending his home from the unfriendly Indians who objected to the white man's entrance into Kentucky.

Zachary was not afraid of the Indians. He was not afraid of anything. Tramping through the woods, swimming in the Ohio River, spending long days in the open, fishing and hunting, he developed a strong and healthy body. As he grew to manhood, he was also known to the settlers as completely honest and straightforward, courageous and quick-thinking— the kind of a man who is good to have around when there is trouble brewing. And the young United States had plenty of trouble on its hands. Our relations with England became more and more threatening. British officials in Canada were doing their utmost to incite the Indians against us.

There was trouble in the South, too, and more and more young Zachary Taylor dreamed of being a soldier. Strong and self-reliant, he was eager to fight the various tribes which were ravaging our frontiers. His first chance came in 1808, when his father secured for him the commission of lieutenant in the United States Army, and he was sent to join our troops stationed at New Orleans.

Zachary was twenty-four then, and soon after his appointment he married Miss Margaret Smith, of Maryland. From the time of their marriage, she shared with him the dangerous and lonely frontier life which he faced all through his long army career.

That career was to continue for forty years, during which Zachary Taylor distinguished himself as a soldier. He fought in the War of 1812; in the Black Hawk War, 1832; and the Seminole War, 1837. Gradually he rose to the rank of colonel. In 1838, Colonel Taylor was promoted to brigadier general, and placed in command of the United States troops in Florida. After two years of warfare against the Seminole Indians, General Taylor requested a change of command, and was placed in charge of the Department of the Southwest.

His troops admired him for his courage. Perhaps, too, they

liked him because he was one of them, a man who understood and shared fully their dangers and hardships. They called him "Old Rough and Ready," a nickname which clung to him all his life.

In the spring of 1845, when Congress passed the joint resolution for the annexation of Texas, General Taylor was directed to have his troops ready for action on the Texas frontier. Meanwhile, Commodore Sloat was sent to the Pacific with seven ships of war, and nearly three thousand men. His secret orders were to seize and occupy San Francisco and other Mexican ports on the Pacific as soon as he received word that war had been declared between Mexico and the United States. No sooner was war declared than Taylor, now a major general, won victory after victory. His most famous battle was that of Buena Vista. There, with about five thousand men, he defeated General Santa Anna and his army of some twenty thousand Mexicans.

When he returned home, he was hailed everywhere as the hero of the hour. Gratitude and admiration were heaped upon him from every side. Even before he left Mexico his name had been suggested for the presidency by various sections of the Union, and soon the idea was taken up by the Whig party.

General Taylor was a soldier; he knew little about politics. He had had no experience in government, and was not, in his opinion, fitted for the presidency. But a large section of the American people wanted to reward the hero of Buena Vista. General Taylor's honesty and integrity only served to increase his popularity.

In June, 1848, the national convention of Whigs met in Philadelphia, and upon the third ballot General Taylor received a majority of votes. He was declared the nominee for President, and Millard Fillmore, of New York, was put on the same ticket as a candidate for Vice President.

In the election which followed, it soon became evident that General Taylor would be elected. The question of slavery was agitating the people and dividing the Union. President Taylor undertook to see that the laws passed by Congress were carried out. But he soon learned that as President he would have to do more than that—he would have to preserve the Union.

California had applied for admission as a state, but this was opposed by the southern members of Congress. The President was in favor of California's admission. It was proposed to give Utah and New Mexico territorial governments, but there again the question of the prohibition of slavery interfered. There was trouble, too, over the Texas boundary, Texas claiming part of New Mexico.

It may well be that if the old soldier had lived, he would have settled these difficulties, but the history of what he might have done will never be written. For about sixteen months after his inauguration Zachary Taylor became ill through a cold and exhaustion. Five days later, on July 9, 1850, "Old Rough and Ready" lay dead at the White House, having served only one-third of his term; and Vice President Fillmore was sworn in to take his place as President.

MILLARD FILLMORE

Another Frontier President

THE name of Abigail Powers is not well-known in American history. Yet this village schoolteacher probably did more than anyone else in guiding Millard Fillmore along the path which finally led to the White House.

When President Zachary Taylor died early in his term, Vice President Fillmore was well equipped by education and experience to step into his place. But if it hadn't been for the good influence of Abigail, Fillmore probably would never have attained office.

He was born on January 7, 1800, in Cayuga County, New York, when that western section of the state was a log-cabin outpost. His parents had come from New England to settle there. His father, who was a farmer, never had much money, and young Millard went to school only now and then. The common schools of the secluded section were not like those we have today. Books were scarce and expensive. The farm boy was bright, good-looking, and eager for knowledge, but he never even saw a history of the country, or a map of the United States, until he was nineteen years old.

When Millard was only fourteen, his father packed him off to the wilderness of Livingston County, and "bound" him, as was the custom in those days, to a clothier to learn his trade. While he was serving his apprenticeship as a wool-carder, the boy fell in love with Abigail Powers, the schoolteacher. She spurred him on, encouraging and helping him, and lending him books. The boy spent all his spare time studying. He read history, biography, and speeches; and in his heart grew the determination to become something better than a wool-carder. His eagerness to get ahead was noticed by a wealthy man, Judge Walter Wood. Judge Wood advised him to give up his trade, and offered him a place in his own law office. He also said he would lend him whatever money he needed to buy off the balance of his apprenticeship.

Millard Fillmore, then a fine-looking young man of nineteen, eagerly accepted. In 1823, when he was twenty-three years old, he was admitted to the court of common pleas and began the practice of law. Three years later he married his schoolteacher sweetheart, Abigail, the great romance of his life.

In the little village of Aurora, on Cayuga Lake, his law practice was limited, and there seemed no opportunity for fame and fortune. But he was beginning to be recognized, and in 1829 he was invited to become the partner of an elder member of the bar in Buffalo. Just before moving to that city, he started on his political career, taking his seat in the Assembly of New York state as representative from Erie County. In 1832 he was elected to the United States House of Representatives; and, after serving four terms, he was nominated for Governor of New York in 1844. He was badly defeated in the election, but he still remained in politics, as a member of the Whig party, and four years later they nominated him for Vice President, on the ticket headed by General Zachary Taylor.

Upon the death of the old General, Millard Fillmore made every effort to be a good statesman and leader. But he made some very grave mistakes in judgment. He had always been outspoken against slavery, but apparently he did not have the courage of his convictions, for when he became President he gave his support to what was called the Great Compromise of 1850. By signing this law—which provided for the hunting down of fugitive slaves who had managed to escape to Northern states, and returning them to their Southern owners—Fillmore became highly unpopular with his own followers in the North. It must be remembered here that the whole slavery question was causing more and more disunity between the North and the South. The population of the free states was rapidly increasing, and the slave states feared they would lose power in government affairs.

President Fillmore served out the term of Zachary Taylor, but was not nominated to run in the next election. He retired from office on March 4, 1853. A few years later, in 1856, Fillmore was nominated for President by the American or "Know Nothing" party. This party was much like a secret society; and its members were instructed, if asked what it stood for, to reply: "I know nothing." Fillmore, however, received the electoral votes of only one state.

His wife, Abigail, who had done so much to help him in his early years, died in 1853. During her stay in the White House, she lamented the lack of books to read. To please her, Congress was asked to set aside some money for a library. This was the beginning of the great library now at the White House.

Millard Fillmore, our thirteenth President, spent his last years in his home in Buffalo. He died there, at the age of seventy-four, on March 8, 1874.

FRANKLIN PIERCE

First President from New Hampshire

FOLLOWING Millard Fillmore, there came to the White House in Washington a man from the North, who, strangely enough, favored the South throughout his years in politics. His name was Franklin Pierce, and he was born at Hillsboro, New Hampshire, on November 23, 1804.

His father, a thrifty New England farmer, was General Benjamin Pierce, who had fought bravely with the small band of Americans at Lexington and Concord in the struggle for independence. General Pierce went right on fighting as a soldier in the Revolutionary War until the victory was won. Then, like so many other colonists during the years of America's beginnings, he continued to serve his country in sharing the responsibilities of government. He had little book learning, but he was a man of integrity and he was highly popular with his New Hampshire neighbors. The state sent him to the legislature, and kept him there for twelve years. Later he served one term as governor of New Hampshire.

Franklin was the sixth in a family of eight children; and, with his father prominent in politics, he heard throughout his boyhood many discussions of state and federal affairs. He was a handsome lad, with an engaging personality and a lively disposition. When he was sixteen he was sent to Bowdoin College, at Brunswick, Maine. There he met Nathaniel Hawthorne, who was also a student, and legend has it that the two boys, along with some of their classmates, were mixed up in many a college prank when they should have been studying their lessons. Franklin and the famous author of *The Scarlet Letter* were close friends as long as they lived, though one chose literature and the other took the path that led to the presidency.

When young Pierce was graduated in 1824, he returned home to Hillsboro. Soon afterward he decided to become a lawyer and entered the office of Judge Woodbury, of Portsmouth, as a student. When he was admitted to the bar a few years later he began the practice of law in his own home town.

In 1829, Hillsboro elected him as its representative in the state legislature, where he served four years. Then, only twenty-nine years old, Franklin Pierce was sent to Congress. There, quiet and modest, he listened carefully to proceedings and learned much from the older and more experienced legislators. He served two terms as a member of Congress; he was elected a United States Senator before he was thirty-three, taking his seat just as Martin Van Buren commenced his administration.

In 1834, Franklin Pierce married Miss Jane Appleton, daughter of the former president of Bowdoin College. After his marriage, he felt that he ought to resign from public office, which paid little in those days, and get back to his law practice where he could make a better living. He resigned from the Senate, later refused a second election, and also declined the nomination for the governorship of New Hampshire. When the appointment of Attorney General of the United States was offered to him, he turned that down.

But he did not hesitate to leave his thriving law practice when the Mexican War broke out in 1846. He enlisted as a private at once, answering his country's call, and in 1847 he was appointed colonel and later promoted to the rank of brigadier general. He took an active part in the battles fought in Mexico, and led an army from Vera Cruz to reinforce General Scott in his attack on the Mexican capital, though illness prevented him from the final triumph of helping to capture the city. He was disabled for a time by the fall of his horse at the battle of Contreras, but remained with the Army until the war ended.

When General Pierce resigned from the Army he returned to Concord, where he resumed his law practice. He was forty-three years old at this time and certainly had no expectation that, within six years, he would be moving into the White House as Chief Executive.

The Democratic Convention met in Baltimore on June 1, 1852, and adopted the two-thirds rule. The roll was called thirty-five times, with none of the presidential candidates receiving the two-thirds necessary for the nomination. On the thirty-fifth roll call, Pierce had fifteen votes. When finally on the forty-ninth call the ballots were counted, all but six votes were cast for this dark-horse candidate from New Hampshire.

Franklin Pierce was elected President of the United States in a sweeping victory, and was inaugurated on March 4, 1853. Both North and South had supported him in the election. The Southern Democrats liked him because he was in accord with their views on slavery. He had supported the Kansas-Nebraska bill, which set apart Kansas and Nebraska and agreed to let the people who settled there decide for themselves whether their states should be free or slave. This bill produced considerable argument because, according to the Missouri Compromise of 1820, all territory north of the southern boundary of Missouri was declared to be "free soil."

But Congress voted to repeal the Missouri Compromise and to allow the people to make their own decision.

During the Franklin Pierce administration, that question of slavery kept the nation in a constant turmoil; arguments flamed higher and higher. Elsewhere in the world slavery was dying out. Great Britain had abolished it in her possessions in the West Indies. Mexico had abolished it. Even Spain, which then owned Cuba, was considering the freeing of slaves on the island.

In the United States, just as soon as the Missouri Compromise was repealed, there was a wild scramble. Settlers flocked to Kansas from North and South, one side wanting it to be a free state, the other side insisting that it be slave. There, with bitter feelings between the opposing factions, the first blood was shed in a struggle which not many years later was to develop to the proportions of civil war.

And Franklin Pierce continued to throw the influence of his high office with those who favored slavery. As soon as he took office, he chose his Cabinet from Eastern and Southern leaders, and that powerful Cabinet he kept all through his four years in the presidency. The whole country recognized at once that their new President was pro-slave, and could not even be expected to remain neutral. In the midst of all this agitation in the United States, he did not neglect our foreign affairs.

During his administration, the United States consular service was reorganized; and the Gadsden Purchase was completed, by treaty with Mexico, adding more than 45,000 square miles to the area of our country. This land is now part of Arizona and New Mexico. A treaty was also signed, in

1854, opening Japanese ports to American trade. Pierce planned the annexation of Cuba, and negotiations were begun for the acquisition of Hawaii and for a naval base in Santo Domingo, and Russia was asked whether she would sell Alaska. He directed America's minister to Spain to consult with James Buchanan and John Y. Mason, American ministers to Great Britain and France, about the annexation of Cuba. They met in Ostend in October, 1854, and signed a report known as the Ostend Manifesto to the effect that since France and Great Britain were busy with the Crimean War, it might be an opportune time for our country to annex Cuba. The report aroused antislavery Americans who were strongly opposed to such a move. The project fell through, and nothing was accomplished concerning Alaska, Hawaii, or Santo Domingo.

While President, Pierce used the surplus in the Treasury to reduce the national debt and urged a reduction in the tariff to prevent the accumulation of another surplus.

As his administration terminated, the "Northern man with Southern principles" grew less popular and the Whig party broke up. Those who opposed the repeal of the Missouri Compromise, and objected to the Fugitive Slave Law, joined with the free-soil party and formed what has since been known as the Republican party, and James Buchanan was elected Democratic President.

With the entire country in a state of unrest, and the dark shadows of civil war spreading across the land, Franklin Pierce retired on March 4, 1857, and returned to his New England home. He lived to see the end of that armed conflict between the North and the South, though he took no part in it.

On October 8, 1869, in his sixty-fifth year, he died quietly and peacefully in the New Hampshire hills, and was buried at Concord.

JAMES BUCHANAN

President of a Divided Nation

IF James Buchanan could have foreseen the future, would he ever have wanted to become President of the United States? He took office at a time of crisis when the North and the South were bitterly attacking each other, and those two fighting words, "slave" and "free," were on every tongue. To be the Chief Executive of the nation in those times took plenty of courage and wisdom, and there are some historians who say that Buchanan had neither. Others who have carefully studied the records of the past believe that he was a devout patriot, but that he relied too much on appeasement. However, in considering the conduct of his administration, all agree that he was faced with tremendous problems.

Buchanan was born in a small frontier town in Franklin County, Pennsylvania, on April 23, 1791. The place where his father's cabin stood was called Stony Batter. It was a wild and beautiful spot in a gorge of the Allegheny Mountains, to which his father had emigrated from the north of Ireland in 1783. Five years later the young Scotch-Irish settler married Elizabeth Spear, and, with his young bride, staked his claim, built a log hut, and opened a clearing. Here James was born and lived for the first eight years of his life. Then the family moved to Mercersburg, where the boy went to school. At the age of fourteen he entered Dickinson College, at Carlisle. At eighteen he was graduated and took up the study of law at Lancaster. He was admitted to the bar in 1812, and had just started his law practice when President James Madison announced the United States was at war with England. Young Buchanan, twenty-one-year-old patriot, thereupon dropped his work and enlisted as a private to fight against the British.

After that was over, James Buchanan was touched by a tragedy which cast an unhappy shadow over his entire life. He fell in love with a young girl named Anne Coleman, the daughter of one of the wealthiest men in Lancaster. They became engaged and all went well until, in the summer of 1819, he received a letter from her breaking off the engagement. Evil gossip, without foundation in truth, had led her to write the letter, and she would not be reconciled. A few months later, while visiting in Philadelphia, Anne Coleman died. The shock and grief nearly broke young Buchanan's heart. He never loved another woman, and remained a bachelor all through his life. When, at his death many years later, executors opened his bank vault, they found among his papers a little package of love letters from his sweetheart of long ago. Written on the outside was his request that they be burned without breaking the seal on them, and this was done.

After six years in state politics, Buchanan, in 1820, was elected to Congress. At that time he belonged to the Federalist party. Later he left that party to join the Jackson–Van Buren Democrats. In 1828, when Andrew Jackson was running for President, he worked actively in the campaign. When Jackson was elected, Buchanan was given an important chairmanship in the new Congress. Four years later President Jackson appointed him American minister to Russia. A year after his return to the United States in 1833 he was elected to a seat in the United States Senate, where he remained for ten years, vigorously supporting the administration.

In the Democratic convention of 1844, James Buchanan was Pennsylvania's choice for President. In that deadlocked convention, he turned his votes to the support of James K.

Polk, the dark-horse candidate who was elected. Buchanan was made Secretary of State in the Polk administration.

In the four years that followed (when Zachary Taylor died in office and was succeeded by Millard Fillmore, his Vice President), James Buchanan remained in private life. His experience and ability, however, enabled him to exert a powerful influence in national affairs. He identified himself with the pro-slavery party, and gave his enthusiastic support to the compromise measures of 1850. And when Franklin Pierce became President, he appointed Buchanan minister to Great Britain.

As minister he received some highly unfavorable criticism through his connection with the Ostend Manifesto of 1854. (As we have seen, this manifesto suggested that the United States buy Cuba from Spain, and that, if Spain would not sell, our country would have every right to seize the island.)

In the meantime, while Buchanan was in England, the controversy over the Kansas-Nebraska bill and the whole question of slavery became more and more bitter at home. President Pierce was widely criticized for his championship of the South.

With all this dissension at home, the Democrats were looking about for a candidate to succeed Pierce. Buchanan had had years of experience; his sympathies lay with the pro-slavery party. They placed his name at the head of their ticket, and on March 4, 1857, James Buchanan was inaugurated President of a United States that was no longer united. Two days later, the Supreme Court handed down its decision on the famous Dred Scott case.

Dred Scott was a slave. His master took him from Missouri to Illinois, permitted him to marry in the free state, and in

1838 took him back to Missouri. After the death of his master, Dred was hired out to various persons in Missouri. He sued for his freedom, but lost the suit. Before this decision was made, the widow of Dred's master deeded him, his wife, and their child, to a relative in New York. Dred, with the aid of white friends, again brought suit. Losing again, he took an appeal to the Supreme Court. This high court declared, in effect, that the Missouri Compromise had been null and void from the beginning, and that Congress had no power under the Constitution to exclude slavery from the territories. Public opinion flamed over the decision.

Civil war already was raging in Kansas; John Brown tried to start a slave insurrection; the Southern states were threatening secession. And while all this was going on, President Buchanan kept changing his mind on every important question which came up. First, he said that no state had a right to break away from the Union, then he stated that the government had no power to prevent secession. He declared it his duty to call out the Army and Navy to enforce federal laws, yet he did nothing. As a result of his inability to make up his mind, both the North and the South lost faith in his leadership. The administration was falling to pieces. Buchanan's Cabinet members were resigning. During the closing months of his administration South Carolina broke away from the Union, and within two months six other Southern states had followed. Buchanan wrung his hands in despair.

During the last month of Buchanan's tragic administration, there were two Presidents in the country. Jefferson Davis, Senator from Mississippi, announced his state's withdrawal from the Union, and then himself withdrew from the United States Senate. Two weeks later, the newly established confederacy chose him as its leader. Davis was a brilliant states-man; he had fought heroically in the Mexican War and served his state long and well.

President Buchanan was unable to hold the United States to-gether; there were many in Congress who sympathized with the Secessionists. Congress adjourned without taking any steps to prevent the dissolution of the United States, and Buchanan marked time, waiting until he could leave Wash-ington and the entire baffling situation to Abraham Lin-coln, who was quietly watching events from his home, stead-fast in purpose and firm for the preservation of the Union at all costs.

Abused by both sides, unhappy and forlorn, the man who bungled the opportunity offered him by destiny retired at the close of his term to his home in Wheatland, Pennsylvania. Seven years later, on June 1, 1868, he died.

A grateful niece, Harriet Lane, whom he had brought up through an orphaned childhood, bequeathed one hundred thousand dollars for the erection of a monument in Wash-ington to his memory. She never wavered in her loyalty to James Buchanan, who left behind him what seems like a record of failure and confusion.

ABRAHAM LINCOLN

"With Malice Toward None"

THE story of Abraham Lincoln is that of a man who walked the earth gently, yet who left a shining imprint on the pages of our history. It is a story that never grows old. It is as much a part of America as the plains and the hills and the rivers. Homely, simple, backwoods-born, reared in poverty as Lincoln was, his achievements are glowing proof that lack of opportunity need not spell obscurity and defeat. Life slapped him down again and again, but in the hard school of experience he overcame obstacles which would have discouraged less hardy souls. And even at the height of his popularity, he did not lose the humility which always strikes a chord of sympathy and admiration in human hearts.

All through his life Lincoln put the interests of the people and the welfare of the nation above his own. Nor did he seek to make himself famous. When biographers came to him, eager for every detail of his early years, his dark eyes twinkled and he laughed aloud. "It is a great piece of folly," he said, "to attempt to make anything out of me or my early life. It can all be condensed into a single sentence, and that sentence you will find in Gray's 'Elegy'—'the short and simple annals of the poor.'"

But Lincoln could not hide the great human qualities which made him a beloved figure. He was revered because he was honest and sincere; remembered, not only as an outstanding American who freed the slaves, but also as a brilliant statesman. He takes his place among the immortals because the principles he lived by and lived for were, and still are, the principles of true democracy. He was a man with a mission—

a man with a dream—who had the faith, the understanding, and the will to turn that dream into reality.

None of Lincoln's ancestors showed signs of greatness. They landed in Massachusetts in the year 1637. With the adventurous spirit of pioneers, they pushed down into New Jersey, then over into Pennsylvania. Later they settled in Virginia, where Lincoln's father, Tom, was born. From there, they went to Kentucky, where Lincoln's grandfather was killed by Indians.

Tom Lincoln was only four years old when his father died. History does not reveal much about his early struggles, but we know he was among the poorest of the poor, that he was never taught to read or write. As soon as he was big enough to work, he went out into the world, a friendless, ragged, wandering boy, who spent his youth as a laborer in the fields of others. He was twenty-eight when he married Nancy Hanks, the daughter of another family of poor Kentucky emigrants, who had also come from Virginia. In 1808 Tom and Nancy Lincoln with their baby, Sarah, moved to a wilderness spot about two miles from Hodgenville, where Tom put up a cabin of logs cut from the nearby timber.

There, in that little one-room cabin, beside a quiet creek in Larue County, Kentucky, their son was born on Sunday, February 12, 1809. "We'll call him Abraham," said Nancy Hanks, "after his grandfather."

Two or three years later the family moved some ten miles to the Knob Creek farm. It was there that little Abe first trudged off to school, to begin his education as he himself said later, "by littles." He went to one teacher for about two months, and to another for three. He had less than a year's schooling all his life. Later, when he went to Congress, he made a joke about that. In filling out a questionnaire, beside the word "Education," he wrote into the blank space a single word: "Defective."

When the boy Lincoln was eight, the family took to the road again. On the seven-day journey to their new home in Indiana, they had to cut their way through the forest to reach the place near Little Pigeon Creek. Once more, Tom Lincoln, with the help of his wife and children, raised a cabin. It was only a rude, temporary shelter—a shed of poles, with walls on three sides, and the front open to wind and weather. But Nancy and the youngsters were accustomed to hardship. They had never known anything else. For a whole year they managed, while Abe and his father set about clearing a little patch of ground for planting corn, and building a better cabin for a permanent home.

But the comforts of life which Nancy Hanks dreamed of were something she was never to know. An epidemic which the pioneers called "the milk sickness" spread through the little community, and it struck her fatally. Little Abe, struggling to hold back the tears which filled his dark eyes, helped his father and Dennis Hanks make the coffin. With a knife the boy whittled wooden pegs to fit into the holes his father bored to hold the rude box together. Abe was ten years old then—too young to understand the tragedy, too old not to feel the deep aching hurt of his loss—as his mother was buried beneath the tree near the cabin.

In the lonely months that followed, Abe and his sister Sally struggled along as best they could without the loving care of the mother they had lost. Dirty, ragged, unkempt, and ill-fed, they must have been a sorry sight to the widow, Sally Bush Johnston, whom Tom Lincoln married thirteen months later. But it was a wonderful day for those neglected youngsters when she came to the Indiana cabin. With her she brought three children of her own, but she took the small strangers to her heart at once. She washed them, combed out their matted hair, and dressed them comfortably in clothing which she had made for her own little ones. She fixed up the cabin with her furniture and made Tom Lincoln put in windows and a door. Within a very short time, order and neatness prevailed. She brought laughter and good cheer into that desolate home, and she brought to little Abe Lincoln his first sense of well-being, making him look, as she herself said, "a little more human." From that time on, a new light of hope burned within him, and he never ceased to adore the step-mother whom he often referred to in later years as his "angel mother."

Earnestly he studied the few books he could get, reading late into the night by the flickering light of the fire. The Holy Bible, the poems of Shakespeare, Aesop's Fables, and Weems's *History of George Washington* opened up a whole new world to his eager mind. And in this world of magic words he found delight. He declaimed aloud as he worked in the fields, and when he was hired out to labor, he made speeches and told jokes as he went about building fires, tending neighbors' babies, splitting rails, and doing all sorts of odd jobs. Everybody liked the tall, lanky youth with the homely face and the quick sense of humor. And hard work seemed to agree with him, for he shot up into a young giant of six feet four, with a huge strength that was the envy of all the lads for miles around.

In April, 1828, when he was nineteen, his first chance came to see the world which lay beyond the green hills of Indiana.

James Gentry was sending his young son, Allen, down to New Orleans on a flatboat loaded with produce. Gentry had noticed how capable, honest, and dependable Abe Lincoln was, and he was glad to hire him to go along on the trip. The two young men floated down the Ohio and the Mississippi into the busy Louisiana port, where Abe was enthralled with the excitements of the busy city. He saw strange people in bright dress—Spanish, French, Mexicans, Creoles, and Indians—chattering and singing in their native tongues. He saw laborers working along the teeming waterfront, and heard their weird, sad songs. There were elegant mansions and immense warehouses, and a church. All these young Lincoln saw; and he saw, too, with troubled eyes, slaves in chains on the auction block, being bought and sold like horses. "If I ever get a chance to hit that thing," he said later, "I'll hit it, and hit it hard!"

On his return home, he found his father getting ready to strike the trail north and west into Illinois. Cheerfully he set to work, helping build the oxcarts for the moving. And at their journey's end in a new settlement near Decatur, he helped to cut the logs for the cabin, split the rails for fences, and plow the fields for planting. As he swung his ax, and made deep furrows in the black soil, he thought tall thoughts. He was twenty-one now—free, and strong, and grown to manhood. When the family was settled, he said good-by, and started off, wearing a faded suit of blue jeans, and carrying his few small belongings in a red bandana handkerchief.

He had no money, but he knew he could earn his keep by the work of his big, strong hands. Coming to the town of New Salem, like "a piece of floating driftwood," as he remarked, he soon made friends. When he wasn't flatboating, keeping store, splitting rails, or doing other chores, he was poring over Blackstone's *Commentaries,* absorbing the fundamentals of law. And whatever he was doing, or whatever he was saying, the plain people with whom he lived and worked noticed him and looked up to him and asked his advice.

When volunteers were called to fight the Black Hawk Indians, in the spring of 1832, Lincoln promptly enrolled. In his company were his neighbors and friends, who elected him captain by an enthusiastic majority. Later on, in each of the two brief autobiographies he wrote, he mentioned that this honor gave him more satisfaction than any other in his life.

The young volunteers saw little of battle, though they were often hungry, weary, and in danger. Lincoln made jokes about his military service after that. Once, in a speech to Congress, he said:

"By the way, Mr. Speaker, did you know I am a military hero? Yes, sir; in the days of the Black Hawk War I fought, bled and came away. I did not break my sword for I had none to break . . . If General Cass saw any live, fighting Indians, it was more than I did; but I had a good many bloody struggles with the mosquitoes!"

The discharged volunteers returned to New Salem only ten days before the August election. Before starting off to war, Lincoln had announced himself as a candidate for the legislature from Sangamon County. He did not win that election, but he received the vote of his own community almost to a man—277 votes against 3—which encouraged him to try again.

In the meantime, he acted as postmaster, did some surveying, and made a few dollars here and there by harvesting, helping at the mill, and splitting rails. He was becoming more and more interested in public affairs and he had very definite ideas against the spread of slavery into the territories. He made simple, forceful speeches which reached out to the people and won their support.

Late in November, 1834, they sent him to the state legislature at Vandalia, which was then the capital of Illinois. During that first term, he looked, listened, and learned much.

When he returned to Vandalia the following year, tragedy waited for him. The world that spring seemed filled with wild happiness. Gentle, blond, little Ann Rutledge was as deeply in love with him as he was with her. Together they made their joyous plans. Ann would go to boarding school the following fall; Lincoln would work hard and pay off his debts; then they would be married. But in August, Ann was stricken with a fever. The doctors could not save her life. For weeks Lincoln wandered about, beside himself with grief. A sadness came into his eyes that never left them through all his later years.

After a time some measure of self-control returned, and in the years that followed (1835-1842) he served for three more sessions in the Illinois state legislature. During his summers, when the legislature was not in session, he continued the study of law, and in the spring of 1837 he left New Salem to hang out his shingle in Springfield. The men and women who took their troubles to his modest law office came away with a new conception of justice—a justice that they felt more in their hearts than in their minds, for Lincoln's logic and experience were mingled always with his great understanding. He knew that laws and rules and writs in themselves are cold and that it is only when a man can *feel* them that he knows them. He never undertook a case unless he honestly felt his client was in the right, and often he gave his services without pay so that justice might be served.

It was in Springfield that Lincoln met pretty, strong-minded Mary Todd. Their courtship did not run smoothly, and Lincoln seemed to be in doubt about wanting to be married. Some said she jilted him; others have told how he failed to appear at the hour set for their wedding. There were quarrels and separations, but friends finally brought them together again, and they were married on November 4, 1842.

Life was going more pleasantly for Abraham Lincoln now. He had a home, a law practice, and he was highly popular, not only in his own community but in the state. In 1846 he was elected by the people of Illinois to represent them in Congress.

Going to Washington must have been a wonderful adventure to the Lincolns and their two small children, but the capital as they first saw it was a sprawling, untidy town. Cows, pigs, geese, and chickens roamed in the unpaved streets and alleys. Pigsties, cowsheds and stables cluttered back yards. Water was supplied by wells, and the only lights at night were oil lamps along a small strip of Pennsylvania Avenue. When Congress was not in session, even those were not lighted. Gangs of slaves, on their way to the auction blocks, shuffled in chains through the streets.

Lincoln served only one term in Congress, then returned to Springfield to settle down to his law practice. But all the time he was becoming more and more excited about the growing controversy over slavery. In a letter to Joshua F. Speed he wrote: "Our progress in degeneracy appears to me to be pretty rapid. As a nation we began by declaring that 'all men are created equal.' We now practically read it 'all men are created equal except Negroes.' "

Lincoln did not hesitate to express himself firmly on the slavery question, or any other, even though his opinions might create political enemies. About the Mexican situation, which was still being hotly argued, he said: "People who claim this war with Mexico is fair and right remind me of an old farmer in Illinois who told me one day, 'I ain't greedy about land, Mr. Lincoln, I only wants what joins mine.' "

It was natural that a man like Lincoln should take this view of the Mexican War. All through his life he amazed his friends and associates by his complete honesty. Shortly after he was elected a Congressman, he returned to his Whig friends $199.25 of the $200 which they had given him to spend on his campaign. "You see, I didn't need it all," he explained. "All the traveling I did was on my own horse. Wherever I went, my friends entertained me. And I only spent 75¢ for a barrel of cider to treat some farm hands."

"Seventy-five cents to get to Congress!" the man said, laughing. "That's pretty good!" And he went off to tell his friends the story of Mr. Lincoln's campaign expenses. No wonder everybody always called him "Honest Abe"!

When Stephen A. Douglas, Senator from Illinois, came out in favor of the Kansas-Nebraska bill (permitting territories to decide for themselves whether they would become slave states), Abraham Lincoln put aside his decision to keep out of politics. He felt strongly that this was his chance to strike out against slavery, and he left his law business more and more often to make speeches against Douglas. The fame of Lincoln began to spread all over the country, and by 1856, the tall, lanky lad who had split rails in the wilderness received 110 votes for Vice President at the Philadelphia convention of the new Republican party. In 1858, when Senator Douglas came up for re-election, Abraham Lincoln came forth as his opposing candidate and captured the attention of the people with his famous statement: "A house divided against itself cannot stand."

Lincoln did not win in the election, but he accomplished something far more important. The earnestness and logic of his speeches made him a compelling figure. Everybody talked about the great man from Illinois who was speaking out against the extension of slavery. Everybody wanted to see him, to hear him. For a year he traveled through the East and the Middle West, and in the spring of 1860 the Republican party nominated him for President. In the fall he was elected.

And even during the convention, Lincoln, in all humility, remarked: "I hope they select some abler man than myself."

While Abraham Lincoln waited gravely to take his place in the White House and shoulder the tremendous burden of office which lay ahead, President Buchanan did nothing about the rising tide of secession among the Southern states. By the time Lincoln took office, the Union seemed to be falling apart. Seven states had seceded and set up a confederate government under Jefferson Davis.

Lincoln refused to recognize secession. No state, he declared, could ever really be separated from the Union. He warned the rebel states that he would tolerate no interference with authority. He yearned for peace, but keeping the states together as one nation was his foremost thought. "My course," he said, "is as plain as a turnpike road. It is marked out by the Constitution."

Secession was only one of the problems which worried the new President. When he was inaugurated on March 4, 1861, he was not greeted with enthusiasm. He was closely guarded because of threats of assassination. Few buildings were decorated in his honor. The people seemed anxious and depressed. Only at the close of his inaugural address did they rouse themselves to applaud him. He stood there in the raw March wind, in his tall hat, new black suit, and white shirt, and his whole heart was in his final words: "In your hands, my dissatisfied countrymen, and not in mine, is the momentous issue of civil war. The government will not assail you. You can have no conflict without being yourselves the aggressors. *You* have no oath registered in heaven to *destroy* the government, while *I* shall have the most solemn one to preserve, protect, and defend it."

In the bloodstained months and years that followed, he never swerved in the carrying out of that oath to preserve the Union. Confederate soldiers opened fire on Fort Sumter on April 12, 1861. Thus the Civil War began.

At first, he was hopeful that rebellion would be brief. But within a few weeks after war was declared, the call went out for more than 80,000 soldiers and sailors. The sadness of war, the weeping of mothers, the hardships, the hospitals filled with wounded, and the long lists of the dead weighed heavily on Lincoln's heart and on the heart of the nation. Lincoln's own little son, Willie, a bright little boy of eleven, was taken ill and died at the White House in February, 1862. Grief and loss were close companions to him. Again and again he visited his generals at the front, and often he went out of his way to comfort a stricken mother, or stop in and see the wounded and speak to them personally.

In his efforts to bring peace and restore unity, he urged the Confederate States to free their slaves, and receive from the federal government the money for which they could have been sold. By this time, though, the South was in no mood for settlement. They would not listen to his offer.

Accordingly on September 22, 1862, he issued the warning that if the states in rebellion did not return to the Union by the following January 1, he would issue a second proclamation declaring the slaves in such states to "be forever free." That warning was ignored, and on New Year's Day, 1863, Lincoln completed the great document on which he had been working for weeks, and signed his name to the Emancipation Proclamation which gave freedom to millions of slaves, and assured freedom for untold millions yet unborn.

The war dragged on. But the tide was turning. Then, in July came the battle of Gettysburg, and General Lee ordered a retreat of the Southern forces to the Potomac. The following November 19, (1863), a soldiers' national cemetery was dedicated at Gettysburg, and Lincoln offered what he modestly called "half a dozen words of consecration."

We all know those immortal words:

Fourscore and seven years ago our fathers brought forth on this continent a new nation, conceived in liberty, and dedicated to the proposition that all men are created equal.

Now we are engaged in a great civil war, testing whether that nation, or any nation so conceived and so dedicated, can long endure. We are met on a great battlefield of that war. We have come to dedicate a portion of that field as a final resting-place for those who here gave their lives that that nation might live. It is altogether fitting and proper that we should do this.

But in a larger sense, we cannot dedicate—we cannot consecrate—we cannot hallow—this ground. The brave men, living and dead, who struggled here, have consecrated it far above our poor power to add or detract. The world will little note nor long remember what we say here, but it can never forget what they did here. It is for us, the living, rather, to be dedicated here to the unfinished work which they who fought here have thus far so nobly advanced. It is rather for us to be here dedicated to the great task remaining before us—that from these honored dead we take increased devotion to that cause for which they gave the last full measure of devotion— that we here highly resolve that these dead shall not have died in vain; that this nation, under God, shall have a new birth of freedom; and that government of the people, by the people, for the people, shall not perish from the earth.

In those few, simple words, the record of his compassion, his simplicity, and his high resolve are written indelibly on the minds of all Americans. Yet, there were many other, less well-known messages which show the great humane qualities of Abraham Lincoln.

He pardoned many prisoners of war. On one pardon he wrote: "If you have not shot Denis McCarthy, don't." And on another occasion: "I think this boy can do us more good above ground than under it."

As Lincoln's first term as President ended, it was clear that he would be re-elected to office. In the summer of 1864, with the South facing defeat, and the entire nation sick of war, there was hope for a just peace. On March 4, 1865, with fighting still going on, Lincoln's second inauguration was held. It was quite a different picture from his first. As he rose to speak, a roar of applause shook the air, and a tremendous shout went up from the crowds gathered to see him. Lincoln had found his place in the hearts of the people, a place which was even more firmly established as he finished speaking, with these words:

> With malice toward none; with charity for all; with firmness in the right, as God gives us to see the right, let us strive on to finish the work we are in; to bind up the nation's wounds; to care for him who shall have borne the battle, and for his widow, and his orphan—to do all which may achieve and cherish a just and lasting peace among ourselves, and with all nations.

That peace of which he spoke so eloquently came one month later, on April 9, 1865, when General Robert E. Lee surrendered to General Ulysses S. Grant at Appomattox Court House, Virginia. Four years of war were over. The eleven states of the South, which had fought a brave, but losing, fight, gave up their dream.

Abraham Lincoln, who had just returned from a trip to the front and a conference with General Grant, heard the glad news before he went to bed that night, his face shining with relief and joy. Next morning, when the newspapers brought the full news of war's end, crowds went trooping to the White House to cheer the man who had saved the Union, emancipated the slaves, and brought victory.

Now, for Lincoln, there lay ahead the task of erasing the bitterness between the Northern and Southern states, of tempering justice with mercy for the defeated South, and straightening out the problems that follow in the trail of war. He knew he would have trouble in trying to persuade the victorious North that the states in rebellion were not enemies, but part of the United States, as they had always been. Yet, through his faith in God and country, he had come thus far. He felt he would have the strength to carry on through the difficult months ahead.

He went to the theater with Mrs. Lincoln on the evening of April 14, just a few days after the war's end. They were thinking ahead to the end of the second term, when they could go back home to Illinois to pass the rest of their lives quietly and happily. As the Lincolns and a group of their friends entered the President's box, the band played "Hail to the Chief." The President bowed. The play, *Our American Cousin,* went on. Then John Wilkes Booth, the assassin, noiselessly opened the door of the box, put a pistol to the President's head, and fired. The cry rang out: "Stop him! He has shot the President!" But no cry came from the lips of Lincoln. Without a sound, he slumped forward. Early next morning, without regaining consciousness, he died.

They carried him to rest back to the soil of Illinois, back home where he had so often longed to go. And a grieving nation mourned its great loss.

We say he died, on that fatal Saturday back in 1865, but look back through the long years. Listen back through the years. All over our land there are statues of the tall, thin figure in the black coat. Down in our nation's capital the massive Lincoln Memorial stands. All over the world there are books about him, and pictures of him. We say he died, but Booth could not kill the soul of Abraham Lincoln with a bullet, any more than bullets ever can kill the souls of free men. The voice of Lincoln still rises clear and steadfast over these United States today, in those words he uttered long ago:

. . . that government of the people, by the people, for the people, shall not perish from the earth.

ANDREW JOHNSON
The President Who Never Went to School

As a shocked and angry people mourned the death of President Abraham Lincoln, Vice President Andrew Johnson was hastily sworn in to take his place. Andrew Johnson, as U.S. Senator from Tennessee, had spoken against Lincoln in the 1860 campaign and had spent his own money to help try to bring about Lincoln's defeat. Johnson was a Southern Democrat of the Jacksonian school; Lincoln a Northern Republican. Johnson had owned slaves, while Lincoln was planning to set them free in the South. Yet, when the main forces of the army of the South had been driven out of Tennessee, and Lincoln needed a military governor, he gave Senator Johnson this dangerous and thankless task. And when Lincoln was preparing in 1864 to run for re-election, and needed a vice presidential candidate, Johnson received the nomination.

This choice, probably, was Lincoln's; he was a farsighted man. One day the war would come to an end, and he would need a Southerner to help "bind up the nation's wounds" and achieve a just and lasting peace. What better man could he find than Andrew Johnson? The Senator was the only Southern member of Congress who had repudiated the secession of his state. He was one of the best-known champions of the common man in the United States. He had been governor of Tennessee. He believed wholeheartedly in the Constitution. He had climbed the political ladder without the aid of a party machine. He had become a loyal supporter of the Lincoln administration. In addition to all this, Johnson was a bold and eloquent speaker and he was in favor of freeing the slaves. As far back as the Buchanan administration, he had denounced secession of the Southern states. That required courage, when you realize that his home was in Tennessee.

Though Lincoln and Johnson were different in temperament, they were alike in many respects. They both believed that the Union was the safeguard of democracy and that if the Southern states were permitted to secede, the government would be labeled a failure throughout the world. They had been born of "poor-white" parents. Each had acquired, during his boyhood, a smattering of knowledge. Johnson never went to school a single day; his father had died when the boy was only five years old. Both Lincoln and Johnson were born in log cabins; and both had known poverty. Both were members of the Thirtieth Congress (1847–1849). They belonged to different political parties, but they had many things in common.

Andrew Johnson, who became the seventeenth President of the United States, was born on December 29, 1808, at Raleigh, capital of North Carolina. His father had been a captain in the state militia; now he was a sexton—and the porter at the state bank. His mother, before her marriage, had been a maid at a Raleigh inn. She supported the boy after his father's death, and at the age of ten he was apprenticed to a tailor.

A Raleigh gentleman (presumably a customer of the tailor) was in the habit of reading to the apprentices as they worked. Mostly he read the orations of British statesmen, such as the younger Pitt and Charles James Fox. Young Johnson thought they were wonderful; he wanted the book, even though he was not then able to read. He offered to buy it; but when the gentleman saw how earnest he was, he gave the book to him. The boy's ambitions were aroused.

By the time he was sixteen, Johnson, having learned his

trade, worked as a journeyman tailor for two years; then followed in the steps of his boyhood hero, Andrew Jackson, and migrated to Tennessee. At Greenville, near the foot of the Great Smoky Mountains, he set up a tailor shop of his own. He had brought his mother; and within two years he was able to buy a home and a small farm for her. He was also able to marry at the age of nineteen; and the girl, Eliza McCardle, was one of a group who had watched him drive into town with his cart loaded with furniture, three years before. She told her friends at the time that she "liked the young man's looks."

The marriage ceremony was performed in May, 1827, by a kinsman of Abraham Lincoln. Eliza was eighteen at the time. She had a fair education, and she set to work at once to teach her young husband to read, write, and "cipher," as they called it in those days. She also read to him as he worked, and encouraged him in his attempts at oratory. Words came easily to young Johnson, once he had learned their meaning, and soon the little tailor shop became the social center of other ambitious young workers. Once a week Johnson walked four miles to and from the meetings of the local debating society, in which he took an active part.

He became so popular with the working people of Greenville that he was chosen alderman, and at the age of twenty-two he was elected mayor. Five years later he was elected a member of the Tennessee House of Representatives; and in 1843 a member of the House of Representatives at Washington. There, for ten years, he represented his state, saw Presidents come and go, and watched the gathering clouds of civil war.

In 1853 Tennessee chose Johnson as its governor and re-

elected him in 1855. He discharged his duties with fidelity
and skill, and proved himself the warm friend of the workingman. This led to his election, in 1857, as U.S. Senator for a
term of six years. During his stay in Congress, he was opposed
to a protective tariff, to giving the government too much
power, to the United States Bank, and to all government
schemes for internal improvements. In 1850, he supported the
compromise measures permitting the citizens of the territories to decide whether or not they wanted slavery; and
calling upon the Northern states to return to the South any
slaves who were caught attempting to make an escape from
their owners.

Johnson came of the same Scotch-Irish strain that gave us
Andrew Jackson. Like Jackson, he was a fighter by nature.
He was about five feet ten inches tall, with a sturdy, well-knit
frame. His dark complexion, bushy eyebrows, and black eyes
gave him an appearance of great determination. He had the
face of the typical Tennessee mountaineer, with his self-
reliance, contempt for danger, and quiet self-esteem.

No one ever doubted Johnson's courage. Once, when he
was campaigning for the governorship of his state, threats
were made that, if he dared to appear at a certain meeting,
he would not leave the hall alive. At the time set, he walked up
on the platform, laid his pistol on the table, and said: "Fellow
citizens! It is proper, when free men assemble for the discussion of important public affairs, that everything be done
decently and in order. I have been informed that I am to be
killed here tonight. I propose that this be made the first order
of business. If any man has come here tonight with that intention, I do not say: 'Let him speak!' I say: 'Let him shoot!' "

Johnson stood by the table, and looked about the room. No

one moved. "Very well," he said. "It appears that I have been misinformed. I shall now go ahead with my talk!"

In 1854, Senator Stephen A. Douglas, Lincoln's old political opponent, had secured the passage of the Kansas-Nebraska Bill, repealing the Missouri Compromise. The people in the South approved of his action, but its effect on the North was to consolidate the Whigs, Free-Soilers, and anti-slavery Democrats into what, in 1856, became the Republican party. As the years went by, the secessionists, encouraged by the Northern politicians, grew more aggressive. At the same time, Senator Johnson became more determined that the Southern states should not be permitted to break up the Union. The North looked with admiration upon the moral courage he displayed in contending, single-handed, against the Senators and Congressmen of the Southern states—including his own.

The issue—as he saw it, and as Lincoln saw it—was not whether the people of the South should own slaves, but whether they should be permitted to bring about the disintegration of the nation. As Johnson expressed it in 1861, in a Senate speech:

"There are two parties in this country who want to break up the Union. They are the secessionists of the South, and the abolitionists of the North."

For his stand against secession, Johnson was burned in effigy in Memphis and, on his return to Tennessee, threatened with lynching. Later, a Confederate court adjudged him "an alien enemy" and confiscated his property.

In March, 1862, President Lincoln appointed him military governor of Tennessee, then occupied by Union troops. Who could restore Tennessee and its loyal inhabitants to their proper relationship with the Union better than the former governor of the state? Lincoln gave Johnson the rank of brigadier general of volunteers—and left him to work out his many problems. One of his first acts was to issue a proclamation granting unconditional freedom to every man in Tennessee—white and black. From day to day, Johnson carried his life in his hands; if the rebels had caught him, undoubtedly they would have hanged him as a traitor to the South.

When, two years later, Johnson was nominated for Vice President, Lincoln was glad to get this "valuable man" as he called him. Johnson had come a long way since Eliza, his faithful helpmeet and teacher, had taken him for better or worse, for richer or poorer. Tailor, alderman, mayor, state representative, state senator, Congressman, governor, U.S. Senator, military governor of Tennessee—and now Vice President of the United States! He was also on the verge of what we now call a nervous breakdown. Johnson had traveled on the uncomfortable trains of the period, day and night, from Nashville to Washington. He was in a state of exhaustion. The Vice President whom Johnson had superseded gave Johnson several drinks. The whiskey affected him, and his condition was noticed by the opposition when he stood up to address the Senate. It was an unfortunate beginning.

The conflict between Lincoln and the radical element of the new Republican party had come to a head on the last day of the 1864 session of Congress, when the radicals adopted a reconstruction plan of their own. Under this plan, Congress would be the final judge of the state governments in the South. Lincoln quietly defeated the bill by a "pocket veto"; that is, he took no action on it before adjournment, which rendered the bill ineffective.

This was only one of the many differences between Lincoln and the radicals. For two years they had been insisting that they, not the President, should fix the terms of peace for the states which had seceded from the Union. Later the radicals refused to admit the Senators and Congressmen from the Southern states.

Johnson succeeded Lincoln as President on April 15, 1865. Lee's surrender had brought the Civil War virtually to an end, so Johnson not only inherited the martyred President's problems, but those brought forward by the end of hostilities. The new President felt himself under moral obligation to continue Lincoln's policies and to retain his Cabinet.

As President, Johnson declared that the Southern states were still in the Union; that they had never been out of it. They should be reorganized by the men who were born and raised in the South and owned property there. The radicals in Congress, on the other hand, declared that the Southern states were outcasts and could return to the Union only by a majority vote of the entire population of the various states, including former slaves and northern "carpetbaggers."

Johnson undertook to do what Lincoln would have done, had he lived. His policy was to treat the Southern states, not as conquered provinces, but as states that had gone astray and were now being welcomed back into the fold. About six weeks after he became President, Johnson issued his reconstruction proclamation, granting persons who participated in the Rebellion (with some exceptions) "amnesty and pardon, with restoration of all rights of property except as to slaves." The main problem was how to protect the former slaves, now that they had been freed, and to admit them to representation, in the constitutional and law-abiding sense. It would be criminal, Johnson maintained, to desert them. Fought primarily to preserve the Union, the war had taken on a larger significance; the rights of man were involved.

The President appointed a provisional governor of North Carolina, just as Lincoln had appointed Johnson to protect the citizens of Tennessee in their rights. If North Carolina wanted to grant former slaves the right to vote, she was free to do so. This was sound, and it was constitutional; it was Lincoln's plan. Johnson's proclamation recognized North Carolina as a state within the Union, subject to the duties, and entitled to the rights and privileges, of a state.

Later the President issued similar proclamations for Mississippi, Texas, Georgia, Alabama, South Carolina, Florida, Arkansas, and Louisiana. By December, 1865, all of the Southern states except Mississippi, Florida, and Texas had ratified the Thirteenth Amendment to the Constitution, abolishing slavery—and Florida joined the procession later in the month. The work of reconstruction had really begun.

The abolitionists in the North and their friends and sympathizers in Congress now set deliberately to work to break President Johnson's power and prestige. They wanted to create, not only a centralized government in Washington (in which Congress was to be paramount over the President and the Supreme Court), but a regime that would divide up the South into five military districts to "protect the life, liberty, and persons of all citizens." In other words, having worked to abolish slavery, the radicals in Congress, led by Thaddeus Stevens of Pennsylvania and Sumner of Massachusetts, and abetted by Wendell Phillips, a professional reformer, set about making the ex-slaves the social, economic, and political equals of their former owners. Not satisfied with keeping the Union from disintegrating as a result of secession, the Northern fanatics seemed determined to humble and degrade the leaders of the secessionist movement.

Johnson's duty, as he saw it, was to take up the task of reconstruction where Lincoln had left off. Because he stood in the path of Congress, they concocted a plot to remove him from the White House and to elect as his successor the president of the Senate. The issue was between Lincoln's idea of constitutional government and military control of the South; between binding up the nation's wounds and keeping them open; between the gradual enlightenment of the former slaves and giving them the vote at once.

Since the radical Republicans had a majority in both the House and the Senate, they overrode the President's vetoes of their legislation. The reconstructed Southern states were outlawed. The ballot was placed in the hands of the former slaves, whether or not they were qualified to vote. A large class of white men were deprived of their votes for disloyalty during the Civil War, and a military government was set up over the people of the South. The Southern states still had no representation in Congress, no voice in the making of the laws.

Another element that helped to rouse enmity against the former owners of slaves was the "carpetbaggers"—those political adventurers who pushed southward as soon as the fighting was over to corral the ex-slaves and get themselves elected to office. Between them, the Southern "scalawags" and the Northern carpetbaggers sowed the seeds of race hatred which flares up occasionally even at this late day. At night the Ku Klux Klan rode their horses and burned their crosses in an attempt to restrain the former slaves from voting.

Soon after the radicals in Congress had passed their own reconstruction bill (over the President's veto), they passed the Tenure of Office Bill. This deprived the President of the power to dismiss his more important appointees, such as members of his Cabinet, without the advice and consent of the Senate. Johnson declared the bill unconstitutional and vetoed the measure. It was passed over his veto. Johnson decided to test the constitutionality of the new law, since it provided for the practical elimination of the Chief Executive and gave Congress supreme power in the government. He dismissed Secretary of War Stanton, a holdover from the Lincoln Cabinet, whom he had long mistrusted. In so doing, President Johnson had as a precedent Madison's contention that the Constitution gave the President the right, without the advice and consent of the Senate, to dismiss any member of his Cabinet. This right had never been questioned before.

President Johnson was thereupon impeached by the House of Representatives for "high crimes and misdemeanors." No crimes were specified; but it seemed that the President's removal of a disloyal Cabinet member constituted a misdemeanor. For the first time in history, a President of the United States had been impeached!

It is doubtful if any trial of importance was ever carried through with as much animosity as the impeachment trial of Andrew Johnson. No weapon was too savage to use against him; no trick too low. One of the Senators charged him with aiding the escape of the son of one of Lincoln's murderers— although Johnson himself (as well as Secretary of State Seward) had been marked for assassination, along with Lincoln! The main question in the impeachment trial was not the vindication of Johnson, but the integrity of the Government.

The trial began on March 6, 1868, with the Senate chamber crowded, and the members of the United States Senate sitting as a High Court of Impeachment. The issue was stupendous: It meant, if Johnson were convicted (with no Vice President in office) and the President of the Senate were elevated to the Presidency, that no future President would be secure in his position! *A political party with a sufficient majority in the House and Senate could depose the President of the United States at any time!* It was without doubt the most audacious move in American history.

Johnson had watched one measure after another being enacted into law over his veto. Now, with his back to the wall, he was still resolved that, come what might, he would "preserve, protect, and defend the Constitution"—as he had sworn he would do. The High Court of Impeachment, on the other hand, was determined to strip him of his power to remove members of his official family.

The South, in particular, was roused to a high pitch of excitement by the coming trial. Virginia, Kentucky, and Tennessee offered to raise 230,000 volunteers and send them to Washington "to preserve the Union and the Constitution." Fortunately for the nation, these volunteers were urged to remain at home, or we might have had another Civil War.

The President's counsel decided that he should not appear as a defendant; they would represent him. Secretary of State Seward was offered a bribe if he would desert the President, which he hotly refused to do. A member of the President's counsel (who resigned soon afterward) intimated that he would call off the attackers if the President would send a gunboat to an island in the Caribbean on behalf of one of his clients, to hold the island by force. To that suggestion,

Johnson replied: "Get out of my office, or, damn you, I'll kick you out!" Fraud and bribery were common. Society itself seemed to have broken down. The radical Senators even tried to pack the High Court of Impeachment by permitting two territories to enter the Union as states in time for their Senators to vote—against Johnson. The attempt failed. They then tried to strip the Supreme Court of its jurisdiction in the case. The President of the Senate, who stood to gain most by the conviction of President Johnson, voted "Guilty" on every count. A conviction would make him President!

There were then thirty-seven states in the Union, each entitled to two Senators. Yet the Senators of ten Southern states had been refused their seats by the anti-Johnson Congress. This placed the President in a precarious position. He needed, and probably would have obtained, their twenty votes. His counsel asked for forty days in which to file an answer to the House's charges; he was granted only nine days.

Thirty-six votes would be required to make the two-thirds necessary to convict. The President himself expected to be convicted; he had packed up and was ready to leave the White House. While he waited, he prepared an address to the American people, setting forth his side of the case.

The trial proceeded. All the President had done, his counsel declared, was to seek a judicial ruling on the constitutionality of the Tenure of Office Law. As they saw it, this law violated the Constitution of the United States, as construed since 1789. Johnson thought it did, too. But the Supreme Court would hand down a ruling. Soon he would have the answer! His principal counsel, Attorney General Stanberry, became ill, but the radical Senators would not agree to a postponement of the trial; it went on without him.

Finally the day came when a vote was to be taken—not on the entire list of charges, but on the single charge considered certain of passage by the radical Senators. It failed—by a vote of 35 to 19—two-thirds of the Senators not having pronounced the President guilty. It was the same with the second charge, and the third. So far, a single vote had saved the President of the United States from conviction. The conspiracy had failed! There was a move to adjourn; and it was so voted. Eight of the charges had not been voted upon—and never would be. A judgment of acquittal was recorded.

President Johnson rounded out the year by issuing a full pardon to all who had taken part in the rebellion of the South, including Jefferson Davis, who had been head of the Confederate States of America. Johnson then retired, at the close of his term, to his home in Tennessee. For the first time in thirty years he was a private citizen. In 1875, however, he returned to Washington as U.S. Senator from Tennessee—the first ex-President to come back to the Senate. Even Johnson's bitterest enemies, observed the New York *Tribune* on that occasion, "were compelled to admit his sterling honesty and unswerving rectitude." And in 1926, almost sixty years later, the Supreme Court, with Chief Justice Taft presiding, ruled in a case similar to the Tenure of Office case that the act in question was unconstitutional.

On July 31, 1875, Senator Johnson died at the home of his daughter. On one occasion, he had said: "When I die, I want no better winding sheet than the Stars and Stripes, and no softer pillow than the Constitution of the United States." His wish was granted, and he was buried on a wind-swept knoll, which he had chosen as his final resting place, in the foothills of the Great Smoky Mountains.

ULYSSES S. GRANT

The President Who Was a Failure at Thirty-Nine

WASHINGTON, Lincoln, Grant
—that is the way the names of our great men were listed:
Washington, who established the republic; Lincoln, who
freed the slaves; and Grant, whose military genius brought
the Civil War to a successful conclusion.

Grant's middle name was thrust upon him by the Congressman of his district. When the Congressman asked for the
appointment of young Grant to West Point Military Academy, he knew him only as Ulysses and assumed that the middle name was Simpson because that was the maiden name of
his mother. At West Point, the young cadet asked to have his
right name entered on the records but was told that it would
be impossible without the consent of the Secretary of War.
That presented a problem. He did not like to upset the routine
in the Secretary's office, so he decided to accept the new name.
Anyway, he reasoned, if the boys at West Point knew that
his real name was Hiram Ulysses Grant, he would be teased
unmercifully for having the initials H.U.G.

At first the cadets translated the initials U.S. into "Uncle
Sam," and they called him that for a time. Then they short-
ened it to Sam, and "Sam" Grant he remained during the
four years at West Point.

The boy's mother was a silent, patient, uncomplaining
frontier wife. His father was a shrewd, hard-working, and
fairly successful tanner. One of the earlier Grants had fought
at Lexington, and on through the Revolutionary War. The
first American ancestor had landed near Boston in 1630.
Almost two hundred years later his descendant, Jesse Grant,
was the foreman of a tannery on the Ohio River about twenty-

five miles east of Cincinnati. The following year, Jesse married Hannah Simpson. Ulysses, their first child was born April 27, 1822. The Point Pleasant, Ohio, cabin which was his birthplace was almost as humble in appearance as the home in which Lincoln was born. Below the village, the Ohio River, then the great highway between Pittsburgh and the Mississippi, curved away into the distance.

When young "Lyss," as they called him, was a year old, his father established a tannery of his own at Georgetown, some ten miles back from the river, where tanbark was plentiful. There the boy grew up with his younger brothers and sisters. By the time he was eight, he had learned to drive a team of horses, and to break up the tanbark in a machine that looked like a giant coffee mill. He also stripped the bark from the oak trees, hauled wood, and did other chores. At ten, he often drove to Cincinnati, forty miles away, to bring home a load of passengers. He seemed to understand horses from the beginning, and they understood him. And no boy was prouder than he when he was permitted to use his father's horses to take the girls on sleigh rides.

Young Ulysses was quiet, short, plump, with a ruddy complexion, brown hair, and steady gray-blue eyes. He was thrifty, too. By the time he was twelve he had earned enough money to buy a horse of his own. And he was dependable, even at the age of thirteen. Once he drove two passengers up to Toledo, on the shore of Lake Erie. There were no paved roads in those days, and few bridges. Many streams had to be forded along the way.

But Ulysses wasn't always working. He had many good times with other youngsters of the village, and at fourteen he was sent off to school in Maysville, Kentucky, where he lived with his Uncle Peter. To him, Maysville was an exciting city. He enjoyed watching the paddle-wheel steamers, and exploring the river and the docks, with their bustling passenger and freight traffic. There, too, he went fishing, boating, and swimming in summer; and coasting and skating in winter.

Two years later, he went back home to take up his plowing and other farm duties. He had made no decision about what he wanted to do in life. His father, talking with him about the future, suggested West Point. It had many advantages, and the tuition was free! To be accepted as a cadet was a great privilege, and there was always an honorable position in the Army waiting for a graduate.

Ulysses was anything but enthusiastic. He was not very much interested in military affairs; he had no love for rifles; and he could not bear to see anything killed. His father, however, had already set the wheels in motion, and the boy dutifully accepted the appointment. Soon he had bought himself a trunk, packed it, and was on the Ohio River steamer bound for Pittsburgh. Traveling from there to Philadelphia, on to New York, and finally up the Hudson to West Point, he was a rather awkward lad of sixteen, with a hundred hard-earned dollars in his homemade jeans.

Life at West Point wasn't any too pleasant at first. He was subject to the orders of the upperclassmen; and required to say "Yes, sir," and No, sir" in replying to them; and to stand at attention and salute. Also there was much drilling, and he had to study and keep his room in order. Sometimes the first-year men were called upon by their seniors to "walk post" all night, or to catch imaginary flies in some lordly young man's tent. The boys never tired of pranks; and they were always hungry.

Their hats were so roomy that it was a simple matter at mid-day dinner to conceal in them a slice of roast beef, a chunk of bread, or a boiled potato. And in the evenings they gathered together, as school boys always do, to have a feast. Sometimes a chicken would be brought in out of the darkness. One night a juicy fowl was being roasted over the fireplace in Grant's room when the tactical officer was heard at the door. The young cadet quickly hid the half-cooked chicken, and gravely stood at attention before the fire. The officer walked about the room, looking mostly at the ceiling and knowing very well what was going on. Finally he said:

"There seems to be an odor in your room—as if something were burning, Mr. Grant."

"Yes, sir," Grant admitted. "I've noticed it, sir."

"Well, be careful that something doesn't catch fire."

"Yes, sir," replied the first-year man, saluting.

It was a good life at West Point. There was plenty of fun and good healthful exercise, and Grant stood well in his classes. On graduation day, he was twenty-one in a roll of thirty-nine. At that time the entire army of the United States numbered less than eight thousand men. Grant still had no great liking for the military side of army life. He looked for-ward to having a wife and a home of his own on some small campus, with a job as instructor in mathematics.

Instead, he was assigned to the infantry and sent off to Jefferson Barracks, near St. Louis. His West Point roommate, F. T. Dent, lived nearby; and Dent had a sister Julia, seventeen years old. There were carefree evenings of dancing and singing at the plantation, and rides through the woods. Grant and Julia became engaged, but the young lieutenants were sent to Mexico, and the wedding did not take place until the Mexican War had ended. Grant was able to save the life of his friend, Dent, during one of the battles, and that endeared the young soldier all the more to his Julia.

As regimental quartermaster, Grant had learned a great deal about army regulations, discipline, and the business of feeding and clothing an army. He was now twenty-five, short and stocky, and looked very mature in his reddish-brown beard. While the regiment went to New York on a transport, he obtained a leave of absence, and journeyed up the Mississippi to claim his bride. The two were happy for a few years, living a rather humdrum existence at an army post. Then, much to his dismay, Grant was transferred to Oregon. The West, then, was still wild country. He knew he could not take his wife and their little boy on the long and dangerous voyage, by way of the fever-laden jungles of Panama.

Lonely, homesick for his wife and child, with too much time on his hands, and living in a period when hard drinking was common among army officers at frontier posts, Grant drifted along with the rest. He tried to earn money by growing potatoes, raising cattle and hogs, and shipping ice to San Francisco—and failed at all three projects.

In 1853, Grant was promoted to captain, and transferred to Fort Humboldt, in California. His new commanding officer made it clear that he strongly disapproved of drinking. Finally, when his warnings did no good, he informed Captain Grant that he must either resign from the army or face a court-martial. So Grant resigned, at a time when he had little money, and no trade or profession. On borrowed money he returned home and built (with the help of neighbors) a log cabin on Colonel Dent's land. When Colonel Dent retired, Grant took charge of the plantation and worked in the fields with the slaves. He tried office work and selling real estate, but failed at that, too.

In 1860, Grant and his family moved to Galena, Illinois, where his father owned a leather business. He was there when the Civil War began, and helped to drill and outfit Galena's company of volunteers. Unknown to Grant, his Congressman had sent in a recommendation to the President that Grant be commissioned a brigadier general. He was appointed and assigned to command the troops of southeastern Missouri and southern Illinois, under General Fremont.

Learning that Southern forces were moving on Paducah, Kentucky, and being unable to reach General Fremont for instructions, Grant took command of the city for the North before the Southern forces arrived. Then he wrote a proclamation, addressed to the residents of Paducah:

> The strong arm of the Government is here to protect its friends, and to punish only its enemies. Whenever it is manifest that you are able to defend yourselves, to maintain the authority of your government, and protect the rights of all its loyal citizens, I shall withdraw the forces under my command from your city.
>
> U. S. GRANT

President Lincoln, reading these dignified words, made a mental note that a general who could take over a Southern stronghold without making enemies of the population was fitted for a higher command.

A few months later, Grant was given command of an army of 200,000 men in the west. With Grant, war was not an adventure, but a duty. He fought grimly and skillfully. Sometimes he wrapped himself up in an army blanket and slept beneath a tree. As for meals, he took them where and when he found them.

Volumes have been written about Grant's campaigns. He captured Fort Henry, on the Tennessee River, and Fort Donelson, on the Cumberland, together with half a Southern army. For this he was rewarded by a major general's commission. He suffered a setback at Shiloh, but later captured the city of Vicksburg. He was made a lieutenant general, and in 1864 he was placed in command of the Northern forces.

In the Virginia campaign, Grant's watchword was: "I propose to fight it out on this line if it takes all summer." Eventually he was able to cut off General Robert E. Lee from the Confederacy, and in April, 1865, to force his surrender at Appomattox Court House, in central Virginia. This virtually brought an end to the Civil War, and to Grant went much of the credit. In 1866, he was named general of the army—a lifetime job at $20,000 a year.

In the 1868 presidential campaign, General Grant was nominated by the Republican party on the first ballot, and elected by a large majority. He was the idol of the people. He had no party commitments, was under no pledges, and was a man of force, decision, and authority.

Certainly, there was need for a strong hand in the White House. Congress had practically destroyed the powers of the states, and was excercising some of the President's prerogatives. The radical Republicans were insisting upon military control of the South, while the South rebelled at the idea of the North passing upon the qualifications of their voters. Grant, who had had no training in government, thought firmness should be used in dealing with the South.

Three years had passed since the end of the Civil War, but still the Union had not been restored. The Southern states were still outside the halls of Congress; they had no Senators or Congressmen in Washington. There remained the questions of Negro suffrage and reconstruction.

From the beginning, Grant's administration was military. He disliked and distrusted politicians. He had a general for his secretary, and majors and captains for messengers. Those who had been kind to him he rewarded with a job of some sort, and he lifted hundreds from obscurity and poverty to well-paid positions. Some of the appointments were made at his suggestion; others by Senators and Congressmen who wanted to curry favor with the President. He was accused by the radical Republicans of accepting expensive gifts from men who expected government favors in return. There was also the charge that thirteen of Grant's relatives were on the public payroll.

The President's recommendation that the Fifteenth Amendment, providing equal voting rights for all citizens, including former slaves, be adopted, was carried through. General amnesty was recommended, and civil service reform was persistently urged upon Congress. Virginia was admitted to the Union, and was followed by Georgia, Mississippi, and Texas. At the request of the governor of South Carolina, Grant tried to disperse the Ku Klux Klan and to protect the Negro in all his civil rights. He was strongly in favor of the settlement and improvement of the lands of the West. The South remembered his offer to General Lee to let the soldiers take home their own horses for the spring plowing, and he ended his first term with a decided gain in the good-will of the Southern people.

Grant knew little of the social graces, and was quiet and reserved at White House gatherings. But he liked young people, and when boys played baseball behind the White House, he often took a swing at the ball, to the delight of the youngsters.

In the 1872 campaign, with Horace Greeley running against him, Grant won an easy victory. He was criticized during his second administration for approving a measure to increase the President's salary and those of the other officers of the government. But the $25,000 salary long had been too little for the President's needs.

In 1874 the Treasury Department was found to be conniving at a fraud in tax collection. President Grant permitted the Secretary of the Treasury to resign. During the following year, it was discovered that certain distillers were, with the help of Treasury clerks and officials, evading payments of the excise tax. General Babcock, the President's secretary, was indicted as a conspirator in the frauds against the government. With Grant's aid, he was acquitted.

With all these clouds hanging over the President's head, his Secretary of War was charged in 1876 with taking a bribe of six thousand dollars a year from a post trader in Indian Territory. The secretary explained the situation to President Grant and resigned, and that was the end of the charge.

Grant had a hostile majority in Congress, and this, in addition to the charges of graft in his second administration, caused his followers to grow fewer and fewer as he came to the end of his term. He was not renominated, although he would have liked a third term.

No real evidence was ever brought out that implicated Grant himself in fraud. It was generally agreed that he lacked political experience and made some unfortunate mistakes. Following the inauguration of his successor, Grant set out on a tour around the world. When he returned, he settled in New York city and entered a Wall Street firm. A young "Napoleon of finance" persuaded him to put what little money he had into the firm—and more than that, his name.

At the end of three years the firm of Grant and Ward failed. Liabilities amounted to more than sixteen million dollars, with assets of less than one hundred thousand dollars. Unknown to Grant, the two other partners had kept a separate set of books, and they were sent to prison for several years. Grant lost everything he owned, and everything his family owned. The crash also wiped out the savings of thousands of old soldiers and others who believed that anything with the General's name attached to it must be safe and honest. So Grant's career ended as it began, in failure.

A little over a year later, on July 23, 1885, Ulysses S. Grant died and was buried in the great mausoleum on Riverside Drive, in New York city.

RUTHERFORD B. HAYES

The Reluctant Politician

FOLLOWING the retirement of President Grant, there came into the White House Rutherford B. Hayes, different in temperament and background from all the Chief Executives who had preceded him.

"Ruddy," as he was called during his childhood, was not born in a log cabin. He had no struggle, either with the wilderness of the frontier or with hardship or poverty. He received a good education, had a happy family life, and made no tremendous effort, either to get into public office or to stay in it. He became President at one of the most critical moments in American history, when North and South were still nursing the hatreds born of Civil War, and graft and exploitation in the hands of party politicians were endangering the welfare of the nation.

Rutherford B. Hayes was descended from good, sturdy pioneer stock. The Hayes branch of the family had been defenders of Scotland as far back as the tenth century. Sophie Birchard, his mother, came from a long line of staunch English ancestors. Both branches came to New England to settle in the seventeenth century. Both grandfathers of our nineteenth President and three of his great-grandfathers, had fought in the Revolutionary War.

In the year 1817, four years after their marriage, Rutherford and Sophie Hayes, with their two infants and Sophie's young brother, Sardis Birchard, set out for Ohio in a covered wagon. After forty days of wandering, they arrived in the vicinity of Delaware, Ohio. Hayes tried farming at first, but found the rugged life too difficult for his family. So he settled in town, where he went into the distillery business. He died within a few years, several months before the birth of Rutherford. The baby was born in a comfortable brick house—the first one in the town of Delaware—on October 4, 1822.

Though he lacked the care of a father, Ruddy was lucky in having Sardis Birchard for an uncle. This young brother of Mrs. Hayes took over the responsibility of the entire family. He never married, and all through his life he was faithful to his charge in looking after Rutherford Hayes. He paid largely for Ruddy's education, helped him later in getting established in his law practice, encouraged him in his marriage, lent him money to build a house, and guided him in every emergency.

Young Hayes was a delicate child, with dark hair, pale skin, and deep-set big blue eyes. His older sister Fanny adored him. She followed him about constantly, joined in his play, and generally mothered him. As he grew older, Ruddy and Fanny read Shakespeare together, and *The Lady of the Lake*. Fanny's influence over her brother's life was most admirable. He loved her more than anyone else in the world—even more than he did his strait-laced Puritan mother, whose severity sometimes troubled him. He went to the district school, skated on the ponds in winter, and in spring and summer often rode horseback with his mother out through the Ohio countryside.

At twelve young Ruddy ventured into the world alone, going to Vermont and New Hampshire to visit relatives. At fourteen he attended Norwalk Seminary. His Uncle Sardis thought nothing was too good for the lad, and so a year later he was enrolled in the private school run by Isaac Webb at Middletown, Connecticut. Isaac Webb was a Yale man who taught in his exclusive academy literature, languages, good manners, and ethics to twenty select young gentlemen whose families could afford $250 per session. At sixteen young Hayes entered Kenyon College at Gambier, Ohio, only forty miles from his home. He was highly popular with his companions, had a sunny disposition, and enjoyed life.

After graduating from Kenyon, young Hayes studied for a few months with a law firm in Columbus, then went on to Harvard to complete his education. He was fond of New England, and of outdoor life. He fished in Long Island Sound; visited Newport, which was just beginning to be popular as a resort; spent a night on Mount Washington so that he could see the glory of the sunrise; and in November, 1848, journeyed with his uncle to Texas to visit an old Kenyon college classmate.

He had tried to enlist in the war with Mexico, but throat trouble interfered, and instead he went to the southwest for his health. The free life of the plains and riding in the open day after day changed him from a rather delicate young man to a vigorous, healthy young man ready to get back to the practice of law. On January 8, 1850, Hayes hung out his shingle in Cincinnati. There he was near his beloved sister, Fanny. She came to see him on the first train of cars to run from Columbus to Cincinnati. Six years later she died, and this was a blow from which Rutherford Hayes never entirely recovered.

As his law business improved, he began to think seriously about marriage. He had had several flirtations, but his mother had long ago chosen Lucy Webb for him. She was popular, warmhearted, religious, and intelligent. Also, she had the advantage of a college education, which was rare among women in those days. On December 30, 1852, they were married.

Hayes was elected city solicitor of Cincinnati in 1858; voted for Lincoln, whom he greatly admired, in 1860; and in the following fateful year he was filled with enthusiasm for the adventure of war. War, then, was still part of the joyous vision of youth. There were no poison gases, high-powered explosives, jet planes, or atom bombs. Hayes was never especially militant, but he was tired of the routine of law books. Here was his chance to get away and enjoy an outdoor life. He believed in the Union cause; he was filled with patriotism; and altogether he liked the idea of marching off to battle. The news of Fort Sumter and Lincoln's call to arms were all that he needed.

But the Civil War proved to be something more than a gay adventure for Rutherford B. Hayes. He saw plenty of action, was shot in the arm, and finally rose to the rank of brigadier general. He had permitted his name to be used as a candidate for Congress, but the post interested him very little. Yet after the war was over, popular acclaim sent him to Congress. He was re-elected in 1866, and resigned his seat in Congress only because Ohio elected him governor in 1867, and re-elected him in 1869.

As governor he did good work on behalf of Civil War soldiers and their families. He was firm in following a pay-as-you-go system, and reduced the state debt considerably. He could have served a third term if he had desired it, but this he refused. Again the reluctant politician repeated that he wanted to get out of public life. Perhaps this very reluctance attracted the people. Perhaps much of his popularity was due to his war record and his reputation as "the soldiers' friend." Anyway, in 1876, he found himself running on the Republican ticket against Samuel J. Tilden of New York, for President of the United States.

The election of 1876 was very close, so close in fact that both sides claimed victory. For a time, it looked as though riot and even bloodshed between the two parties could not be avoided. Finally, the decision was put up to Congress, which appointed a commission to look into the subject. After investigation, the commission conceded the election to Rutherford B. Hayes by a vote of eight for him as against seven for Tilden.

The new President announced in the beginning that he would serve only one term. In that one term, he demonstrated to the South that a man from the North could give them honest and efficient government. He did much to win the South by removing federal troops which had been stationed there since the war. He fought graft and the spoils system and used his influence toward establishing a Civil Service Commission. With the country struggling under the financial panic of the Grant administration, Hayes helped to restore the money market and put the nation on a more stable basis. At the end of four years he had the satisfaction of seeing it on the road to prosperity, and seeing a closer approach to real peace and friendliness between the North and the South.

Though history does not record him as one of our outstanding Chief Executives, Rutherford B. Hayes was zealous in promoting the welfare and amity of the entire nation, and in reorganizing the government on honest foundations. When he left the White House in 1881 he had more friends among the people than when he took office in 1877.

In the final months of his administration, he looked for-

ward eagerly to getting back home. He spent the last twelve
years of his life there, working to help his soldier friends,
striving for better prison conditions, and making more public
schools available.

He died at Spiegel Grove, his Ohio home, on January
17, 1893, and was buried there with honors at a state funeral
attended by many great dignitaries and military men.

JAMES A. GARFIELD

Another "Dark Horse" President

ALL night long Abram Garfield fought the raging fires that surrounded his log cabin and threatened the twenty acres of wheat growing on his land. When the flames died down and the battle was won, he sank wearily to a little three-legged stool at his doorstep. He was completely exhausted and his lungs were full of smoke. The damp, fresh air of early morning cooled his face and his sweating body. Suddenly a chill seized him. The Ohio pioneer had saved his wheat crop, but he was to pay for it with his life. Shortly afterward he died, leaving a wife and four young children.

The baby of the family was James A. Garfield, who became our twentieth President. He was born on November 19, 1831, in the cabin at Orange, Cuyahoga County, Ohio, and he was not quite two years old when his father died.

Eliza Garfield, his mother, was faced with sorry prospects after her husband was buried. With two sons and two daughters to feed and clothe, all she possessed in the world was the small farm laden with debt, and the land only partly cleared. Her few neighbors were as poor as she was. Eliza Garfield was only thirty years old then, and small and frail, with no one to turn to for help. She decided, above all, that she would keep her children together. Resolutely she set to work. She rose early and went to bed late. Her older son, a young boy, helped her in the fields. Her older daughter helped with the housework and cooking. The young orchards which her husband had planted flourished amazingly. Cherries, apples, plums and berries, along with the corn, potatoes, and wheat, helped to feed the family, and all of them, working together, found happiness and contentment. They had no luxuries, but somehow they managed. The mother helped her children with their studies during the long winter evenings, and read to them nightly from her Bible.

Little James grew strong and healthy. He had blue eyes, a round rosy face, and reddish-blond hair. As soon as he was big enough, he began doing his share of the work, picking apples, bringing in wood, and doing such other chores as a boy could handle. His one great desire was to help his mother, and his sisters and his older brother felt the same way. They were good children, never lacking in appreciation for the sacrifices their mother was making for them.

As the boys grew older, conditions began to improve for the Garfield family. They weren't rich, or even well-to-do, but they never went hungry. When James was twelve he worked in the fields from sunrise to sunset. He didn't like farming. He grew weary of plowing, planting and hoeing. But he kept plugging along, just as his ancestors had done before him.

His father's people and his mother's ancestors had been among the early settlers in New England. They were of pioneer Yankee stock, with plenty of courage and a capacity for hard labor, and young James Garfield inherited those qualities. At an early age he did a lot of wood chopping, and he longed to be a carpenter. When his mother decided that they could afford something a little better than the log cabin in which he was born, work was begun on a new house. It was to have four rooms, and that sounded like luxury to the Garfield children. Working with the builders early and late, James had his chance to learn carpentry. By the time the new house was completed, he had gathered a few tools together and was the proud possessor of a workbench of his own. Soon he was earning a little money at his trade, and every penny he received was turned in to his mother to help support the family.

There wasn't much time to devote to an education. For a few months during the winter, James went to the village school, and in the evenings he read and reread the few books his mother owned. The book that fascinated him most was a tale of adventure called *The Pirate's Own Book*. The more James read it, the more eager he was to become a sailor. Day after day, as he chopped wood for the neighbors, or helped in the hayfields at home, he dreamed of going to sea. When he was sixteen, he finally prevailed upon his mother to let him go. And he started off on foot for Cleveland and the boat docks along Lake Erie. There was only one ship in port, and the young adventurer boarded her and asked for the captain. The captain, however, was in an ugly mood. With a volley of oaths he greeted the boy who wanted to sign on his ship as a hand. Frightened, hurt, and discouraged James got away from the vessel as fast as he could. But he was not completely beaten. Maybe he could get a job on a canal boat. The *Evening Star* was tied to the bank, and Captain Amos Letcher was impressed at once with the sturdy, earnest lad who wanted work.

Work on the canal, however, wasn't any more exciting than farming. James Garfield drove the horse along the canal path while the barge moved along slowly with its load of coal. Working on the decks wasn't any better. Again and again, the new hand fell overboard while handling the ropes. He could not swim a stroke and there wasn't always someone handy to fish him out. One dark rainy night, when a rope gave way, he nearly lost his life in the cold, dark water. That was too much even for James Garfield. He said to himself: I will go back home, get an education, and become a man. And that is exactly what he did.

Lean years and struggles followed, but Garfield worked, studied, and saved his money. He taught a country school for twelve dollars a month and his board. He worked his way through Hiram College, serving as janitor until somebody discovered he could teach English literature just as well as he could tend fires.

It was at Hiram that he first met a sweet-faced girl with dark eyes and hair, named Lucretia Rudolph. She was the daughter of a Maryland farmer, and she shared Garfield's love of books. When, at the age of twenty he entered Williams College, in Massachusetts, Lucretia went to Cleveland to teach in the public schools. They planned to be married after his graduation.

In 1858 he was made president of his old Hiram College. Shortly afterward he and Lucretia were married, and set up housekeeping in a neat little cottage on the campus. They didn't have much money, but they were ideally happy.

While Garfield was president at Hiram, he was elected to the Ohio state Senate. For two years he had been interested in public affairs, he was a vigorous speaker, and was opposed to slavery. He took high rank in the legislature at once. He had completed his law studies and had just been admitted to the bar when President Lincoln called for troops to fight in the Civil War. Garfield enlisted immediately.

He fought valiantly in the battle of Shiloh and at Chicamauga, and at thirty he was one of our youngest brigadier generals. While he was at the front, in 1862, he was elected by Ohio Republicans to the Congress of the United States. He took his seat in the House of Representatives in December, 1863, and was re-elected every two years after that until 1879, when he was promoted to the Senate. He never did take his seat in the Senate, however, for much to his own surprise he was nominated for the presidency by the Republican convention of 1880.

At the convention a group of politicians called Stalwarts were determined to bring Ulysses S. Grant back to the White House for a third term. Other leaders, opposed to a third term for any President, supported James G. Blaine or John Sherman. Ballot after ballot was taken without reaching an agreement. Then somebody mentioned the name of James A. Garfield, who was present at the convention but had no idea he would be considered for the highest office in the land. On the next roll call there was a stampede to him. He was nominated on the thirty-sixth ballot, with Chester A. Arthur as Vice President; and in November, 1880, he was elected.

President Garfield's term of office began under unhappy circumstances. His own party was not united in his support, and there was still considerable bitterness over the unexpected turn of events at the convention. When the new President appointed James G. Blaine as Secretary of State and made William Robertson collector of the port of New York, the Stalwarts turned completely against him. They disapproved his appointments and were angry because they had not been consulted.

But all these disagreements were soon forgotten in the events which followed. Whether President Garfield could have straightened out his difficulties will never be known. Less than four months after his inauguration, while he was waiting in the railroad station at Washington for a train to take him to a reunion at Williams College, President Garfield was shot down by Charles J. Guiteau, a disappointed office seeker. With a shout of triumph, the crazed assassin screamed: "I am a Stalwart! Arthur is now President!" Then he fired again.

In the anxious months that followed, Garfield put up the greatest fight of his life—for his life. But it was a losing battle from the beginning. After careful nursing at the White House for eleven weeks, he was carried out of the summer heat of the capital to Elberon, New Jersey, where he died on September 19, 1881.

For the second time an assassin's bullet had struck down a President of the United States, and the nation mourned. He was buried in Lake View Cemetery, Cleveland, Ohio.

CHESTER A. ARTHUR

Son of a Vermont Minister

AT the death of President Garfield, Vice President Chester A. Arthur, a man with two strikes against him at the start, was sworn in as the Chief Executive of the United States. First, the position of a Vice President who inherits the presidency by the accident of death is not easy. He does not enter the White House as a man chosen by the people to govern them. Second, Chester A. Arthur had another handicap. Little was know about him by the general public, except that President Hayes had removed him from the office of collector of the port of New York only three years before. Besides, he had been an active member of the Stalwarts, and when Garfield was shot, the American people were indignant at the idea that Arthur, political boss of his party, was now to be put into the White House.

But Chester A. Arthur, party boss and shrewd politician, became a very different man when he was installed as President. He surprised everybody by putting aside party politics. Perhaps that is because, from his earliest childhood, he had been brought up in an atmosphere of religion and high ideals.

His father, William Arthur, was born of English-Irish parents in Antrim, Ireland. A graduate of Belfast College, William Arthur fulfilled his dreams of emigrating to the great new land of opportunity across the ocean. When he arrived in the United States, he began the study of law. But as he studied, his religious convictions were stirred. So he prepared for the ministry instead and was ordained in the Baptist Church.

The young minister married Malvina Stone, also a New Englander, and on October 5, 1830, in a log house in Fairfield, Vermont, their son Chester was born.

Chester's boyhood, like the boyhood of most sons of preachers, was enlivened by a series of moves. The family lived first in one town, then another—wherever the Baptist Church called the Rev. William Arthur. Chester began his schooling at home. There he was taught religious principles and heard many discussions about the political questions of the day. He grew to be tall and strong, and fond of outdoor sports. With a mind as active as his young body, he quickly learned his lessons. After attending the village schools, he was ready, at fifteen, to enter the sophomore class of Union College at Schenectady. Three years later, in the summer of 1848, he was graduated.

No doubt, during his school and college years, he dreamed about what he would become in life. He was sure he didn't want to enter the ministry, but he had always been interested in debates. He decided that he would become a lawyer; and, after a few months in a law school at Ballston Spa, he was sure his choice was right. Looking about for a way to earn his living while going on with his studies, he became a school-teacher. He prepared boys for admission to college and did so well that, in 1851, when he was only twenty-one years old, he was made principal of the academy at North Pownal, Vermont. All this time he continued studying law. While teaching school, he saved up five hundred dollars with which to start in business. When he was admitted to the bar in 1853, his father's old friend, E. D. Culver, then a successful lawyer practicing in New York city, was glad to make the promising young man a junior member of the firm.

Chester Arthur took up his new work with enthusiasm, and gained public attention with his first big case. Before the year 1855, Negroes were not permitted to ride with white passengers in the street cars of New York city. In 1855 a colored girl named Lizzie Jennings, thinking she might escape notice, entered a car of the Fourth Avenue line; but she was quickly discovered and was put off.

The firm of Culver, Parker, and Arthur decided to make a test case of it. They sued the company for damages. Chester Arthur appeared as counsel for Lizzie Jennings, and won her case in the state supreme court. That was a great victory for the young attorney. He obtained damages for Lizzie Jennings. Moreover the right of all Negroes to ride in public conveyances was never afterward challenged within the jurisdiction of New York state. Chester A. Arthur began to attract attention as a leader.

He was a strong, good-looking young man with a friendly manner, and he took a deep interest in military affairs. As a member of the National Guard, he became judge advocate of the second brigade. He was also, at this time, working steadily in politics as an active member of the Whig party.

On October 29, 1859, Arthur married Ellen Herndon, of Fredericksburg, Virginia. The rising young lawyer now had a home, a wife, a good law practice, and a recognized position in the affairs of his political party.

But war was rapidly coming closer. Arthur now held the rank of brigadier general in the state militia. He was not destined to become a war hero or to command an army, but when Fort Sumter was fired upon in April, 1861, and President Lincoln called for 75,000 men, General Arthur was made acting quartermaster general of New York state. He had charge of all matters connected with outfitting, training, and forwarding troops, and was prompt and efficient in carrying out his assignments.

After the war ended, he resumed his law practice. In 1871,

President Grant appointed him collector of the port of New York; and reappointed him in 1875. This most important home appointment in the gift of the President of the United States was an official honor which ranked above all but a very few positions abroad. It also carried considerable powers of appointment, and the collector often used those powers to reward members of his political party.

When Hayes became President in 1877, he was determined that the New York customhouse should be separate from partisan politicians and the spoils system. He issued an order forbidding the civil servants of the government to take an active part in political management. General Arthur was at that time chairman of the Republican Central Committee of New York city. He ignored the President's order. In September, 1877, Arthur was asked to resign. He refused. In 1879, at a time when Congress was not in session, President Hayes removed Arthur from office.

General Arthur then returned to his law practice, and apparently his reputation suffered little injury. For in 1880 he was nominated for the vice presidency on the ticket with James A. Garfield.

President Garfield and Vice President Arthur entered upon their official duties on March 4, 1881. Just a few months later, in September, the President, shot by an assassin, lay dead; and Vice President Arthur stepped into the White House.

Thus the man who had been removed from the office of collector of the port of New York, accused of ethics none too high in the discharge of his duties, now became President of the United States. But if his party expected that, as President, he would continue to be influenced by the spoils system, they were to be sadly mistaken.

President Arthur was deeply affected by the death of Garfield. He was also impressed with the importance of his own position. Having taken the sacred oath of office, he courageously faced his duties and obligations. The public, at first incensed at having him as their Chief Executive, gradually became convinced of his integrity and his efforts to serve, not a political party, but all the people of the nation. He was handsome, tall, graceful, and dignified; and as President, he announced that he would follow the policies of his predecessor. Following words with action, he began at once an attack on the spoils system. He struck his first blow in 1883 by signing the Civil Service Reform Act. He also vetoed a Chinese exclusion bill which would have violated a treaty with China; and he followed this by vetoing a river and harbor bill which carried extravagant and wasteful appropriations.

He made one grave mistake when he insisted on the nomination of Judge Folger, his Secretary of the Treasury, for governor of New York. The Democrats denounced his interference in state elections and nominated and elected Grover Cleveland instead. In all other respects, President Arthur served out his term with integrity and ability.

While there is no outstanding accomplishment to record during his term in office, he left the White House with the respect and admiration of the American people. In March, 1885, Chester A. Arthur returned to his home in New York city. He was then fifty-four years old. Less than two years later, on November 18, 1886, his career was suddenly ended by apoplexy.

He was buried in the family cemetery at Albany, New York.

GROVER CLEVELAND

The President Who Upheld the Gold Standard

IN less than four years, Grover Cleveland emerged from comparative obscurity as a citizen of Buffalo, New York, to become the twenty-second President of the United States. He was elected mayor of Buffalo in 1881, governor of the state of New York in 1882, and President in 1884.

He was the son of a Presbyterian minister and one of the strongest personalities we have ever had in the White House. He was an honest and independent politician who despised grafters, a conservative lawyer who took the city of Buffalo as his client and freed it from the control of an aldermanic "ring." He carried out drastic reforms in the city, the state, and the nation which are still remembered. He upheld the gold standard and thus saved the country from what might have been a disastrous business depression.

The first of his name, Moses Cleveland, landed on our shores in 1635. Grover's father was graduated from Yale with high honors. His mother was the daughter of an Irish merchant. Stephen Grover Cleveland was born in Caldwell, New Jersey, on March 18, 1837; he dropped the "Stephen" in his early youth. Before he was sixteen, his father had moved the family three times—to Fayetteville, Clinton, and Holland Patent, New York. The boy grew up a chubby youngster, large for his age, round faced and blue eyed. He was fond of outdoor games, swimming, and nut gathering; but he liked fishing best of all. Even as President of the United States, Grover Cleveland was known and admired as an expert fisherman.

There were two older brothers and two older sisters. They

—and Grover's parents—spared no effort to lay a solid foundation for his character. He did his share of wood cutting, weed pulling, and hoeing in the garden. For, as a clergyman, Grover's father earned, on the average, less than a hundred dollars a month.

At Clinton the boy entered a preparatory school to fit himself for college. There followed an interval of two years when the family fortunes were at a low ebb, and it was necessary for him to take a job as a clerk. This brought him fifty dollars with board and room the first year; and one hundred dollars the second. Then his father died. That loss changed the whole course of Grover's life. There were his mother and several younger children to support. For two years he worked with his older brother as a clerk. Then he decided to go to Cleveland, Ohio, where opportunities looked more promising. One of his father's old friends loaned him twenty-five dollars and offered to put him through college if he would become a minister. But the boy wanted to be a lawyer.

Off he started for Cleveland, but as things happened, he did not complete his journey. Stopping off at Buffalo to visit an uncle, he remained a year, working on his uncle's herd book. In the fall of 1855, the uncle, who was very much pleased with the lad's ability and good character, introduced him to the members of a Buffalo law firm, Rogers, Bowen, and Rogers. There Grover began the study of law and was paid four dollars a week. Even at the age of eighteen, he took his profession seriously and felt that he had no time for social affairs. Within a year he was completely self-supporting. Before he was twenty-one he was earning five hundred dollars a year. And at the end of four years he passed his bar examination, and was admitted to practice.

Cleveland must have been tempted to hang out his shingle without delay; but he remained with the firm for another four years. Meanwhile, he had become a staunch Democrat and acted as a volunteer worker in helping to get out the Buffalo vote. He took no part in the Civil War. When he was drafted, he happened to be assistant district attorney of Erie County. Following the custom of the period, he provided a substitute. Cleveland was earning a thousand dollars a year with the law firm at the time of his appointment, and the county job paid only five hundred dollars. But he might become district attorney later; he might even be sent to Congress! By this time he had definitely decided to go into politics.

Cleveland received the nomination for district attorney, but was defeated. So he formed a law partnership with Isaac K. Vanderpoel, which lasted three years; later he associated himself with the firm of Lanning and Folsom. In 1869 he was elected county sheriff. Here he found an opportunity to "clean house" and, incidentally, to save some money for the first time in his life. In the three years that followed, he straightened out some rather crooked practices, saved the taxpayers a considerable amount of money, and established a high standard of business and official procedure.

The exuberant and jovial ex-sheriff, thirty-seven years old and a bachelor, became in 1874 a member of the firm of Bass, Cleveland, and Bissell, which soon became known as one of the leading law firms in Buffalo. Cleveland had his living apartments on the floor over his office. He often worked all night on a case, took a shower, ate a hasty breakfast, and appeared in court that morning, looking as fresh and healthy as though he had had a good night's sleep. In court he was forceful, deliberate, and impressive, a heavy man, with blue eyes, brown hair, and a mustache. He was highly popular and was elected president of the local bar association. Among his clients were the Standard Oil Company, the Merchants and Traders Bank, and the Lehigh Valley Railroad. When his former partner, Folsom, died, the court appointed Cleveland administrator of the estate. From that time on, he felt that he owed Mrs. Folsom and her daughter, Frances, a special duty. Eleven years later, when Frances was twenty-two and Grover Cleveland was President of the United States, they were married in the White House!

Cleveland was not yet forty-five years old when the voters thought the city administration of Buffalo ought to be "hauled over the coals" and that Cleveland, with his honesty and determination, was the man for the job. Not long before, he had been asked to become chief counsel in western New York of the New York Central Railroad. He could have increased his income by $15,000 a year, but Cleveland declined the offer. It was a fateful decision. For, if he had consented, he would not have been asked to run for mayor—and it was the fine reputation he made as a reform executive that led to his nomination for governor, and (two years later) for President.

As mayor, Cleveland attacked the custom of allowing the county treasurer to pocket the interest on public funds placed in his care. He routed the professional money lenders by arranging for city laborers to be paid weekly, instead of monthly. He defeated an attempt to rob the city of more than one hundred thousand dollars on a street-cleaning contract and saved Buffalo another eight hundred thousand dollars on a sewer contract. Throughout his term of office, supported by public sentiment and his own party, he kept up a barrage of vetoes against the ring of Buffalo councilmen.

Mayor Cleveland soon was known throughout New York state for administrative ability and integrity. He fought constantly for right and justice. He even appeared before the governor on behalf of a man who had been (as Cleveland thought) unjustly convicted of first-degree murder. When the man's counsel asked for commutation of sentence, after a two-hour argument, the governor, tired and irritated, refused, and told the lawyer to sit down. "It is a waste of your time and mine to discuss this matter further," said the governor.

Cleveland sprang to his feet, towering over the governor in his swivel chair. Quoting Blackstone, he said: "The King himself condemns no man, but leaves that rugged task to his courts!" The governor was angry at this challenge of his authority. The room was hushed, but Cleveland was permitted to take up the argument where the lawyer had left off— and the governor listened. In the end, sentence was commuted.

Reform was the issue of the day, not only in New York state, but all over the country. In 1882, Cleveland, rugged and independent, was elected governor without piling up political debts. When his own party undertook to reorganize the fire department at Buffalo, in order to provide a few more jobs "for the boys," Governor Cleveland vetoed the measure. He had co-operative insurance companies placed under the control of the state, abolished political assessments upon state employes, urged laws for the further protection of the Adirondack forests, and established a court of claims. His breach with Tammany Hall, of New York city, caught the imagination of the public; they flocked to his standard. As the outstanding Democratic governor of the year, it was predicted in

1884 that he would be nominated for President—and he was.

The opposition of the Democratic bosses brought Cleveland's complete fearlessness to the country's attention. The Republican party had been in power for twenty-five years; and its presidential candidate stood accused of using his position as Speaker of the House to obtain favors for a certain railroad, and of profiting thereby. Prominent Republicans were condemning this man (Blaine) and calling upon the Democrats to nominate a candidate whom they could support. The candidate was Cleveland.

In the election, the "mugwumps" (independents) decided the issue in favor of Cleveland. The powerful groups which had obtained land grants for their railroads, subsidies for their industries, pensions for thousands of healthy (or non-existent) Civil War veterans—all these had overreached themselves. The country was ripe for a change—and Cleveland was the kind of man the people wanted.

As President, he applied the same principles that had won him fame as sheriff, mayor, and governor. In one bureau in Washington he found there were 40 per cent more employes than were needed. Of 125,000 government employes, at least 110,000 were political appointees. Party heads were forcing officeholders to contribute a percentage of their salaries to the campaign chest. East and West were divided on the currency problem. Banks and trust companies were steadily depleting the stock of gold in the Treasury. The government was compelled to accept silver from its debtors, while it paid out gold to its creditors. Any other course would have ruined its credit.

At the same time, the government was expected to maintain a reserve of at least one hundred million dollars in gold to protect the redemption of greenbacks; and this reserve,

Cleveland found, was getting dangerously low. The problem was to keep silver money and gold money at a parity. One way would be to stop the coinage of silver money, but this would bring a strong protest from the silver-producing states.

In his annual message of 1885, Cleveland declared that abandonment of the gold standard would impair confidence in the government, cancel a large part of the savings of thrifty people, disrupt business, and reduce the income of the farmer and the workingman. For seven years the government had been buying silver bullion, coining it at the rate of two million dollars a month, and paying for the silver with gold from the Treasury reserve. These idle silver dollars were added to the mass already burdening the government's vaults.

The West, of course, was eager to obtain the free and un-limited coinage of silver. But Cleveland maintained that if silver buying continued long enough, the result would be the substitution of silver for all the gold the government could apply to this purpose. The nation would thus be forced to adopt the silver standard of Congressman William Jennings Bryan, in which sixteen ounces of silver would be equivalent to one ounce of gold. In his annual message, therefore, Cleveland made this blunt suggestion to Congress: "I recommend the suspension of the coinage of silver dollars, directed by the law passed in February, 1878."

Cleveland faced other problems in the West, where the government still owned a million square miles of mining, timber, grazing, and desert land. Tens of millions of acres, set aside by the government as subsidies for the transcontinental railroads, were lying idle because the railroads were lax in making their selections. If a homesteader happened to file a claim, and the railroad came along ten years later and decided that it wanted the land—with all its improvements—it laid claim to it.

Such injustice was intolerable to President Cleveland. He proceeded to throw open millions of acres to homesteading. Cattle barons and lumber companies prevailed upon their employes to "homestead" 160 acres—and turn the property over to their employers at a nominal price. Cleveland "cracked down" on them, too. Once he used his executive authority to revoke an order of the previous administration, whereby a land company was authorized to graze two hundred thousand head of cattle on an Indian reservation. This violated our treaty with the Indians. Cleveland gave the company sixty days to vacate the land.

During his first year in office, Vice President Hendricks died. The law of succession to the presidency thereupon came up in Congress, and a bill was passed, providing a long line of succession (Vice President, Secretary of State, etc.) which Cleveland signed. He also signed a measure regulating the counting of the electoral votes, so as to render impossible a repetition of the dispute of 1876.

Cleveland recognized the South by appointing three members of his Cabinet from that section. Bureau heads in the Treasury, War, and Navy departments were not removed merely because they were Republicans. He also ordered his Secretary of the Treasury to look into the systematic undervaluation of imports at the customhouses. This, he claimed, had been going on for fifteen years—at the expense of American merchants and the Treasury. He also insisted upon a reorganization of the civil service.

The President found time, in 1886, to set a precedent as the first Chief Executive to be married in the White House.

During the first year his sister, Rose, had been mistress of the Executive Mansion, but on June 2 Cleveland married charming young Frances Folsom, daughter of his former law partner. She herself created a precedent, for she was the first college-bred mistress of the White House.

President Cleveland realized that a rapid transition in naval equipment, from old to new, would have to be brought about. Wooden ships would have to be abandoned for steel. The Navy Department would have to be placed on a more efficient basis—like a huge corporation. We would have to make our own 14-inch guns and armor plate, instead of depending upon Europe to supply them.

There was a Republican majority in the Senate, and the new Democratic President and the Senate confronted each other in open battle. The tariff, free coinage of silver, and individual pension bills were the three problems that worried Cleveland most. The pension claims were in many cases fraudulent, and Cleveland was the first President in a quarter of a century to give them his personal attention. Except for the interest charges on the public debt, veterans' pensions accounted for the largest annual Treasury outlay. Presidents from Johnson's time to Cleveland's had not found it politically expedient to veto individual pension bills; but Cleveland, on the theory that, although the people support the government, the government should not support the people, vetoed one piece of pension legislation after another.

The tariff question was still bigger. The Republicans claimed that the revenue necessary to finance the government should be provided chiefly by duties on importations. Under successive Republican regimes and high customs duties, the income of the government had been far in excess of its needs.

The Cleveland administration decided that, since high tariffs brought this money into the Treasury and in their opinion impoverished many American industries and favored only a few, the tariff should be lowered. They believed that hoarding money in the Treasury, instead of keeping it in circulation, was a dangerous practice. Also, the tariff law laid a tax on some four thousand items. According to Cleveland, the worker and the farmer bore the heaviest burden in this form of taxation.

Tariff revision thus became the big issue. The country was aroused by discussions on the tariff to a pitch of excitement never before known. A reduction in the tariff would relieve the people of the tax. The great tariff debate began in April, 1887, and lasted well into July, when the House passed the Democratic measure.

When we come to appraise Cleveland's first administration, we must admit that he set up in Washington a new standard for men in public life. His boldness and independence encouraged mayors and governors everywhere. His vetoes toned up the politics of the nation. His broad-mindedness is shown by the fact that he approved the Interstate Commerce Commission measure, which the Republicans had initiated. Most of the Democratic leaders disliked him because he was difficult to manage and because he did not distribute patronage freely.

The first Cleveland administration, under favorable business conditions, built up the government's gold reserve from one hundred and twenty-five million dollars to one hundred and fifty-one million dollars. Cleveland issued the first message to Congress on the subject of organized labor in our history. Under his administration provisions were made for the arbitration of railway labor disputes and investigation of labor quarrels.

He was the outspoken champion of settlers' rights in the West. The land-grant railroads, the cattle barons, and the land syndicates had had things very much their own way for twenty years; they had well-financed lobbies in the capital, and crafty lawyers. Yet, by the end of Cleveland's first administration, the government had regained more than eighty million acres of railroad and other land, and had thrown it open to homesteading.

Two other accomplishments of the first Cleveland administration were the creation of a Department of Labor and the negotiation of a treaty with Great Britain, defining the rights of American fishermen in Canadian ports and waters and removing the friction between American and Canadian fishermen.

President Cleveland had put in a busy four years as the head of the nation. When he was defeated by Benjamin Harrison, the Republican candidate, in 1888, Cleveland returned to the practice of law. Though he had lost in the election, he was glad to get back into the life of a private citizen and enjoy some of the freedom and relaxation he had missed as Chief Executive.

BENJAMIN HARRISON

Patriot and Soldier

NO American boy was ever born with a finer heritage than Benjamin Harrison, who became our twenty-third President. His family had been prominent in the building of America since early in the seventeenth century. His great-grandfather took an active part in the Revolutionary War, was one of the signers of the Declaration of Independence, a member of the Continental Congress, and governor of Virginia. His grandfather was William Henry Harrison, one of the heroes of the War of 1812 and later the ninth President of the United States. Benjamin's father, John Scott Harrison, was a well-informed and active citizen, and served two terms in the House of Representatives.

The Harrisons settled originally in Virginia. When William Henry was a young man he built a house on a tract of land near North Bend, Ohio. There Benjamin Harrison was born on August 20, 1833. At this period the Harrisons did not have much money; and the boy, at an early age, began to help on the farm, plowing, haying, and harvesting. He went to school during the winters at the little log-cabin schoolhouse on his father's property.

Later, he attended Farmer's College, near Cincinnati, for two years; then enrolled at Miami University. While there he fell in love with young Caroline Scott, and they became engaged. Benjamin was only eighteen at that time. He was graduated before he was nineteen, married a year later, and he and his bride started life together in a small three-room cottage in Indianapolis.

Benjamin was quiet and serious, quite ready to shoulder responsibility, even though he had almost no money. He went to work as a court crier, for which he received $2.50 a day. Shortly after his marriage he was admitted to the bar. Not having funds for an office of his own, he secured the use of a desk in the office of a friend, and there he began the practice of law.

The young attorney was shy and nervous at first, but soon he found that he could throw away his notes and speak convincingly and without embarrassment before the court. As time went on, he was able to get enough business to make a good living; and, being an ambitious youth, he further increased his income by acting as clerk of the supreme court of Indiana. He also joined the newly organized Republican party and became one if its principal speakers.

When, in 1861, President Lincoln called for an army to defend the Union, Benjamin Harrison put everything else aside to help fight the Civil War. The following year he raised his own company of volunteers, and was commissioned a colonel and placed in command of the Seventieth, an Indiana regiment. Like his ancestors, Harrison was an ardent patriot and a brave soldier. He showed outstanding courage and skill in several battles; he fought at Kenesaw Mountain, Peachtree Creek, and Nashville. He was with General Sherman on his march to the sea.

At the close of the war Harrison returned to his law practice, and before long he was earning an average of ten thousand dollars a year, which was considered unusually large at that time. With his family background of public service, and his Civil War experience, it was natural that he should become more and more active in national affairs. He worked enthusiastically for the election of General Grant to the presidency in both campaigns. In 1876 Harrison ran for governor of Indiana, but he was defeated by the Democratic candidate. He received so many votes, however, and attracted so much favorable attention by his speeches that the leaders of the Republican party began to consider him seriously for higher office.

In 1880 Harrison actively supported Garfield, and was chairman of the Indiana delegation at the Republican convention. As President, Garfield offered him a Cabinet post. Harrison declined that honor since he had just been elected to the United States Senate.

At the end of his six years as Senator, he was defeated when he ran for re-election. He returned to Indianapolis and to the practice of law. A few months later, in 1888, he was nominated for the presidency, running against President Cleveland. Tariff revision became the big issue, and since Harrison was believed to be cautious and conservative, he won the election. He was inaugurated as President of the United States on March 4, 1889.

Now a second Harrison was in the White House, and he was recognized as a man of integrity and ability. But he was not a good mixer and did not practice the arts of the politician. Instead of being benefited by the fact that his grandfather, William Henry Harrison, had been President many years before, Benjamin Harrison was often pictured in cartoons as a little man wearing a hat many sizes too large for him. He was small in stature, it is true, and he was highly sensitive. He determined from the beginning to prove that he himself could be a good President and was not leaning on the fame of his ancestor.

During his administration he signed the McKinley high-tariff bill and the silver-purchase act which more than doubled the purchase of silver by the Treasury. He expanded the pension list, suppressed the Louisiana lottery, and aided in the admission to statehood of North and South Dakota, Montana, Washington, Idaho, and Wyoming. He supported the Sherman Anti-Trust Act, and presided at the first Pan-American Congress, held at Washington to encourage more friendly relations with neighboring countries.

President Harrison did much to help industry and to reduce the public debt, but the controversy about tariff and free silver was still agitating the entire country as his term came near to its close. There were serious labor difficulties; the farmers were crying out against inflation; and housewives all over the nation were complaining bitterly about the high cost of living.

Once more the people began to turn toward ex-President Cleveland, whose policies on tariff and silver were exactly opposite to those of President Harrison. In the bitter struggle which followed in the campaign of 1892, Cleveland was again elected. Harrison returned to his home in Indianapolis in March, 1893.

There, in addition to his law practice, he wrote a series of articles for the *Ladies Home Journal* on the nature of the federal government. These were later revised and published in book form under the title *This Country of Ours*. For many years the book was used as a standard reference work for schools and colleges.

Public life again claimed Benjamin Harrison in 1899, when he was invited to act as senior counsel for Venezuela in its boundary dispute with Great Britain. The arbitration tribunal met in Paris. Before Harrison was half through his argument, the British counsel admitted defeat. Once again the man who had been President proved himself a good lawyer and an eloquent speaker.

An able and upright man, he served his country honorably and well, both in war and in peace.

On March 13, 1901, Benjamin Harrison died at the age of sixty-seven in Indianapolis, and was buried there.

The President Who "Came Back"

PRESIDENT CLEVELAND'S greatest single service to the nation during his first administration was, without doubt, his stubborn fight to maintain the gold standard. The Republicans, on the other hand, demanded the free and unlimited coinage of silver and the use of silver as legal tender for all debts. When, in 1890, President Harrison signed the bill that required the government to purchase four and one half million ounces of silver each month and issue notes based on it, this meant absorbing almost the entire output of all the silver mines in the United States. It also indicated the widely different opinions of Republicans and Democrats as to sound financing.

The 1892 campaign between Harrison and Cleveland was a bitter struggle between East and West, high-tariff and low-tariff forces, debtor and creditor, the gold-standard and the silver forces. In the four years that had passed, the Northwest had been strengthened by the admission of six new states: Idaho, Montana, North Dakota, South Dakota, Wyoming, and Washington. Three of these were silver-producing states. Silver-mine owners, railway promoters, cattle barons, and timber and land speculators, already enriched by government bounties, preferred to see the government in Republican hands.

Cleveland won the 1892 election, however, and for two years the Democrats had a majority in both the Senate and the House. Many changes were taking place in the American economy. The Socialist Labor party had launched an independent national campaign, in which it advocated government ownership of public utilities, inheritance and income taxes, universal and equal suffrage, abolition of child labor, and the secret ballot. American farmers, trying to defend themselves against inflation, joined with the Socialists, and the Populist farmer-labor party that resulted polled more than a million votes in the 1892 campaign.

When Cleveland took office in March, 1893, the entire country was in a state of unrest over the two questions: silver and the tariff. Cleveland considered Harrison's silver-purchasing law to blame for the unsettled financial situation. Early in August he called a special session of Congress to deal with the emergency. The silver-purchasing law was repealed; and Cleveland turned his attention to a reduction of the tariff. Trusts and combines, he declared, would be curbed; and the standard of value of the currency would be maintained against depreciation.

The high-tariff law of 1890 apparently had not interfered with prosperity, and to the people generally, and manufacturers in particular, Cleveland's talk of lowering tariffs and curbing big business was disturbing. The tariff bill that the House and Senate passed fell so far short of President Cleveland's ideal that he refused to sign it; it became law without his signature. It contained an income-tax provision, aimed at the rich, most of which the Supreme Court found unconstitutional.

While President Cleveland was sorely tried by all this dissension, he and his charming wife enjoyed their return to the White House. Electric lights instead of gas had been installed during their absence, and now there was a telephone switchboard instead of a single telephone. Soon they were to share the comforts of the mansion with their baby daughter— the first child of a President to be born in the White House.

Two months after Inauguration Day, the long-pending storm broke upon the second Cleveland administration. The vague feeling of distrust on the part of industry had grown into a full-fledged agricultural and industrial depression, the worst in fifty years. One railroad, with debts of one hundred and twenty-five million dollars, went bankrupt. The buying of silver had been inflating the currency by about fifty million dollars annually, and approximately the same amount of gold had been shipped abroad. The stock market collapsed. The value of the dollar, in the opinion of one well-known financier, dropped to fifty-three cents. The year closed with prices of many products the lowest ever known, with millions of men out of work, and with suffering and starvation in all our cities.

The gold reserve in the Treasury fell below the established minimum, and people feared that the Secretary of the Treasury might redeem outstanding notes in silver. President Cleveland issued a statement that gold payments would be maintained, but the public mind was in a state of panic and a crash was inevitable. Imports were vastly in excess of exports. Runs on the banks developed in all parts of the country. A total of one hundred and fifty-eight national banks, one hundred and seventy-two state banks, forty-seven savings banks, thirteen loan and trust companies, and sixteen mortgage companies went down in the general crash, according to the 1893 figures of R. G. Dun and Company. The South and the Middle West were in the grip of ten-cent corn, six-cent cotton, and ten per cent mortgages.

Many blamed the Cleveland administration, but it is not likely that an authoritative explanation exists for the panic of 1893. We do know the West had been colonized too rapidly for its own good. Men who lacked both farming experience and capital had pushed into the homesteading country. Railroads, steamship lines, and farm machinery had been developed so rapidly that the world's food markets were overstocked. Farmers had gone heavily into debt for land and equipment, and when they could not sell their grain, beef, and pork, foreclosure resulted.

President Cleveland still clung to his original ideas. He began a long, hard, and determined fight to maintain the gold standard. Almost alone he upheld it all through his second administration, as he had during his first. Bond issues were required to replenish the Treasury. The first sale—fifty million dollars at 4 per cent interest—was announced. When it became clear that the public would not buy the bonds, the Secretary of the Treasury was sent to New York city to plead with the principal bankers. They took the bonds at a price on which they later lost money.

The shutting down of mills, mines, and factories continued. At the end of the long winter, serious labor trouble broke out at the Pullman works in Chicago and spread westward. President Cleveland's Attorney General advised the use of federal troops and a court injunction: The mails must be moved and interstate commerce must be maintained. Cleveland rejected the idea of using troops, but the government obtained an injunction against the strikers. Meanwhile the situation grew even more alarming. Passenger trains were stopped, freight cars were burned by the hundreds, railway switches were smashed and switchmen driven from their towers.

It required tremendous courage for the President to call out troops. The governor of Illinois and the mayor of Chicago had done more than anyone else to help Cleveland carry their state in the 1892 campaign, and both opposed the use of force. To go against the wishes of these men would mean the disruption of the Democratic party in Illinois. Cleveland realized that. But he realized also that the strikers were getting out of hand and that the railroads of the entire country were threatened. He issued a statement: *"If it takes the entire Army and Navy of the United States to deliver a post-card to Chicago, that card will be delivered!"*

The injunction issued by the court, and Cleveland's firm stand, turned the tide. But organized labor felt that the President had taken the side of capital.

Another situation greatly disturbed Cleveland. During his first administration he had offered the help of the United States in arbitrating a boundary dispute between British Guiana and Venezuela. Nothing came of the offer, and the boundary question had not been settled. Great Britain seemed about to take matters into her own hands, when there occurred a rupture between the British and Nicaragua. Several Britons, including a vice consul, had been arrested and expelled from Nicaragua, and the Foreign Office had demanded a payment for damages amounting to seventy-five thousand pounds.

Angered by the delay, Great Britain sent three warships to Nicaragua, landed several hundred troops, and seized a customhouse. Nicaragua paid the indemnity and the British forces left the country; but the incident worried President Cleveland. There was a possibility that she might ignore the Monroe Doctrine and deal with Venezuela in the same high-handed manner. In reply to a forceful note from the British Foreign Office, Cleveland asked Congress to appropriate money for a commission to determine the true Venezuelan boundary. He further declared that it would be the duty of the United States to maintain this boundary against any aggression.

The warlike tone of the Cleveland message has been criticized, but it helped to bring about a satisfactory settlement of the dispute—and a broader acceptance of the Monroe Doctrine. American public opinion, suddenly awakening to the importance of the nation in world affairs, approved of vigorous action in our foreign relations. Besides, the atmosphere having been cleared, the two world powers were found to be firm friends after all.

Cleveland was still haunted by the draining off of gold reserves. Another bond issue brought sixty-five million dollars into the Treasury; and the export of gold to Europe was stopped. A year later some sixty-six million dollars' worth of bonds were sold. It is generally agreed that if the nation had not been on the gold standard, the bonds could not have been marketed.

Taking advantage of the depression, strikes, unemployment, and increasing economic distress, the Populists captured the Democratic convention in 1896. The Cleveland administration was virtually repudiated by its own party, and a young politician from Nebraska, who believed in the ratio of sixteen ounces of silver to one of gold, was nominated as the Democratic candidate for President. He was William Jennings Bryan, who in a stirring address, declared: *"You shall not crucify mankind upon a cross of gold!"*

In the White House, Cleveland carried on his negotiations

with Great Britain. The result was a treaty between the two great English-speaking nations, pledging them to submit to arbitration all disputes which they might fail to settle by diplomatic means. But in spite of all Cleveland's efforts, the treaty failed in the Senate.

In the matter of Hawaii, where the Queen had been compelled to abdicate and American and other interests had formed a republic, Cleveland was firm. A treaty of annexation had been signed by President Harrison, but in the early part of Cleveland's second administration he blocked the project. He felt it was unfair to take away from Hawaii the right to its own rule. He also declared, with regard to a proposed canal across Nicaragua, that any canal which might be built must not be dominated by a single power, but must be for the benefit of the entire world.

Cleveland's strength of character made him an outstanding figure in public affairs. He restored honesty to government and planted deep in the American mind the idea that special privilege ought to be abolished. In a period of stress and confusion, his dogged determination saved the nation's money standard. By his firm handling of the Nicaraguan, Venezuelan, and Hawaiian problems, he said, in effect: "No foreign power or combination of powers shall deprive any country in this hemisphere of the right to govern itself or to shape its own destiny."

At the end of his term, President Cleveland took his family to Princeton, New Jersey, where he had bought a colonial mansion. In 1901 he became a trustee of Princeton University.

He died at Princeton seven years later, on June 24, 1908.

WILLIAM McKINLEY

The Third Martyred President

THE administration of William Mc-
Kinley, twenty-fifth President of the United States, will stand
in history as one of the greatest transition periods in the
country's history. The presidential election of 1896 seems, as
we look back, to have ushered in an era of faster tempo in
American life. It was a time of heavier gold production and
greater business prosperity than the nation had ever known.
There were bigger and more powerful trusts. The first automobiles were appearing on the roads; the first motion picture
theaters were opening. There was more travel, and therefore
wider horizons and more education. Already the people were
beginning to forget the panic of 1893.

The campaign in which McKinley, Republican, opposed
William Jennings Bryan, Democratic advocate of "sixteen to
one" silver, aroused the country as no other campaign had
done since Lincoln's. On Bryan's side were the voters who
were against concentrated wealth and big business. They were
the Socialists, single-tax adherents, and organized labor leaders. Those who favored McKinley believed in a protective
tariff, the importation of labor from Europe, and the expansion of railroads and steamship lines. All the continental
territories except three (Arizona, Oklahoma, and New Mexico) had been admitted to the Union. The United States had
grown into a nation strong, lively, and filled with confidence.

With the aid of an ever increasing list of inventions, beginning with the cotton gin in 1793 and such mechanical improvements as the tin-plate mill in McKinley's own day, the
United States produced more farm commodities and manu-
factured more articles than the people could use. Businessmen

declared that the nation must have new outlets for her surplus. Led by Marcus A. Hanna, a Cleveland industrial magnate, they elected McKinley on sound-money, protective-tariff issues.

The early ancestors of William McKinley were Scottish Highlanders, one of whom migrated to Ireland in 1690. It was the son of this "MacInla" who settled on a three-hundred-acre Pennsylvania farm in 1743. His grandson fought in the Revolutionary War, and his great-great-grandson became President of the United States. William McKinley, father of the President, was an iron founder. He emigrated westward to Ohio, and in 1829 married Nancy Allison, whose ancestors had come from Scotland. William, Jr., their seventh child, was born in Niles, Ohio, on January 29, 1843.

At that time, Niles was a small hamlet. There were no railroads in the region—and few wagon roads. If Mrs. McKinley wanted to visit her relatives, thirty miles distant, she rode on a horse, and usually carried one of her children with her. Niles was also lacking in schools. When the future President was nine, therefore, his father decided to move to Poland, Ohio. Here young William went swimming with the other boys in summer, and skating in winter. Here he learned his lessons at the little schoolhouse, and after a year entered the local academy, which he attended until he was seventeen.

By this time, every other member of the family was working. Times were hard; so William, at the age of eighteen, taught school at twenty-five dollars a month and board. When vacation time came, he worked in the Poland post office. Then came the Civil War. The youth was not in robust health, but he enlisted, and maybe the rugged outdoor life was what he needed. For, though he knew nothing about army routine and was not accustomed to physical hardships, he gained strength as he went along. He was soon promoted to sergeant. On one occasion he marched 104 miles in a little more than three days, in order to take part in a battle which cost the regiment nearly two hundred men. When the war came to an end, McKinley found himself a major at twenty-two, with an enviable record and better health than he had ever known.

McKinley had proved his natural ability as a speaker, and in 1866 he entered the Albany Law School. The "Major," as he was always called, had the knack of getting along with people. In the spring of 1867 he moved to Canton, a thriving city of five thousand, and was admitted to the bar. One day he was asked by a prominent attorney to take charge of a case. The lawyer wanted to size up the young stranger. He watched McKinley win the case, and decided to take him in as a partner. From that time forward, William McKinley never lacked a client. Two years later he was elected county prosecuting attorney.

It was in Canton, the county seat, that he met Ida Saxton, daughter of a pioneer banker and newspaper publisher. They were married on January 25, 1871, and within the next three years became the parents of two baby girls. Before she had been married six years, however, Mrs. McKinley lost her health, her two children, and her mother. For the rest of her life, she was an invalid. Nevertheless, she took a deep interest in her husband's career, and urged him to campaign for General Rutherford B. Hayes, his former commanding officer. Hayes was elected governor in 1875 and President in 1876.

McKinley was now well known as a political orator. He was elected to Congress in 1876, and served seven successive terms in the House (with the exception of 1882), rising to the chairmanship of the powerful Ways and Means Committee and leading the fight for a high tariff to protect American industries. From the time of his first speech in Congress to the end of his life, William McKinley advocated tariff protection. "Self-preservation," he said, "is the first law of nature—as it is, and should be—of nations."

Congressman McKinley was the sponsor of the tin-plate industry in America. Capitalists were ready to launch a business that would "employ thirty-three thousand men" in this industry, provided they were guaranteed adequate tariff protection. McKinley got it for them. The cost of tin plate was reduced from $6.75 per box to $2.99 in eighteen years. In 1896 the United States *imported* nearly four hundred million pounds; in 1912, the United States *produced* more than two billion pounds. The American industry was less than twenty-five years old.

Marcus A. Hanna, Cleveland magnate, recognized McKinley as the foremost exponent of protection in America. He was so anxious to see the Ohio Congressman in the White House that he gave up his business interests, and devoted his entire time and fortune to running McKinley's campaigns. First, there was the governorship of Ohio. This high office did not appeal to McKinley, for the governor had no veto power and therefore no direct influence upon legislation. However, since he had lost his seat in the House, he entered the race, and won.

Though McKinley led a busy life, he never allowed public duties to interfere with his devotion to his invalid wife. On entering the grounds of the Ohio state capitol on his way to his office each morning, the governor would turn around and raise his hat in a smiling farewell to Mrs. McKinley, who sat at her hotel window across the street. And, at exactly three o'clock each afternoon, even if he happened to be in a conference, he excused himself, walked to the window, and waved his handkerchief. Mrs. McKinley would be watching for this greeting. They never forgot.

In Congress, the election of 1894 revealed a Republican majority of 142 in the House; the Senate also became Republican with a margin of 12. The Republican skies all over the country were getting brighter. Hanna lost no time in getting the McKinley band wagon rolling; two years would not be too much time to build up McKinley throughout the United States and secure his nomination for President. More than McKinley himself, perhaps, the shrewd campaign manager long had realized that the governorship was merely a steppingstone to the White House.

In the 1896 campaign, the methods of the two candidates, McKinley and Bryan, were widely different. Mr. Bryan toured the country in a special train (although Hanna and the Republicans were usually caricatured as literally rolling in wealth). McKinley chose the more dignified course of sitting on his front porch and letting the people come to him. When he spoke to a crowd of visitors on his front lawn, he could be sure that his speech would be carried in the country's newspapers and reach a wide audience.

McKinley's victory, which was predicted as early as October, was considered a triumph for both tariff protection and sound money. On Inauguration Day, there was a courteous transfer of authority from Democratic President Cleveland to his younger Republican successor. For each man had a genuine feeling of respect for the other.

McKinley found that the gold reserve in the Treasury was

low. He also found that the 1894 low-tariff law had unsettled manufacturing and commercial interests. It had failed to produce enough revenue for the expenses of the government. Another problem was the fear, on the part of the people, that the gold standard would not be maintained. This fear led them to present a tremendous amount of legal-tender notes for redemption, which caused further depletion of the Treasury's gold reserve. The immediate problem was to bring in more money than the government was spending.

McKinley's policies almost immediately restored confidence. He called Congress into special session soon after he was inaugurated and sent a message urging an increase in the revenue through higher duties on imports. When the Senate got around to passing the tariff bill some four months later, the rates were even higher than McKinley thought necessary. Under its operation, however, the country prospered as never before. The new tariff did not ruin our foreign trade, as opponents of protection declared it would. On the contrary, both exports and imports increased enormously.

Early in the McKinley administration the republic of Hawaii submitted its Constitution, which had been framed by elected representatives of the people, and asked for annexation to the United States. In June, President McKinley sent to the Senate a new treaty of annexation. The Senate rejected the treaty, declaring that the United States had no moral or legal right to annex the territory of an independent state.

The President now turned to the Cuban problem. He would have preferred to continue Cleveland's policy of neutrality, but newspaper reports of atrocities committed by the Spanish rulers of the island and stories of the Cubans fighting for liberty and independence (as our forefathers had fought in the Revolutionary War) stirred the people of the United States. Incensed by the sinking of the battleship *Maine* (by a submarine mine in Havana harbor while on a friendly mission), Congress passed a resolution empowering the President to use the armed forces of the United States, if necessary, to expel the Spanish government from the island. This was, in effect, a declaration of war; and under it, war began.

Our Navy sank the Spanish fleets in both Cuban and Philippine waters early in the summer of 1898, and the war was over by August. Cuba was freed from Spanish dominion and the United States later paid Spain twenty million dollars for all claims to Puerto Rico, Guam, and the Philippines. Cuba gained her independence; but two years afterward she agreed to an American protectorate over the island.

Dewey's victory over the Spanish fleet in Manila Bay was followed by the occupation of the islands by American forces. It was not until 1935 that President Franklin D. Roosevelt started the Filipinos on the road to independence.

The victory in Manila Bay caused Congress to see the projected annexation of Hawaii in a new light. The strategic value of the islands to the United States could not be overlooked. An annexation treaty could be ratified only by a two-thirds vote of the Senate, and that would take time. Meanwhile, European nations might complicate matters, on the theory that unattached islands in the Pacific were fair game. A joint resolution of Congress, on the other hand, required only a majority vote in both Senate and House. Such a resolution was passed in June by the House, and in July by the Senate, and Hawaii became a Territory of the United States in the summer of 1898.

The war with Spain had taught Americans the value of a

canal that would connect the Atlantic and Pacific oceans. An old treaty with Great Britain provided that that country should share equally with us in any canal which might be built across Nicaragua. But public opinion in 1898, both in and out of Congress, favored a canal built, owned, and operated exclusively by the United States. A second treaty with Great Britain was made, in which that country withdrew and left the field entirely to the United States. Thus the Nicaragua project was abandoned in favor of the Panama Canal.

In this new era of international responsibility, President McKinley definitely helped the United States, then developing from an isolated nation into a world power, to a friendlier and more secure footing with such nations as Germany, Japan, Russia, Great Britain, and France. He sent our armed forces to join theirs in rescuing foreign legations from a siege of Chinese revolutionists in Peking. This was the first instance in which American forces joined other powers in a military expedition.

This incident led indirectly to a new policy in China—the policy later known as the Open Door—in which the nations having certain "spheres of influence" in China agreed to refrain from interference with the treaty ports or the special interests of the other powers. Thus Americans acquired, as a result of the Boxer uprising, equal trading rights in China with British and other nations. In a few short months we had become a world power.

At home, Congress, mindful of the Republican campaign promise to "preserve the existing gold standard," established a reserve fund of one hundred and fifty million dollars in gold, instead of one hundred million dollars, and provided that notes, once redeemed, should not be paid out except for gold. This was one of the most important financial reforms in the history of the United States. For more than a generation it was the rock upon which rested the stability and safety of our financial system. The same act definitely established the gold standard, specifically the dollar, which consisted of "25.8 grains of gold, nine-tenths fine."

In 1900 the Republicans re-elected McKinley, together with Theodore Roosevelt as Vice President. The President had made a good record and hoped to open, in his second term, a new era of expansion for American trade and shipping. On September 6, 1901, however, while welcoming citizens to the Pan-American Exposition in Buffalo, N.Y., he was shot down by Leon Czolgosz, an anarchist, and died on September 14.

William McKinley went to the White House when this nation was weak in foreign prestige; when he left it, the United States enjoyed the respect of the entire world.

THEODORE ROOSEVELT

"Rough Rider" President

ON the back porch of a spacious house in New York city a small boy with pipe-stem legs bent and stretched. His light brown hair was moist on his pale forehead. There was dogged determination in the firm set of his jaw and in his nearsighted blue eyes, as he worked with dumbbells and Indian clubs and pulled back his frail shoulders in a mighty effort at deep breathing.

The Civil War was over, and President Andrew Johnson was struggling with the problems that always follow war, but the nine-year-old boy was too young to be deeply concerned about the affairs of the nation. He was engaged in his own private war—a battle for health and strength. Many years later he would become President of the United States, but in 1866, he had only one objective. He would build up his frail little body so that he would be strong like other boys.

His name was Theodore Roosevelt. He was thin, pale, and short of breath because of the asthma which had troubled him since babyhood. It was a great moment for him when his father first led him to that outdoor gymnasium, and said: "You have the brains, Theodore, but brains are of little use without the body; you have got to make your body, and it lies with you to make it."

The boy's eyes brightened and he set his prominent white teeth in firm resolve. Never once after that did he pause in his struggle for strength. It was dull, hard, lonely work. Yet most people probably thought he was a very lucky boy. His father was a rich man. Tutors were at hand to look after his education. In summer he was taken to Maine, where he could roam through the woods and breathe the healing fragrance of pine-scented air. He tramped for miles, he learned to paddle and row, and he chopped wood. Lincoln had to split rails to earn his bread; Theodore Roosevelt chopped wood to develop his muscles. And at his father's country home at Oyster Bay, Long Island, he learned to ride and swim and play tennis.

His determination was tremendous, and the trait was strong in his ancestors. On his father's side he came from a race of sturdy Hollanders, who first settled in New York (or New Amsterdam, as it was then called) in 1650. The family name then was Van Rosenvelt. It did not take its present spelling of Roosevelt until a century after those early Dutch settlers came to America. Theodore's mother, Martha Bulloch, was descended from a prominent Southern family. Her great-grandfather, Archibald Bulloch, was the first governor of the state of Georgia during the Revolutionary War.

Theodore Roosevelt was born in the house on East Twentieth Street, in New York city, on October 27, 1858. When he was twelve he was taken to Europe. From the age of thirteen he always wore heavy spectacles. At sixteen his family bundled him off to Algiers, in the hope that the air there would help his weak lungs. With his brother Elliott and his sister Corinne, he was then taken to Dresden, Germany, where they lived in the home of a tutor. Theodore, or "Teed," as he was often called, was not fond of lessons, but he liked natural history and enjoyed drawing. He also kept faithfully at his physical exercises.

As he grew older he took up boxing, fencing, and even jujitsu, and, when he entered Harvard, he had almost won his battle for health. He was able to take part in most of the sports, such as wrestling, sparring, and running. "I never came in first," he used to say, "but I got more out of the exercise than those who did."

Unlike most rich men's sons of the period, his lodgings near Harvard were fitted up simply. His room was decorated with stuffed birds and small animals which he himself mounted, and stones he had collected during his travels. His practice of keeping strange pets threw the rooming house into disorder one day when an enormous tortoise which had escaped from his quarters sauntered down the hall. On another occasion, some live lobsters he was carrying on a street car from Boston for scientific study broke out of their package and almost caused a panic.

At twenty-one, Theodore Roosevelt was graduated from Harvard, and was ready to face the world—a young man five feet, nine inches in height, with wavy brown hair and keen blue eyes behind heavy spectacles. His smile framed his prominent white teeth, and he smiled often. He was bursting with enthusiasm to get things done, whether in work or in play. At Island Falls, Maine, where he spent many happy vacations with his friend and guide, Bill Sewall, the villagers loved young Theodore for his unfailing good humor and democratic ways. "He was as plain as a spruce board," they said, "and as square as a brick."

During his college days, he had fallen in love with Alice Hathaway Lee, of Boston, and they were married just a few months after his graduation.

Although he did not have to worry about earning a living, young Theodore had no intention of living a lazy life. Before he was twenty-three, he was the author of a *Naval History of the War of 1812*. He had been one of the editors of his college paper and he enjoyed writing. The *Naval History* was the first of several books which he wrote as the years went by. He, like other young men he knew in New York city, was much interested in politics. That led him naturally to the law, and though he never had any intention of becoming a lawyer, he took up the study of law at Columbia College. It was a steppingstone for more active participation in government affairs.

He was twenty-four when he took his seat at Albany as the youngest member of the state Assembly. Before long his independent spirit and his fighting qualities attracted attention. He was re-elected, and served during 1883 and 1884. When the legislature was not in session he spent most of his time in the open. One of his trips led him out to what was then the Wild West, to the little frontier town of Medora, North Dakota, and his stay there influenced his entire life. In the West he met his first cowboys and ranchmen, hunted buffalo, slept under the stars with his saddle for a pillow, and found joy in the broad prairies, the snow-capped mountains, and the rushing rivers. He wrote a book about it later, called *The Wilderness Hunter*; and, before his first visit ended, he bought the Chimney Butte Ranch. But there was still work to be done at home. He never believed because he was a rich man's son that he could afford to be idle.

He joined the New York National Guard and became a captain. As chairman of the Committee on Cities in the legislature, he suggested many reforms in New York's government that put an end to high salaries and extravagant expense accounts. When he was twenty-five, he went to the Chicago convention as the head of the delegation from New York state. He had become a prominent figure in politics and ardently supported the Republican party. The Republicans, however, were beaten. Theodore Roosevelt decided to leave politics.

He was beginning to learn that life does not always run smoothly. His father, his mother, and his young wife had passed away. Roosevelt turned once more to the West. Ranching now became a business with him. He sent for his old friend, Bill Sewall, bought another ranch, and went to work in earnest. He spent days in the saddle, riding herd and rounding up cattle. And in the quiet times he read and wrote. His best writing was inspired by his life on the plains.

In the autumn of 1886 as he sat before his open fire at Elkhorn, he read in a New York newspaper that he had been nominated for mayor by the Independent party. He started at once for the East, where his own party gave him the nomination. But the Republican party again went down in defeat. Roosevelt sailed for England. There in 1886 he married Edith Kermit Carow, whom he had known since boyhood. Several months later, he brought his bride to New York. Once again he took up his literary work and plunged into politics. He campaigned for General Harrison in 1888, and the newly elected President gave him a place on the Civil Service Commission in Washington. It was a thankless job, but he attacked it with his usual energy, uncovering graft, fighting the spoils system, and getting measures adopted so that public employment would be within reach of the people, regardless of their politics. He did this work with such fearlessness and zeal that he began to worry his political opponents. When after six years of labor in Washington, he was appointed president of the board of New York's police commissioners, he attacked this new job with the same enthusiasm and honesty. No amount of political pressure could stop him. He made a clean sweep of the Police Department. He showed the people of his city that graft was not a necessary evil, that corruption could be wiped out, and that inefficiency was not to be excused.

Roosevelt had been in public life for more than fifteen years, and he liked it. In fact, he liked nothing better than a good fight—a fight against wrong and injustice. Political leaders of both parties, however, were afraid of him. He was honest and patriotic, but so impulsive and independent that they never knew what he might do next.

During the McKinley administration he was given a place as Assistant Secretary of the Navy. He felt that the United States would soon be in a war with Spain. The Cubans were begging for our protection. So he set to work to build a stronger American Navy, and reorganized the Department from top to bottom. His militant spirit both alarmed and amused those in high office. But when the battleship Maine was destroyed in Havana harbor, he left his desk. "There is nothing more for me to do here," he said. "I must get into the fight myself . . . I have no right to ask others to do the fighting while I stay at home."

Never was a more widely assorted company of soldiers gathered together than Colonel Roosevelt's famous Rough Riders! He was besieged by volunteers. There were educated men, members of the most fashionable clubs of Boston and New York, polo players, track athletes, tennis champions, football players, policemen who had admired him when he was police commissioner, and his good friends among the cowboys of the West, all eager to serve under his command. Side by side, these young men from every walk of life charged up San Juan Hill together. They took San Juan, and that led to the capture of Santiago which brought the war to an end. American newspapers were filled with accounts of the heroism of "Teddy" Roosevelt and his Rough Riders. Roosevelt, in talking about it later, often remarked with a twinkle in his blue eyes: "It wasn't much of a war, but it was all the war we had!"

It was a little war and a short one, but it brought Theodore Roosevelt home to glory. The political bosses now had more than an enthusiastic young reformer to deal with. He was a war hero, and the admiring eyes of the nation were upon him. He was elected governor of New York, and continued his policy of honesty and his fight against the spoils system. Most of the people in the state liked his vigorous methods. But the bosses and the politicians wanted to get him removed to some spot where he would have little to do. Having him nominated for Vice President seemed a good idea, and when McKinley was re-elected President, Roosevelt was swept into the office of Vice President.

Those who feared him sighed with relief. But they had not reckoned with the accident of death. Within six months after taking the oath as Vice President, Theodore Roosevelt was elevated to the highest office in the United States. McKinley had been shot in Buffalo, and not long afterward he died.

The people, after their first shock and grief over the loss of McKinley, admired their new President. Roosevelt was only forty-two years old, years younger than any President the country had ever had. And he was youthful in spirit. Within three years he had become a war hero, the governor of the Empire State, the Vice President, and now he was the Chief Executive. The people liked his frank way of speaking. He was democratic, friendly, eager, and a champion of the right.

234

"The door of the White House," he announced, "shall swing open as easily for the poor as for the rich, and not one bit easier." He never departed from that policy. What's more, he got things done.

Theodore Roosevelt fought vice and crime. He settled the Alaskan boundary dispute. He broke up powerful trusts and regulated the railways. He favored imposing income and inheritance taxes; he favored forest conservation and irrigation in the Far West. He instituted the Pure Food Law and government inspection of meat. He dispatched a fleet of battleships around the world to show our naval strength, and he appointed delegates to the second Hague Peace Conference. He went down to Panama to inspect the progress of the building of the new canal. In informal, neighborly fashion he talked with Russia and Japan and persuaded them to end the war they were waging, for which service he won the Nobel Prize in 1906 as the world's foremost peacemaker.

A year before the Republican national convention was to meet, he frankly expressed his desire to extend his stay in the White House. And when election day came he received a popular vote three times greater than any candidate had ever received. He had succeeded to the office of President in the beginning. Now he was chosen by the people.

The doctrine Theodore Roosevelt preached was threefold: the square deal, the big stick, and the strenuous life.

"The labor unions shall have a square deal, and the corporations shall have a square deal," he said, "and in addition all private citizens shall have a square deal."

"There is a homely old adage," Roosevelt said at another time: " 'Speak softly and carry a big stick; you will go far.' If the American nation will speak softly, and yet build and keep at a pitch of the highest training a thoroughly efficient Navy, the Monroe Doctrine will go far."

Many forgot the admonition to "speak softly," but the term "the big stick" caught on. Cartoonists around the world pictured the bespectacled Teddy Roosevelt with gleaming white teeth, a wide smile, a Rough Rider hat, and in his hand the "big stick."

He made it known at the beginning of his second term that he would not again be a candidate at the end of his four years' term. On March 4, 1909, he gave his blessing to the new President, William Howard Taft, his friend and former Secretary of War.

Within a few weeks, Roosevelt was off to the wilds of Africa on an expedition for the Smithsonian Institution. After an absence of fifteen months, he landed in New York, where he was greeted warmly and urged to run again for President. "My hat is in the ring," he smilingly replied. He fought hard for the nomination, but it went to Mr. Taft, and Teddy was nominated by the Progressive party. In the end both lost out through the split in the Republican party. It was the Democratic candidate, Woodrow Wilson, who was elected.

Roosevelt took his defeat like a good fighter and was off again to South America, where blood-poisoning and fever attacked him. He was never quite so strong and vigorous after that.

When World War I came, he tried in vain to get into it. He saw his four sons go off to war, and lost his youngest, Quentin, who was a fighter pilot.

On Monday, January 6, 1919, Theodore Roosevelt died at his home in Oyster Bay. There, after a severely simple service in the little church, he was laid quietly to rest in the village cemetery, according to his wish.

Perhaps his own words furnish the most fitting epitaph for his active life:

> I wish to preach, not the doctrine of ignoble ease, but the doctrine of the strenuous life—the life of toil and effort. Far better it is to dare mighty things, to win glorious triumphs, even though checkered by failure, than to take rank with those poor spirits who neither enjoy much nor suffer much, because they live in the gray twilight that knows not victory or defeat.

WILLIAM H. TAFT

The President Who Wanted to be Chief Justice

WILLIAM HOWARD TAFT

only man in the history of America who held both the highest executive and the highest judicial office in the government. It was natural for his thoughts to turn, at an early age, to public office. His father, a lawyer, served as Secretary of War and Attorney General under President Grant, and later was sent by President Arthur as minister to Russia. "Will" Taft grew up in a household where national affairs were constantly being discussed, and he was eager to follow in his father's footsteps.

The boy who was to become the twenty-seventh President of the United States was born on September 15, 1857, in Cincinnati, Ohio. They called him Willie from the beginning. The name exactly fitted the round, dimpled baby. "He is very large for his age," wrote his mother when he was seven weeks old. "He spreads his hands to anyone who will take him, and his face is wreathed in smiles at the slightest provocation."

As Willie grew older, he was still fat and smiling. Excess weight was something he had to bear all through his long life. As a boy he went to the public schools. Before he was eighteen, he became Bill Taft of Yale. The tall, huge-bodied lad, with blue eyes, fair skin, light hair, and a sunny disposition quickly made friends at the university. He laughed with the boys who made jokes about his size. He played football and baseball; and, though he was never overstudious, he stood second in scholarship when he was graduated with his class of 1878.

Alphonso Taft, his father, was a wealthy man, but he had always worked hard, and he saw no reason why his sons should take life easy. Will enrolled at the law school of Cincinnati College when he returned home from Yale, and began reading law in his father's office. Two years later, having completed his course, he was admitted to the bar.

Now, at twenty-three, he was ready to set up a law office of his own. Instead, he went to work as a reporter on the Cincinnati *Commercial* and was assigned to cover court cases. There he gained plenty of experience in the workings of justice. Also, he wrote so well that his editor urged him to make journalism his career. Will Taft, however, laughed at the idea of giving up the law. Even then, he was dreaming of taking his place as a member of the Supreme Court of the United States. That, to him, was a higher honor than being in the White House as President.

His first position in public office came in 1881, when he was appointed assistant prosecutor of Hamilton County. A year later President Arthur made him collector of internal revenue, with headquarters in Cincinnati. Will Taft found the routine work dull. He belonged with the law, not in a tax office. Within a year he resigned.

Ambitious, enthusiastic and with a keen sense of justice, he turned his attention to the Cincinnati courts. They had long needed cleaning up. Will Taft did exactly that, and his good work won for him the assignment of assistant county solicitor.

Along about this time a new experience tore at his heart-strings: Will Taft fell in love. Helen Herron was good looking, witty, and intelligent. She was also highly popular with the boys. Taft was filled with humility; he doubted whether this beautiful and talented girl would even consider him. Helen was slow in making up her mind, but on June 19, 1886, the two were married. They toured France, England, and Scotland that summer. By autumn they were back in Cincinnati, living in their new house. And Will Taft was happier than he had ever been in his life.

One promotion followed another as the years went by: Judge of the Superior Court; U.S. Solicitor-General, Federal Circuit Judge. Nobody could have been more astounded than Taft when, in 1900, President McKinley decided to send him to the Philippines. Taft was comfortable and contented in his office. He was dismayed at the idea of leaving Cincinnati. He knew as much, or as little, as the average American about the islands in the Pacific which Spain had just ceded to the United States. He could not speak the language of the natives, and he was uncertain about his ability to straighten out their tangled affairs. Yet, as always, he regarded any government appointment as a sacred duty.

In the spring of 1901 he began the difficult job of governing the islanders. They were bewildered and suspicious, but Taft saw their need and understood their problems. He won their confidence by giving them schools, roads, and courts of justice. Through him they learned the principles of democracy and freedom. He improved sanitation and living conditions. He protected their rights. For them he sacrificed the big chance for which he had been waiting all his life—the chance to become chief justice of the United States. Theodore Roosevelt, who had become President, offered him the appointment and urged him to take it. It must have cost William Howard Taft a battle with his conscience to turn down that opportunity, but turn it down he did. His work in the Philippines was not completed. For three years he served as governor general. During that time he went to Rome and, in a personal interview with the Pope, arranged for a transfer of lands which had been owned by the Church in the Philippine Islands. For several years the natives and the priests had been quarreling over those lands. Taft was so earnest in pleading his cause that he persuaded the Church to sell the lands to the United States; and Congress voted $7,239,000 to pay for them.

During his stay in the islands, Taft, who was burdened by many pounds of excess flesh, was far from well. The broiling sun and the tropic heat were none too kind to a fat man. Officials in Washington were concerned about his health and urged him to rest. In the summer of 1903, accordingly, he went to a mountain resort in the Philippines, and in a cable to the Secretary of War, he said: "Stood trip well; rode horseback twenty-five miles to five thousand feet elevation." Senator Root, reassured and seeing in his mind's eye a picture of the 300-pound governor general riding up the mountain trail, sent this cable in reply: "Referring to your telegram, how is the *horse?*" This joke became famous. It was told and retold by Taft himself, who always enjoyed as big a laugh over it as the general public did.

It was 1904 when Taft returned to Washington to become Secretary of War, and when he left the Philippines he had the satisfaction of knowing that he had established loyalty and democracy there, and had won the enduring devotion of the people of the islands.

As Secretary of War, he supervised the construction of the Panama Canal, straightened out affairs in Cuba, and traveled to Japan on a mission of peace and reassurance. President Roosevelt was so enthusiastic about his ability that he used all his influence and had Taft nominated as his successor.

William Howard Taft was elected in 1908, and took up his

presidential duties on March 4, 1909. During his term he urged the adoption of an amendment to the Constitution to permit the levying of income taxes. He recommended to Congress the setting up of a national budget. He fought monopolies and trusts and tried in every way to revise the tariff. He did manage to lower the scale on import duties, but his four years in the White House were far from happy. When, during the last year of his term, he felt he wanted to continue in office, his enemies opposed his renomination, calling him reactionary and too conservative. He had also lost many political friends by removing from office some of the men appointed by Roosevelt. Taft was not good at playing the game of politics. He did not hesitate to replace those whom he considered inefficient, and this did not increase his popularity with some of the Republican leaders.

His chances for a second term as President did not seem too bright. They seemed even less bright when his one-time close friend and champion, Theodore Roosevelt, decided to run again for the office. This caused a definite split in the Republican party. Taft won the nomination, but because of that split, his party was defeated, and the Democrats elected Woodrow Wilson.

Taft was much too active to consider retiring. When he left the White House, he became a professor of law at Yale University. In addition, he was elected president of the American Bar Association in 1913. He stood firmly on the side of President Wilson in opposing America's entry into World War I, and later, after the close of that war, he agreed with Wilson in favoring the League of Nations for world peace.

William Howard Taft still looked longingly toward the Supreme Court, but as the years slipped by, he almost despaired of getting his wish. Then, on the death of Chief Justice White in 1921, Taft finally reached the goal he had set for himself when he first began to study law. President Harding chose him to be Chief Justice of the United States!

For nine years he presided with dignity and wisdom over the Supreme Court, enjoying more real satisfaction in his work than in any other service he performed for his country.

Because of illness, he reluctantly resigned the post in 1930. A few weeks later, on March 8, he died and was buried in the nation's capital which, for so many years, had been the center of his hopes and dreams.

WOODROW WILSON

Writer, and Maker, of History

WE naturally think of Woodrow Wilson, twenty-eighth President of the United States, as a Virginian. And he *was* born at Staunton, December 28, 1856, as Thomas Woodrow Wilson, son of a Presbyterian minister. But "Tommy" Wilson, as he was known until he graduated from Princeton University, was barely able to toddle when his parents moved to Georgia, and he did not return to the state of his birth until he entered the university for a two-year course. So he lived, in all, less than three years in Virginia.

The boy's education and training were cosmopolitan, and he was the product of no section. His father and mother were born in Ohio, of Scotch and Irish forebears; and the boy grew up in Georgia, South Carolina, and North Carolina. His college years were spent in Maryland, Virginia, North Carolina, and New Jersey; and he taught history, politics, and government in three different colleges—Bryn Mawr, Wesleyan, and Princeton, located in Pennsylvania, Connecticut, and New Jersey. Woodrow Wilson was a representative American. Certainly he managed to get around. He was the first President in history to cross the Atlantic Ocean while he was in office.

Most boys start going to school at the age of five or six; Woodrow Wilson was nine before his father, Rev. Joseph R. Wilson, placed him in a school in Augusta, Georgia. His real teacher was his father—then and afterward. They were constant companions. The father saw in his son his own ambitions and ability. He inspired Tommy to think for himself, to use well-constructed phrases in voicing his thoughts, and to consult the dictionary for the real meaning of the words he

248

used. Father and son played with words as others enjoy a game.

Joseph R. Wilson and Janet Woodrow had met back in Ohio when the former, an ordained minister, was teaching in Steubenville. They were married on June 7, 1849. The home in which their two daughters and the boy grew up was just a comfortable American home, no matter where it happened to be. Woodrow (he dropped the "Thomas" and chose his mother's maiden name at the age of twenty-three) was a lithe and active boy, fond of baseball, horseback riding, debating—and study. As the years went by he devoted even more time to studying history and political economy than he did to baseball. His life was simple and uneventful. At the age of fourteen, he moved with his family to Columbia, South Carolina.

His father was pastor of the First Presbyterian Church at the state capital and also taught at the seminary. The two salaries, and a legacy which Mrs. Wilson received at the time, enabled them to build a rather luxurious home. The school which Woodrow attended was just across the street; and, after he became President, he admitted that he looked back upon the years spent at Columbia as the happiest of his life.

Two years after the move to Columbia, he entered Davidson College, near Charlotte, N.C., where each student cut his own wood, made his fire, kept his room neat, and carried water from the school pump. It was a new experience, but Woodrow liked it. He went in for debating, wrote some good essays, and stood well in his classes. He played shortstop on the college team, and was rated a good hitter. His father meanwhile had moved to Wilmington, N.C.; and when the boy, never very strong, needed building up, he dropped out of school for a year and spent the time with the family. He and his father became better friends than ever, and he was coached in Latin and Greek by a local teacher who assured him, as many boys have been assured by their teachers, that "one of these days you are going to be President." He is chiefly remembered in Wilmington as the first person who owned and rode a bicycle in North Carolina.

Wilson, at nineteen, was awkward, but quite mature in mind and character. When he entered Princeton in September, 1875, he joined the Whig Society and was considered its best debater. He specialized in English, the science of government, and kindred subjects; sang in the Glee Club; was made one of the editors of the college paper; and in due course became the managing editor of *The Princetonian,* as well as president of the Athletic Committee. His ambition was to study and write about government, American history, political economy, and the interpretation of the Constitution of the United States. He planned to make public affairs his life study.

After his graduation, Wilson went to the University of Virginia to study, not merely law, but law as it related to government. He was not conceited, but conscious of his superiority of intellect. At the same time, he had a sense of humor. According to Josephus Daniels, Secretary of the Navy in both Wilson administrations, Wilson used to tell this story of his father: "A parishioner said to my father once: 'How come, Preacher Wilson, you have such a slick hoss, an' you is so skinny yo'self?'

" 'Oh, that's easy,' my father replied. 'I feed the horse—but the congregation feeds me!' "

Wilson was a member of the University of Virginia Glee

Club in 1880 and 1881, and a photograph shows him with a mustache. He joined the debating society, and was elected its president. His health still was not good, however, and at the end of the year he returned home and spent another year in recuperation and study. Then he formed a law partnership with a former student, and they established an office at Atlanta. In a few months, Wilson reached the conclusion that teaching and politics, not law, should be his life work, so he went to Johns Hopkins University for a two-year course in history and political economy.

Before Wilson left Atlanta, however, he met Ellen Louisa Axson, who was visiting his cousin. They became engaged; but the wedding, they agreed, could not take place until he had finished his course and had found a teaching job. So it was not until he was in his twenty-ninth year that the future President acquired a job and a wife at the same time. He became an associate professor at Bryn Mawr, where he and his bride set up a home and remained three years. The young couple spent the next two years at Middletown, Connecticut, where Professor Wilson taught history and political economy. In 1890 he was offered the chair of jurisprudence at Princeton University, and from that September until he became governor of New Jersey, Wilson was connected with Princeton —from 1902 until 1910 as President.

Wilson was not aware, as he delivered lectures at Princeton and made speeches throughout the country, that he was under observation. But George Harvey, a magazine editor of New York city, had for some time considered him a promising candidate for the presidency of the United States. Harvey was a Democrat; and he knew that a strong current was running against the Republican party. He and his Wall Street friends believed that Wilson could swing the Democratic party back to the conservatism of Grover Cleveland. Two years in the governor's chair would enable Wilson to put into practice his theories of government.

The New Jersey Democratic machine made overtures to the expert on government. Wilson agreed to accept the nomination, on condition that he was bound by no political promises or obligations. This, to the political bosses, was fine campaign talk. It probably did not occur to them that Wilson meant what he said. One of them soon learned that the candidate had all the attributes of a buzz saw. During the campaign, this political boss, bowing to the express wishes of the voters, announced that he would not be a candidate for the Senate. But as soon as the election was over and Democratic success was assured, he sought the pledges of the new members of the legislature. (At that time, Senators were elected by the state legislature.) He even tried to get Wilson's support. When Wilson could not induce the boss to withdraw, he took the fight directly to the voters in the man's own community, and in two political meetings, denounced him as the head of a selfish system and entirely lacking in consideration for the interests of the people of the state. Wilson also went directly to the members of the legislature, and told them the entire story. The boss was not elected.

Wilson's majority was 50,000; the Democrats also carried the legislature. Working together in 1911 and 1912, the governor and the legislature made over the election, corporation, public utility, and labor laws of the state of New Jersey. These reforms, accomplished despite the desperate efforts of the well-intrenched political machine, made a deep impression on the country at large. People began to say that this was the type of man needed in the White House. Harvey, of course, had come to that conclusion several years before; and now he published at the masthead of his weekly: "For President: WOODROW WILSON!"

Wilson's political astuteness (except, perhaps, in sizing up Senate Republicans years afterward) has never been questioned. He realized immediately that the conservative support of Harvey and his Wall Street friends would be embarrassing, to say the least. Being a forthright person, he bluntly asked Harvey to withdraw his support. Wilson's name was taken from the masthead, and the governor and his manager went ahead with their own campaign for nomination and election. At the Democratic convention in Baltimore they were aided in obtaining the nomination by the rather belated support of William Jennings Bryan. Colonel Edward M. House, of Texas, also attached himself to the Wilson entourage, and his advice was of inestimable value to the candidate. To the end of his active life, Wilson and Colonel House were in constant consultation on government matters.

Wilson won the presidential election in 1912 through the division of Republican voters between Roosevelt and Taft, candidates of the Progressive and Republican parties, respectively. In that year the Senate yielded to the House and approved a resolution calling upon Congress to submit to the people an amendment to the Constitution providing for the popular election of Senators in a regular and constitutional manner. The amendment was then sent to the states for action. The Seventeenth Amendment was ratified by the requisite number of state legislatures and went into effect during the first year of the Wilson administration.

Of all the problems that confronted the new President on

March 4, 1913, the most urgent was the revolt in Mexico. Important business interests had invested large sums in Mexican mines, railroads, oil refineries, and ranches; and some of these financiers asked for intervention by the United States. Wilson, however, adopted the policy of "watchful waiting." Since the Mexican dictator had gained his position by force, Wilson believed our foreign policy required us to withhold recognition. In 1914, partly to prevent the sale of arms and ammunition to Mexican revolutionists, the President ordered the landing of marines at Vera Cruz as a temporary expedient. Again, in 1916, he sent General Pershing at the head of American troops into Mexico. The result of this foray was inconclusive.

Once in office, Wilson assumed the leadership of the Democratic party. Unlike President Grant, who considered his Cabinet a glorified general staff, Wilson looked upon the members as executive counselors. From the very beginning of his administration, he gave them free rein—and held them to strict accountability. By the same token, he stood back of them when they were unjustly criticized. As for himself, he adopted the attitude of a member-at-large of both the House and Senate. Often he met Senators and Congressmen in the President's Room, which adjoins the Senate chamber, to talk over legislation. He also broke a precedent when, instead of sending his annual message to Congress to be read by a clerk, he appeared in person on April 8, 1913, to deliver the first message Congress had heard a President read since 1796. These were two instances where a little unbending on the part of the President resulted in better teamwork between the executive and legislative departments.

The first Wilson administration, therefore, was able to

conduct an astounding amount of legislative business. This included a revised tariff law, the establishment of the Federal Reserve System, a graduated income-tax law, establishment of the Federal Trade Commission, repeal of the law that allowed some American ships to use the Panama Canal without paying toll, the regulation of trusts and monopolies, thirty arbitration treaties, the eight-hour law for trainmen, the Federal Loan Act, the LaFollette Seamen's Act, the Merchant Marine Act, the Child Labor Law, the purchase of the Danish West Indies, legislation for the building of the Alaska Railroad, and a good-roads program that benefited the entire country.

Late in Wilson's second administration, the President called upon Congress to pass the suffrage amendment to the Constitution. With the aid of Republicans, the requisite two-thirds majority was obtained for the Nineteenth Amendment (giving women the right to vote) in June of the following year. Three-quarters of the state legislatures promptly ratified the amendment, and it went into effect before the presidential election of 1920.

At the beginning of August, 1914, the European War broke out; and on the sixth President Wilson's wife died. In the midst of his anxiety over her health, he had issued a proclamation declaring the neutrality of the United States in what was to become World War I. He thought the matter out carefully: how we would be affected by the catastrophe and what we should do about it; how we should protect Americans on the high seas and bring home stranded travelers from Europe. (This subject is covered in the chapter on Herbert Hoover.)

Most people, including the President, felt that the war

would be over in six months; but that was not to be. Early in 1915 a number of vessels were attacked by German submarines, and several Americans were lost; the sinking of the *Lusitania* alone cost the lives of more than a hundred Americans, including women and children. In a note to the German government, President Wilson put our case so bluntly that William Jennings Bryan, Secretary of State, resigned in protest. Robert Lansing was advanced to take his place.

The people of the United States were startled when it became known that Germany was behind a movement to embroil Mexico in a war with this country. There was also considerable unrest in Haiti and San Domingo; and both were occupied by quotas of troops by order of the President. Numerous British acts, as well as German, invaded the rights of Americans on the high seas. The President was both caustic and impartial in the notes he sent to each government.

In the 1916 presidential campaign, the Republicans nominated, as Wilson's opponent, Charles Evans Hughes. The election was close; at first it was reported that Hughes had won, but later returns gave the victory to Wilson.

Early in 1917, after Germany had promised not to engage in unlimited submarine warfare, she withdrew that promise. Wilson thereupon dismissed the German ambassador in Washington, severed relations with the German government, and asked Congress to declare war. Four days later (April 6, 1917) the resolution was passed with few dissenting votes—fifty in the House and six in the Senate. A great armed force was raised by a draft. Loans were floated running into billions. Extraordinary powers were conferred upon the President. Men and women workers were regimented. Never before in the United States had life and property been subjected to so many restrictions.

World War I lasted until November 11, 1918. During those nineteen months, almost two million American soldiers were sent to France and an additional two million were trained at home. Our casualties were: Dead, 126,000; wounded, 234,300. On October 5, 1918, when the German government asked for an armistice, President Wilson sharply replied that such a request would have to come from a government controlled by the people. The German kaiser could not meet this requirement. Thus the German and Austrian emperors were toppled from their thrones by the former professor of political economy.

During World War I, President Wilson was married to Mrs. Edith Bolling Galt, widow of a Washington jeweler. At the end of the war, Wilson, as the sponsor of the terms to which the Allies and Germany had agreed, decided to go to Europe himself to attend the peace conference. He took Mrs. Wilson with him.

The President deeply believed that a League of Nations was absolutely essential to insure future peace in the world and that it must be an integral part of the peace treaty. The Assembly agreed; and a committee, of which President Wilson was chairman, was appointed to draw up the constitution for the proposed League. The first draft of the Covenant of the League was accepted on February 14, 1919. The next day the President sailed for the United States. The Treaty of Versailles, including the Covenant, was laid before the Senate for discussion and action. It was a blueprint for a world association. A few determined Senators undertook to defeat

American participation in the League. The debate over the League became entangled with debates over foreign and domestic affairs.

There were some Republican and Democratic Senators who were willing to vote for the League if some modifications were made in its plan, but President Wilson held out against any compromise. The treaty was therefore laid before the Senate July 10, 1919. On March 19, 1920, both the treaty and the League failed, by eight votes, to receive a two-thirds majority required by the Constitution of the United States for adoption.

President Wilson no doubt realized, in the summer of 1919, that this might happen; but he determined to fight to the end. He would appeal to the people, as he had done in New Jersey to defeat the boss! But he had underestimated the influence of "a little group of wilful men," as he called them, in the Senate. He maintained that a League of Nations was the only method of preventing another World War; these Senators thought otherwise. World War II began exactly twenty years to a day after Woodrow Wilson set out from the Middle West on his speaking tour to the Pacific Coast on behalf of the League of Nations.

The President returned from this uncompleted trip in a state of exhaustion, and soon became a semi-invalid. Cerebral thrombosis (a blood clot in one of the blood vessels in the right side of the brain) impaired the motor nerves of the left side of his body, and he was unable to walk by himself. For years he was a pathetic figure, attended by his wife and his personal physician.

Woodrow Wilson found release in death on February 3, 1924.

WARREN G. HARDING

Seventh President Born in Ohio

THOSE who read the Marion, Ohio, *Star* on November 26, 1884, found this announcement on its masthead: "We have purchased the *Star* and we will stay." It was signed by three young men, whose names were Sickle, Warwick, and Harding. The youngest of these three, who had persuaded his friends to rescue the bankrupt newspaper from the hands of the sheriff, kept that promise to the year of his death. He was Warren Gamaliel Harding, nineteen years old; and all through his life, the *Star,* for which they had paid three hundred dollars and assumed a mortgage, was his greatest pride and pleasure.

As a child, Warren was not outstanding. He gave no sign that he would make good. He disliked hard work, and had no great zeal for making money. If the pay was attractive and the labor light, he did odd jobs now and then. But mostly he was just one of the boys who hung around the town skating rink or the corner drugstore.

Warren G. Harding was born on November 2, 1865, in an old frame house on the edge of the town of Corsica, Ohio. His grandfather had built the house and cleared, plowed, and planted the land surrounding it. There, George Harding, Warren's father, was born and grew up, tending the farm, studying medicine with a neighboring physician, and becoming in time known as "Doc" Harding.

The Hardings moved on to Caledonia when Warren was a small boy, and then to Marion. Little was known of the family when they arrived in Marion, except that they seemed poor. They moved into a house in the shabby section of town. Warren, the oldest of eight children, went to school along with the others, and when he was fourteen he entered Ohio Central College at Iberia. It was not like the colleges we know today, but it gave him the equivalent of a high school course.

Young Harding was graduated three years later, a husky young giant more than six feet tall. He had been editor of his school paper and played the alto horn in the college band. He thought his band was just about the best in the state, and was filled with youthful pride when it won third prize at a contest in Findlay, Ohio. Warren, however, had to begin thinking less about tooting a horn and more about how to make a living.

He taught school for a term, but the handsome, pleasure-loving young man was anything but happy as a schoolmaster. "It was the hardest job I ever had," he said later. Working as a reporter on the Marion *Mirror* suited him better, though that job did not last long either. His employer complained that Warren spent too much time at Republican headquarters instead of sticking to his work. The cub reporter insisted that the editor, who was a Democrat, had other reasons for objecting to him. The young man appeared at the office with a gray plug hat. The new hat was the symbol of allegiance to the campaign of James G. Blaine, Republican, and no one wore it more jauntily and defiantly than Warren G. Harding. He joined a Blaine club, marched in processions, and made rousing speeches for his candidate. And he lost his job.

What next? Warren was nineteen, and so far he had not made much of a success in life. His heart was set on newspaper work, but the *Mirror* had failed to appreciate him. Naturally his thoughts turned to the bankrupt *Star*. He wanted that paper more than anything in the world. And when he and his friends managed to get together the money for it, and brought out their first edition on that November day in 1884, Warren Harding felt he had found his place in life.

To publish a paper had been his ambition since, as a boy of six, he did the chores in the office of a small-town weekly of which his father was part owner. He was fascinated by the type and the printing press. He was a born news gatherer. He felt that the *Star* was his great opportunity. He enjoyed roaming about the streets, dropping into the courthouse or the city hall, and exchanging gossip with the citizens of Marion. They were always welcome in the *Star* office. Businessmen, farmers, politicians, and others dropped in often. They knew they could count on a genial smile, a slap on the back, and a friendly word from the tall broad-shouldered editor who thought his town, his state, and his country represented all that was best in life.

It was the shrewd, practical young widow he married in 1891, however, who did more than anyone else to make the *Star* the highly successful paper it later became. Florence Kling was five years older than Warren Harding. She was neither beautiful nor affectionate, but she proved herself a devoted wife. Not long after their marriage, when her husband was not well, she offered to lend a hand on the paper. "I went down there," she told an interviewer many years later, "intending to help out for a few days, and remained fourteen years."

Harding himself picked up news, wrote stories, set type, and labored for long hours day and night. Getting out among the people as he did, and working with the Republican party, it was logical that he should enter politics. He was a good mixer and an engaging talker. With the backing of an Ohio Senator, Joseph B. Foraker, Harding ran for the state Senate

in 1900, and was elected and re-elected. Then he became
lieutenant governor. He met his first political disappointment
in 1910 when he ran for governor. Failing to win that election,
he almost decided to give up politics. But, in 1912, he was
chosen to present Taft's name for the Presidential nomination, and once more he was deep in the affairs of his party.

He made his genial entry into the United States Senate in
1915. With World War I raging in Europe, and everybody
looking to President Woodrow Wilson for leadership and
wondering what part the United States might have to play in
the struggle, Senator Harding took up his duties in Washington. He was not altogether happy about his situation. He disliked writing letters, and often refrained from voting on various bills which came up in Congress. He followed his party
implicitly and tried to stay out of controversies. He remained
in the Senate all through the war and until 1920, when he was
elected President.

He favored the Prohibition Amendment in principle,
though it was well known that, at that time, he was not a
total abstainer. When the war ended and President Woodrow
Wilson was pleading earnestly for the League of Nations,
Harding bitterly opposed it.

As Chief Executive, however, Harding did agree with his
Secretary of State, Charles E. Hughes, who sensibly proposed
a naval holiday among the big powers in battleship building
and arrived at an understanding with Great Britain and
Japan to limit their armaments accordingly. The President
arranged the Conference for the Limitation of Armaments,
and the foreign powers accepted his invitation. That meeting,
as we know, did not bring about lasting world peace, but it
created good will and succeeded at a time when the nations of

the world were having difficulty agreeing on peace plans. Another outstanding achievement of his administration was the establishment of a federal budget system with a director of the budget.

When Warren Harding was inaugurated on March 4, 1921, he was humble about the position he was to occupy as leader of the nation. He was not a devoutly religious man, but he said to a close friend of his, before he left for Washington:

"I have been thinking a lot about these things, as I have come to a realization of the tremendous responsibilities which rest upon me. It is my conviction that the fundamental trouble with the people of the United States is that they have gotten too far away from Almighty God."

Did he later forget those words? President Harding's administration was sharply criticized during his years in office, and in later years. One of his weaknesses was his loyalty to his friends. As Chief Executive he appointed many of them to important positions of trust. Some were merely inefficient; others, unfortunately, were dishonest.

Two years after the World War I Armistice, the United States had more than 300,000 wounded and disabled veterans to be cared for. The President and Congress did not forget them. They set up the United States Veterans Bureau, but Harding was unwise in his choice of a head. The graft and corruption that marked the conduct of the bureau resulted in a public scandal. While the people generally trusted the President, they were indignant at the graft and dishonesty which went on during his administration in the handling of public resources. They blamed President Harding for permitting his appointees to remain in office and for refusing to recognize their betrayal of trust.

With considerable scandal, rumors, and gossip beginning to circulate about conditions in the nation's capital, it is no wonder that President Harding was losing his popularity with honest American citizens. Yet, with all his faults, there was a genuine kindliness about him which endeared him to the people. Because he understood human frailty, he was always ready to forgive others. He pardoned many prisoners during his administration. Outstanding among these was Eugene V. Debs, leader of the Socialist party, who was serving a ten-year term in the penitentiary at Atlanta, having been convicted of obstructing the conduct of the war. He was not inclined to check the actions of friends in government posts.

Harding's goodness of heart was well known to those who worked for him on the Marion *Star*. During thirty-five years of ownership, he never discharged an employe or reduced a wage. His newspaper is said to have been the first daily in the Middle West to initiate a profit-sharing system by the distribution of stock among its employes.

Early in 1923, realizing that he was losing his popularity, and thinking of a second term, President Harding decided to make a tour of the country. He described this as a "voyage of understanding." He wanted to explain his position and his policies to the people, and he hoped that by personal appearances he could win back their confidence and regard. Though still a strict party man, a change was taking place within him. He seemed to have a deeper sense of responsibility to the nation as a whole than he had when he first entered the White House.

On that journey across the country, he was a weary and worried man. He could not rest. He visited west-coast cities, and was the first Chief Executive of the United States to visit

Alaska. He was also the first President to visit Canada in his official capacity.

When he returned to Seattle and began the trip down the west coast, the doctors knew he was a sick man. His heart was bad and, added to that, pneumonia set in. He had planned to go home by way of the Panama Canal, but he got no farther than San Francisco.

There he died, on August 2, 1923.

As his funeral train passed through the cities and towns on its way eastward, thousands of people gathered beside the tracks, scattering tributes of flowers. Church bells tolled. Whatever the faults or shortcomings of Warren G. Harding during life, they were forgotten as the nation mourned his death.

At the White House in Washington, formal and elaborate funeral services were held. Three Presidents, William H. Taft, Woodrow Wilson, and Calvin Coolidge (who had at once taken the oath of office), were present among the mourners. Then, after all the pomp and ceremony were over, the body was taken on its final journey to Marion, Ohio.

Warren G. Harding had come home, to rest in peace.

CALVIN COOLIDGE

Yankee Farmer from Vermont

THE little village of Plymouth, in the Vermont hills, slept peacefully. The six or seven farmhouses, the church, the cemetery, the blacksmith shop, and the general store and post office were dark and still under the stars. Shortly past midnight a car drove up to one of the houses. Its occupants jumped out and one of them knocked at the door.

Colonel John Coolidge, who was a poor sleeper, lighted a kerosene lamp and went to greet the unexpected callers. Then he climbed the narrow stairs to the bedroom where his son lay sleeping, and called: "Calvin!" The old man's voice trembled, for he was bearing a message which embodies the greatest desire of any father. His son, Calvin Coolidge, had just become President of the United States. In his hand, Colonel Coolidge held the official message that President Harding was dead in California.

Calvin Coolidge read the telegram carefully. Then he washed in the china bowl, dressed quickly in a dark suit with a black tie, and knelt in his old-fashioned bedroom to pray. He was small of stature, and looked almost boyish with his pale angular face, his russet-blond hair, blue eyes, and broad high forehead. Downstairs, the parlor was already filling with excited people. The news was spreading fast.

First he dictated a reassuring message to the people of the United States, wrote a letter in longhand to Mrs. Harding, and issued a written statement for the reporters who had gathered there.

After he had talked on the telephone with the Secretary

of State and other officials in Washington, he turned to his father and asked: "Father, are you still a notary?"

"Yes, Cal," was the response.

"Then I want you to administer the oath."

Colonel Coolidge stood erect, facing his son across the mahogany table which had been cleared of everything but two oil lamps and the family Bible.

It was shortly before three on the morning of August 3, 1923. Colonel Coolidge adjusted his glasses, cleared his throat, and solemnly went through the ritual of swearing in his son to execute the office of President, and to preserve, protect, and defend the Constitution. Then, by the glow of the lamps, the oath was signed. Calvin Coolidge laid his pen aside, and his father affixed the seal. For the first time in America's history a father had administered the qualifying oath of the highest office in the land to his own son, and was the first to address him as "Mr. President."

If either of these two New England men was excited, it was not apparent in that moment, though they knew well the responsibilities involved. With the calm inward strength of his ancestors, the new Chief Executive would fulfill his obligations to the nation with the help of God.

None of Calvin Coolidge's forebears had risen to prominence in his state. Most of them were farmers. John Coolidge, born in Cambridge, England, came to Massachusetts around 1630. Captain John Coolidge, who fought in the Revolutionary War, left the state in 1781, shortly after his marriage to Hannah Priest and the birth of his eldest son Calvin, and settled in Plymouth Notch, Vermont. Captain John had enough land at his death to leave a farm to each of his five sons. He did his share in building up the community and farming the rocky New England soil. Soon a flour mill and a sawmill were built. Log cabins were replaced by sturdy frame houses, and a general store supplied the simple wants of the farmers. Life in Plymouth Notch was going smoothly by the time old Captain John died.

It was running as smoothly and quietly on Thursday, July 4, 1872, when Mrs. John C. Coolidge gave birth to a son. Their home was used both as residence and as store. The baby was named John Calvin after his father. His parents always called him Calvin or Cal; and, when he was old enough, his mother taught him his letters from a set of wooden blocks.

That mother (Victoria Josephine Moor) died before Cal was thirteen, leaving her boy lonely and grief stricken; but during her life she instilled in him a love for what was right and honest, and a contempt for what was wrong. Grandfather and Grandmother Coolidge, who had a farm close by, continued to watch over his character, and to keep an eye on his material needs.

Though little worldly excitement reached the quiet village, there were many pleasant things to fill the days of young Calvin. There were husking bees, quilting parties, church "sociables," and county fairs. And on the rare occasions when the circus came to Ludlow or Rutland, Calvin and his sister Abigail started out with the family long before daylight to drive to town in time for the big parade.

Calvin was expected to do his share of work on the farm. Early in the spring he helped to make maple syrup, and later he helped with the planting, mended fences, dug potatoes, picked apples, and chopped wood against the long cold winter. By the time he was twelve he could handle a plow without help from the hired man.

Although his father had been in the state legislature and was fairly prominent among the local citizens, Calvin carried apples and popcorn balls to town meeting and sold them, as his ancestors had done before him. His first long trousers were cut down from a pair his grandfather had discarded. His first money was earned sawing wood; and he had a boyish ambition to run a store, as his father had done, but nothing ever came of that.

He was educated at the district school near his father's farm; then at Black River Academy twelve miles away in Ludlow. Later he went to St. Johnsbury Academy, which prepared him for college, and on September 17, 1891, entered Amherst as a freshman. When he was graduated in June, 1895, just before his 23rd birthday, young Calvin said: "I am only sure of one thing—that I'm a Republican."

The winter of 1895 found him studying law in the Northampton, Massachusetts, office of Hammond and Field, and two years later he was admitted to the bar. He opened an office of his own in 1899, and that year he was elected a councilman. From then on he occupied one position after another as he climbed the political ladder—city solicitor, clerk of the courts, member of the legislature, mayor of Northampton, state senator, lieutenant governor, and finally governor of Massachusetts. He didn't draw cigars from his vest pocket or slap people on the back; he made no promises which he could not keep; and when he spoke he said something worth while.

While he was still playing a minor role in politics and had a modest law practice, young Coolidge married Grace Goodhue, the only girl who had ever attracted his attention. They lived economically and were very happy, starting housekeeping in a small rented house in Northampton. The Norwood

Hotel there was closing, and Mrs. Coolidge bought a large part of her household supplies from its stock. For years the linens and plated silver of the thrifty pair bore the mark "Norwood Hotel."

Coolidge served as mayor of Northampton in 1910 and 1911; and thus began a period of continuous office holding which did not end until after he had retired from the presidency. By the summer of 1913 he was a leading Republican. He hated graft, extravagance, and immorality, and believed that government should help to improve the lot of the common man.

As governor of Massachusetts, Calvin Coolidge was efficient and honest. During the Boston police strike of 1919 he attracted the attention of the entire country and strengthened the confidence of the people by his stand for orderly government. Governor Coolidge made this blunt statement: "The forces of law and order may be dissipated; they may be defeated. But so long as I am commander-in-chief, they will not be surrendered." Then he wired the head of the American Federation of Labor: "There is no right to strike against the public safety by anybody, anywhere, any time."

His stand in the police strike brought him the nomination for the vice presidency. When on March 4, 1921, he took office with President Harding, Calvin Coolidge faced an entirely new life. He knew little about Washington, but he soon learned. Being invited by the President to sit in at the Cabinet meetings, the new Vice President listened quietly, was loyal to his superior, kept his own counsel, and adhered to the principles of honesty and truth which had always guided him. The upright New England Yankee must have done some tall thinking as he sat around the table week after week with

Cabinet officers Fall and Daugherty, who were later proved to be dishonest. But he did not condemn them, or gossip about what was going on around him during the Harding regime.

The training he was getting in national government stood him in good stead on that August day when, after Harding's death, he became President of the United States. As President, he stressed his favorite subject—economy. In three years, he reduced the national debt by two billion dollars. He opposed the League of Nations; approved the World Court; showed great political courage in vetoing the Soldiers' Bonus Bill, which passed over his veto; and, in 1924, he was elected President in his own right by a huge majority. As his good friend and adviser, Frank W. Stearns, put it: Everybody was against Coolidge—everybody, that is, except the voters!

The people of the United States were tired of inefficiency and graft. What they wanted was honesty, idealism, and common sense. They found all these in Calvin Coolidge. He did not recommend any major reforms or shifts in policy, but he saw the nation, during his term in the presidency, enter a period of peace and prosperity greater than it had ever enjoyed before. The buying power of the nation increased. By 1929 there were twenty-four million automobiles on the roads where ten years before there had been less than seven million. The wage earner was better off; savings banks deposits increased. The average family lived well, and had such luxuries as a car, radio, oil heater, electric refrigerator, washing machine, and telephone. It seemed from 1925 to 1929 as if unemployment, poverty, and human misery were definitely on the decline. Lindbergh's dramatic solo flight across the Atlantic in May, 1927, made him a national hero. Prohibition was in force. The stock market was booming. Broadcasting was coming into its own. And while all over the nation people were spending and living well, the Coolidges clung to their New England ideas of thrift.

A prosperous nation seemed completely satisfied with the administration of the silent President who never used two words where one would do. They enjoyed his dry humor and his rugged independence as much as they enjoyed their increasing prosperity. Then, like a bombshell, on August 2, 1927 —exactly four years after he had taken over the Presidency upon the death of Warren Harding—came the President's announcement: "I do not choose to run for President in 1928." Nothing could have stirred the country more. Persuasions could not move Calvin Coolidge. He had stated his intention and he stuck to it.

In the eyes of the people, he had been an excellent Chief Executive. They never held him responsible for the oil scandals, involving Secretary Fall and Doheny and Sinclair, oil executives, in the leasing of the Navy oil reserves in California and the Teapot Dome reservation in Wyoming; this was a burden Coolidge had inherited from the Harding administration. Coolidge had appointed special counsel to investigate the corrupt situation, and had declared that every law would be enforced and every right of the people and the government protected. He had kept that promise.

As President, he worked to reduce income taxes, to reduce expenses, and to reduce the national debt. He believed in flood control and authorized appropriations of three hundred and twenty-five million dollars for that purpose. He seldom interfered with the members of his Cabinet, but consulted them daily. In the competent hands of Secretary Mellon was the Treasury. Herbert Hoover could be relied on as the Secretary of Commerce. And Secretary Kellogg handled foreign affairs. One of President Coolidge's great secrets of success was the placing of responsibility in the hands of those he could trust, those he knew to be efficient in promoting the welfare of the nation.

As his administration drew to a close, he was happy in the thought that prosperity was established and increasing. The year 1928 set a new record for profits as well as for the production of goods. He could return now, in the satisfaction of a job well done, to his friends and neighbors in the New England hills.

When his term of office was ended, on March 4, 1929, he and his family returned to Northampton, Massachusetts, and his old law office. For a time they lived in the simple house where he and his wife had gone when they were first married. Later, he bought a larger, more secluded home called The Beeches. During the long summers he found rest and quiet at Plymouth, the scene of his childhood.

He did a great deal of writing during those peaceful years, for newspapers and magazines; and like Van Buren, Grant and Theodore Roosevelt, he set down his autobiography.

Then, on January 5, 1933, quietly and without suffering, he died in his home at The Beeches in Northampton. Later he was buried on a rugged hillside at Plymouth, Vermont, to rest among those he knew and loved best.

HERBERT C. HOOVER

Quaker President from Iowa

H

ERBERT CLARK HOOVER

was the first native son of our great prairies to occupy the White House. He was the first President whose ancestors became known as Pennsylvania Dutch; also the first to follow the profession of mining engineer—a profession that led him to far places. He was the first Chief Executive to be born in Iowa; also the first of Quaker faith. With all these "firsts," the story of the life of our thirty-first President presents a different pattern from those who preceded him.

Hoover was not born in a log cabin, though the one-story frame house in the little village of West Branch, Iowa, was severely plain, without porch or decoration. There were no sidewalks along the street before it. Oil lamps lighted the few rooms, and they were furnished with strict simplicity. It was a cosy, cheerful home, nevertheless; for it reflected the serene and happy life of its owners, Jesse and Huldah Hoover. Their small son, Theodore, was three years old when, on August 10, 1874, his brother arrived. The new baby was chubby and dimpled. They named him Herbert Clark Hoover, but they always called him Bert, and he dropped his middle name early in life.

His mother's family, the Minthorns, had settled in New England fifty years before the Boston Tea Party. Some of them later went to Pennsylvania, the colony settled by the great Quaker leader, William Penn. The ancestors of Herbert Hoover's father settled in Philadelphia in 1739. The first to arrive was a young German boy named Andreas Huber, who in the course of time became Andrew Hoover.

When the gold rush to California began, thousands of

families packed their covered wagons and started for the West. In 1854, Jesse Hoover and his family followed the westward trail until they came to a spot in Iowa where they decided to settle. They called it West Branch. There the people built their homes and a meetinghouse, and began life in the traditional way of Quakers. If one member of the community was in need, his neighbors "tided him over." If one enjoyed a larger crop than the others, he shared with those around him.

Here the Minthorn and Hoover children grew up. Young Jesse Hoover became a blacksmith. Huldah Minthorn, who had attended the University of Iowa, devoted herself to religion. On March 12, 1870, the two were married and went to live in the little house where Herbert Hoover and his older brother were born.

Bert was a friendly, healthy child. He toddled around his father's blacksmith shop, his eyes shining with excitement as he watched the sparks fly and heard the ring of the anvil. Before the boy was three, Jesse Hoover closed his blacksmith shop and became a salesman of farm implements. He was so successful that a year later the Hoovers moved into a fine new home.

When Bert was six, his father was killed by a falling tree. He left little money, and Mrs. Hoover took in sewing to help support her children. Her Quaker sermons, too, were in demand and the congregation often gave her cash and food supplies. After a few years the sturdy Quaker mother also passed away, and Herbert Hoover went to live with his uncle, Allan Hoover, on a farm just outside of town. There he helped with the chores, as he was expected to do, and when he had a chance he stole away to the old swimming hole or sat on the bank of a stream fishing with a willow pole, a piece of string, and a penny fishhook. Then came an exciting visit to another uncle who was a commissioner out in Indian territory. There the eight-year-old boy from Iowa became friendly with the Indian boys, who taught him camping and scouting. And wherever he went, young Hoover hunted for the shiny stones in the ground which influenced his whole life.

His first real job was with his uncle, Dr. Minthorn, out in Oregon. The doctor, in 1888, took charge of the Oregon Land Company, and Hoover, at fourteen, having finished grammar school, became office boy. There he picked up typewriting, studied geometry, and pored over maps and land reports. There, too, one day, he met a mining engineer who spoke of rocks, strata, lodes, and ores. The boy listened, entranced. From that day on, he knew what he wanted to do in life.

In the summer of 1891, Herbert Hoover entered Stanford University, in California, to study mining engineering. He earned his way through college by peddling papers, running errands, and doing all sorts of odd jobs. He became laboratory assistant, and during summer vacation, when the geologists needed a field man, he went joyfully into the Ozark Mountains. One map he had made won a prize of two hundred dollars in 1893 at the Chicago World's Fair.

The tall, broad-shouldered young man tried other ways of making money, too. During his college years, when Paderewski, the great Polish pianist, was on a concert tour in California, Hoover figured he could rent a hall at San Jose, pay Paderewski's fee of two thousand dollars, and sell enough tickets to make a profit. But Holy Week was a bad time to bring out a large audience. When Hoover frankly admitted to the pianist that he hadn't even enough money to pay his fee, the good-natured Paderewski came to his rescue. He accepted only a small sum, after the expenses were paid, and allowed the young man a profit besides. After that, Herbert Hoover decided that he'd better stick to engineering.

In 1895 he was graduated with honors. At first he had to go out with pick and shovel as an ordinary miner at $2.50 per day, but before long he met Louis Janin, a San Francisco engineer, who recognized Hoover's worth. Soon he was entrusted with engineering jobs in Wyoming, Idaho, Arizona, Colorado, and New Mexico. Then came the big chance which sent him to London, and on to the gold fields of far-off Australia. His reputation became international; wherever mining men got together they talked about young Herbert Hoover.

When the head of the Chinese Bureau of Mines offered him a position as director general of mines, Hoover made up his mind quickly. He sent off two cables, one accepting the job in China; the other to Lou Henry of Monterey, California, which said: "Will you marry me?" The answer which came back a few hours later was even more brief: "Yes." He joined her as quickly as possible.

Herbert Hoover and Lou Henry were married on February 11, 1899, and sailed for the Orient that evening. They arrived during the Boxer Rebellion. Though they lived in a protected Western settlement, shells shrieked overhead and they were in constant danger. Mrs. Hoover became chief aide to the doctor in charge, and her husband managed the dwindling food and water supplies for their little group.

In the years that followed, the Hoovers journeyed to every continent and to almost every country. In 1903, their first son was born, and they took him with them twice around the world during his first year.

Herbert Hoover was sometimes thought of as hard and

unapproachable because he was not talkative. In reality he was home loving, gentle, and sympathetic. In his work, he encountered the most difficult problems. As soon as he had solved them, he moved on to further adventures.

Between 1907 and 1912, Hoover's professional work took him to South Africa, to Peru, to Siberia, Mexico, Korea, and the Straits Settlements. He also spent some time in Central America and New Zealand. He developed modern placer-gold mining methods in California, and the potash deposits of Death Valley. Wherever mining problems came up, there Hoover was most likely to be found. Mrs. Hoover usually went with him, and after thirteen years of married life they bought a house in Stanford, California, which was the spot they always loved best.

Herbert Hoover found little time, however, to enjoy himself at home. He was in London when World War I broke out, and so were thousands of his fellow-Americans. Their letters of credit and their travelers' checks were useless; nobody had gold or credit to buy tickets home. Hoover put aside everything else to help them. With a group of his friends, he organized a relief agency for the stranded Americans, putting in more and more of his own money, arranging steamer transportation. Finally, when danger seemed imminent, he sent his wife and boys back to the United States. He himself stayed on to distribute the million-dollar fund sent by Congress.

Hoover's volunteer relief organization distributed a million and a half dollars to homeward-bound Americans, and when all the accounts were settled, the amount not paid back was less than five hundred dollars. In all these operations, Hoover himself refused to accept one penny for his services, even when he became chairman of the Commission for Relief in Belgium and supervised what developed into the greatest charitable effort in the history of the world up to that time.

As United States food administrator during the war, he took up the burden of feeding the hungry. Here at home he enforced a strict food-conservation program to supply the needs of our armies abroad and their families in the United States. He urged all Americans to share with the citizens of other countries overseas, and gave us a new conception of responsibility—not only to our own people in America but to the needy peoples of the world. The boy who had been brought up among the good Quakers of West Branch, Iowa, never forgot their teachings. Sharing with those in need was natural because it was right.

When the war ended, though the fighting and killing were over, the hunger, sickness, and want which always follow war continued. When Congress appropriated one hundred million dollars for European relief, Hoover was put in charge of that work. Later much more money was appropriated, not only by the United States but by other countries as well. Through the European Children's Fund which Hoover established, millions were helped. And throughout the years of his service, he continued to refuse to accept one cent of compensation.

When Hoover was called back home, it was as Secretary of Commerce in President Harding's Cabinet, an office he continued to occupy under President Coolidge. He worked to standardize production and increase our exports, and he inspired radio regulation, through the Radio Board, to preserve freedom of the air for the public.

All this time, Hoover was becoming more and more of a

national figure, and on the first Tuesday of November, in 1928, he was elected President on the Republican ticket with one of the greatest majorities the voters had ever given any man.

Herbert Hoover was not tempted to office by money or fame. He was already a world figure as a humanitarian, and as a mining engineer he had become a millionaire. He knew nothing of the political game. He had endorsed President Wilson's stand at Paris for a League of Nations, and as Secretary of Commerce he was useful and efficient, but he had never served in any elective office of the government before going to the White House.

Prohibition was then a big issue, and President Hoover emphatically favored continuing it. He began at once to carry out the policy of military withdrawal of American intervention in the Caribbean, and he reached an agreement in the London Naval Conference for the limitation of armaments. At home he set up a Farm Board to help restore agriculture; and, though Congress plunged into a long wrangle about the tariff, "Coolidge prosperity" was keeping the nation generally happy. Across the Pacific, the Japanese were preparing to seize Manchuria from China, in defiance of the Kellogg-Briand Peace Pact. The "Hoover Doctrine" speedily made it clear that the United States would not recognize any transfer of territory or property in violation of the Kellogg Pact. The majority of other nations agreed with Hoover's stand, and peace among nations seemed a little closer.

Then a catastrophe occurred here in the United States which shook the entire world. One October day in 1929, the American stock market collapsed, when more than sixteen million shares of stock were dumped on the exchange. In that crash vast fortunes were swept away overnight. The entire country, so lately confident of prosperity, was plunged into a mounting panic as business concerns closed, unemployment increased, and money markets tumbled. Abroad, the situation was equally bad, or worse. European markets were collapsing. England, France, Germany, Belgium, Italy, and Japan had looked to the United States for huge loans to help them over the postwar period. What was to be done?

Hoover proposed a year's moratorium on the payment of all war debts. Even with the depression on, the American people backed him in that generous gesture. During the weeks that followed, however, world depression became more acute, and European nations began to go off the gold standard. With England taking this drastic course, the dollar alone was left intact in a world of devalued currency.

Within a month, foreign financiers withdrew seven hundred million dollars in gold that had been stored here. Americans, fearful for their own money, drew it from the banks, and banks that had not already failed began to close. President Hoover called upon stronger banks to organize a credit fund for the protection of weaker ones. His recommendation to Congress set the Reconstruction Finance Corporation in operation. He submitted other proposals to check the growing deficit in the Treasury, which toward the close of his administration reached four billion dollars. But the Republican party had lost control of the House of Representatives and Hoover did not have full power to carry out his ideas. He did plan an increase in federal public works, however, and called upon state and local governments to follow this example.

But the Democrats were insisting that the country must have a new President. In 1932, when Hoover ran for re-election, he was defeated by Franklin D. Roosevelt.

Before Hoover's term expired, a bill to give independence

to the Philippines was passed over his veto. Another, repealing the Eighteenth Amendment and prohibition, was passed, and presented to the state legislatures. Relief measures which the President suggested got nowhere. In February, the governor of Michigan ordered all banks to close their doors for a "bank holiday" of eight days. Other banks followed suit. The affairs of the nation were in a state of extreme crisis as Hoover saw his successor inaugurated.

Herbert Hoover was fifty-eight years old when he left the White House, but as elder statesman of the Republican party, humanitarian, and public servant, he was not ready to retire.

During his administration he had initiated the Boulder Canyon project (Hoover Dam) and supported relief measures in the Farm Loan Bank, Home Loan Banks, and the Agricultural Credit Corporation. He gave his official salaries to charities and underpaid government officials.

President Truman appointed him coordinator of the European food program in 1946 and the German food program in 1947. In 1948 he was placed at the head of a Committee on Reorganization of the U.S. Executive Departments.

In later years, almost up to the time of his last illness, Hoover continued to keep busy. He wrote several books; among them *An American Epic,* a four-volume study of the efforts of the United States to relieve famine around the world.

In 1962 serious illness overtook the great humanitarian and elder statesman. Herbert Hoover died on October 20, 1964, at the age of ninety and was buried in West Branch, Iowa, the little town where he was born.

FRANKLIN D. ROOSEVELT

The "New Deal" President

B Y Inauguration Day, March 4, 1933, bank holidays, following the most disastrous stock-market crash in history, had virtually paralyzed banking in the United States. And less than three weeks before, at Miami, Florida, President-elect Franklin D. Roosevelt had narrowly escaped death at the hands of an assassin.

Certainly this was not a happy beginning, especially for a President as badly handicapped as "F.D.R." For more than twelve years he had been afflicted with infantile paralysis. As governor of New York state, he had faced for the last three or four years the same problems which the financial panic brought to President Herbert Hoover. And since election day, back in November, Roosevelt had waited, while the "lame duck" Congress dragged its way toward the finish and Hoover tried, against overwhelming odds, to keep the country from disintegrating. Leadership seemed to have been destroyed—in business, as well as in politics. Twelve million men and women were unemployed.

Roosevelt's first American ancestor, Claes Martenszen van Rosenvelt, came from Holland to New Amsterdam in 1649. The branch of the family from which F.D.R. was descended had settled in Dutchess County, on the Hudson River, and had always been wealthy. His father was vice president of the Delaware and Hudson Railroad. His mother's people had landed at Massachusetts Bay in 1621. Franklin, the only child of James and Sara Delano Roosevelt, was born on January 30, 1882, on the Dutchess County farm near what is now Hyde Park, N.Y.

He was a lonely, shy boy from the very beginning, with a

nurse, a tutor, a doting mother, a bow and arrow, a sled, a pony, a boat, and just about everything a child could desire—except playmates. From one high point on the estate, he could see a ten-mile stretch of the Hudson River. Sometimes he and his parents visited the other branch of the family—the New Amsterdam branch—which had furnished a President of the United States, Theodore Roosevelt. Sometimes he played with his distant cousin, Eleanor.

Franklin was less than a year old when he was taken on his first voyage to Europe. In fact, until he was fourteen he spent portions of eight years abroad. With this background of travel, French and German tutors, and home study, Franklin entered Groton at fourteen, and there he remained four years. At eighteen, more than six feet tall, slender, and fine looking, he was ready for Harvard. During his freshman year he went in for rowing and football, and later became a reporter on *The Crimson,* editor, managing editor, and finally president of the college paper. History and government were his principal studies.

F.D.R. graduated in 1904; and in the following year, on March 17, he married his cousin Eleanor. She was twenty, and he was twenty-three and a law student at Columbia University. In 1907 he took his degree and entered the New York city law office of Carter, Ledyard and Milburn. Like Woodrow Wilson, whom he admired, young Roosevelt began to yearn to put some of his theories of government into practice. He had been accustomed to having practically everything he wanted, and now he wanted to be a state senator. He had a friendly smile, a persuasive voice, and he talked the language of the farmers.

From the start, the odds were against him, for Dutchess

County was a Republican stronghold, and the young politician was a Democrat. Nevertheless, nominated to fill out the ticket with a name that would draw votes, he won the election easily. This was 1910, and he was twenty-eight. Once in Albany, he quickly showed the politicians that he was not going to be run over by that steamroller known as Tammany Hall.

Two years later, young Roosevelt was re-elected state senator and was serving his second term when President Wilson appointed him Assistant Secretary of the Navy. He served through World War I, and was still in the Navy Department when he ran (unsuccessfully) in the New York primaries for U.S. Senator on the Democratic ticket. He then went to the Democratic convention in 1920 to battle for the policies of Woodrow Wilson, particularly the League of Nations. Much to his surprise, F.D.R. received the nomination for Vice President. When the Republicans won, he became the head of the New York office of the Maryland Fidelity and Deposit Company.

In 1921, Roosevelt, at thirty-nine, was a fine, tall robust man. Then, without warning, while on vacation, he was stricken with infantile paralysis, was brought back to New York on a stretcher, and spent the next month in the hospital. At first his hands and arms, as well as his legs, were partially paralyzed. Gradually he regained the use of his hands and arms and developed broad shoulders; but his legs remained useless. Then and there began F.D.R.'s fight to get back his health. It was the most important fight of his life—bigger than politics, bigger than money, bigger than fame. Three loyal people fought that battle with him every step of the way.

They were Eleanor Roosevelt, his wife; Sara Delano Roosevelt, his mother; and his secretary, Louis Howe, a former newspaperman.

Little by little, through exercise and determination, Roosevelt learned to walk with the aid of braces, a cane, and crutches. He also learned to drive a car equipped with special hand controls, to swim, and to play water polo. When standing, he gripped a desk or leaned on someone's arm. But these handicaps did not keep him from an active life. He became a law partner of D. Basil O'Connor, an association which continued until Inauguration Day, 1933. Meanwhile, he went to Warm Springs, Georgia, for whatever benefit he could get from swimming in the healing waters. In 1928, and again in 1930, he was elected governor of New York.

Governor Roosevelt was now in an excellent position to obtain the nomination for President in the 1932 campaign. His health had stood the test; and he had polled an exceptionally large vote in the governorship race. Governor Alfred E. Smith had received the presidential nomination in 1928, but had lost to the Republicans. Now, however, Roosevelt felt that the situation had changed. The great depression had begun, and each year the federal deficit grew. Despite the Reconstruction Finance Corporation, which Hoover had set up, railroads continued to go into receivership; hundreds of thousands of tenants were turned out when they could not pay their rent; and other hundreds of thousands of owners lost their mortgaged homes. Farms by the million were foreclosed. England went off the gold standard; world trade shrank. As the economic plight of the United States grew steadily worse, with cotton selling at six cents a pound and wheat at thirty-two cents a bushel, the political prospects of the Democrats looked brighter. The people were looking for a change.

The Roosevelt forces, under leadership of State Chairman Farley, went into action; and by the beginning of 1932, Governor Roosevelt was the obvious favorite in the presidential race. His pledge was a "New Deal for the American people." He still held to his 1910 objective: to help make life better for the average man and his family. He promised a lower tariff, economy in government, a sound currency, federal aid to the needy, regulation of the stock market, and control of the production and marketing of electrical power. He was known as a progressive.

Two days after Roosevelt was nominated at the Democratic convention, he and his wife and two of their sons were flown to Chicago, where the governor accepted the nomination in person. Thus he became the first presidential candidate in history to deliver his acceptance speech to the convention which nominated him. To F.D.R. it was the logical thing to do. Why, he asked, should he wait several weeks, and cause the notification committee the trouble and expense of a trip to Albany? In November, he was elected by an overwhelming majority and the Democrats won more seats in the House and Senate than had ever been held by any party.

Roosevelt created another precedent when, for the first time, a Cabinet was nominated, confirmed, sworn, and called into session on Inauguration Day. Such speed and efficiency, known throughout the nation over-night through radio and newspapers, was not lost on the general public; the people began to take hope.

On March 4, 1933, the new President found hundreds of

banks failing. State governments had closed others as a precautionary measure. He began with a new appeal for confidence. "The only thing we have to fear is fear itself," he said in his Inaugural Address. By proclamation, the President closed all banks of the United States, including the Federal Reserve Banks; only the Postal Savings Banks remained open. The withdrawal of gold and silver was forbidden. When Congress, called into special session, met on March 9, a banking bill was ready for it. It gave the President power to open banks that were wholly solvent.

For a man fifty-one years of age and supposed to be an invalid, Roosevelt gave the impression that he actually was enjoying the opportunity to deal with the country's greatest emergency since the Civil War. He met the whole body of state governors who had come to Washington for the inaugural. He secured the promise of Congressional leaders to act swiftly on his program. He demanded that the federal budget be balanced; that veterans' pay and government salaries be cut. He set up an embargo on gold. On March 12, he gave the first of his "fireside chats" over a nation-wide radio hookup, reporting to the people that the first battle with fear had been won. His voice lent itself remarkably well to radio, though he had never had a lesson in diction or public speaking.

The President did not accomplish these miraculous results all by himself. Months before he had formed what newspapers, hostile and otherwise, called a "brain trust." The original group consisted of Professor Raymond Moley, Professor Rexford G. Tugwell, and Judge Samuel I. Rosenman. Later Adolph Berle was brought into the group; and sometimes Dr. Joseph McGolderick and General Hugh Johnson were consulted. Under Roosevelt's direction, a multitude of measures were adopted, such as control over banking and currency; federal credit to property owners and corporations in financial difficulties; relief to farmers; the legalization of 3.2 per cent beer; regulation and stimulation of business enterprise; systematizing the rights of collective bargaining for organized labor; and social security for certain groups against unemployment, poverty, and old age.

In the very beginning, banks were put under closer federal supervision. Credit was extended to banks that were financially sound; the others were liquidated. The gold standard was abandoned. Gold and silver coins and bullion were called in and deposited with the government, and the right of citizens to demand gold and silver coins in exchange for paper money was abolished. The farm loan banks were reorganized. Billions of dollars were loaned to homeowners, banks, railways, insurance companies, industries, and enterprises in general that were in need of money.

Surpluses of wheat, corn, cotton, meat, and other farm products could not be sold to a bankrupt Europe; but surpluses, in future, could be prevented. The Agricultural Adjustment Act and later amendments organized the farmers, persuaded them to reduce production, and paid them for the losses they incurred under this plan. Trade agreements were made with other countries, furnishing new markets for our farm products. Billions of dollars were authorized for the construction of public works. The Civilian Conservation Corps was formed to provide work, shelter, food, and clothing for young men who were beginning to roam through the United States in discontented groups. They built roads, trails, and bridges in the forests and national parks, prevented soil erosion and floods, and often sent the greater part of their thirty dollars a month home to their dependents.

Some five hundred million dollars was advanced to the states—not as a loan but as a gift from the taxpayers—to be disbursed by relief agencies, with the proviso that the states raise three dollars for every dollar they received. The President offered a breathtaking plan for the development of power dams in the entire Tennessee Valley, stretching out into Virginia, Ohio, Tennessee, North Carolina, Alabama, and Mississippi. And the man who sparked the group that produced these measures had to propel himself in a wheelchair along the corridor which led from the Executive Mansion to the office building!

By December 5, 1933, the requisite number of states had brought about the repeal of the Prohibition Amendment. The bootlegger and the racketeer were obliged to go to work. The President now turned his attention to a moral and financial reform of the stock market, and the Securities and Exchange Commission came into being. Its duty was to license and regulate stock exchanges.

In such a whirlwind of action, it was quite natural that there should be mistakes and failures. But the country seemed to be well on the road to recovery. Farmers, for example, found themselves better off than they had been in several years, and a noticeable amount of gold began to arrive in the United States from Europe.

Meanwhile, our foreign relations were not neglected. Roosevelt watched the rise of Adolf Hitler to power, established diplomatic relations with the Soviet Union, observed the steady march of Japan in Manchuria, and proclaimed the independence of the Philippine Islands.

President Roosevelt took the oath of office for a second term on January 20, 1937, the new date fixed by the Twentieth Amendment, which went into effect December 5, 1933. Although in 1935 the Supreme Court had declared unconstitutional nearly all of the National Industrial Recovery Act, the President's second administration was stormier than the first. Now the Court upset the Agricultural Adjustment Act. At least six million men and women were still out of work, and business was still far below the peak of 1928. To add to the administration's embarrassment and worry, sit-down strikes against employers began in Michigan and quickly spread across the nation.

In 1937 another crisis struck the stock market, and prices again went tumbling. Relief rolls increased, and the national debt mounted a billion dollars at a time. New Deal "experts" advocated a policy of borrowing and spending for increasing industrial and farm production.

In October of that year, the President, speaking at Chicago, startled the country by denouncing, without naming them, Germany, Italy, and Japan for bringing on "the present reign of terror and international lawlessness." He denied that the United States could keep out of war, if it came, when he said: "Let no one imagine that America will escape, that it may expect mercy, or that this Western Hemisphere will not be attacked." Inside of two years, Germany launched her invasion of Poland, thereby setting off World War II.

At home, the President was not seeing eye to eye with the Supreme Court. The country was shocked by his request of Congress for authority to appoint new Justices to offset those who were eligible for retirement. His contention was that the advanced age of some of the members was responsible for their conservative leanings, where New Deal legislation was concerned, and that the economic situation called for new and drastic experimentation. Senator Wheeler, of Montana, however, saw in the President's move an attempt to destroy the independence of the judiciary. In due course, three of the conservative Justices retired on a full pension, and two died. So Roosevelt was able to appoint five new Justices of liberal viewpoint.

In the 1938 Congressional elections, the President marked out some of his opponents for defeat at the Democratic primaries; and in Georgia, Maryland, and New York he openly supported candidates who were trying to unseat those in office. The Republicans gained in the election. Business failures increased, and conservative critics believed it was because of the government's hostility. Industry also resented the Roosevelt policy in favor of organized labor, which had swung its votes—and contributed its funds—to the Roosevelt campaign. Others criticized him for failing to keep his promise to balance the federal budget. Naturally, the administration did not agree with this fault finding.

As 1940 drew near, it became evident that the President was going to permit the Democratic convention to nominate him, despite the unwritten law against a third term. On the Republican side, Wendell Willkie, darkest of the dark horses, received the bid. Both promised to keep the nation out of war! Even when Roosevelt had won the election, and the Lend-Lease Act permitted him to send ships, destroyers, guns, and tanks to friendly nations such as Great Britain and Russia, the sponsors of the Lend-Lease Bill in Congress assured the people that it was intended to keep the United States out of the war!

In October, 1940, the first United States peacetime compulsory military service was inaugurated; and in July of the following year, our troops and British forces jointly occupied Iceland, at the invitation of that country. In August, Great Britain and the United States agreed upon measures to be taken to provide for the safety of their respective countries against the Rome-Berlin-Tokyo Axis. In October, German submarines attacked our shipping and a destroyer. On December 7, the Japanese attacked Pearl Harbor, Hawaii, while negotiations between our State Department and two Japanese envoys were being carried on in Washington.

At last we were in the war! Italy was knocked out first. Germany hung on until early in May, 1945; and Japan surrendered in August of that year.

The primary task of the Roosevelt administration, of course, was to preserve our democratic government. So the war determined the character of the third term. For a time the Roosevelt critics were silenced. Tens of thousands of women were recruited as volunteers, put into Army or Navy uniforms, and used both at home and abroad where they could release men to fight. Millions of men were transferred to war industries. Almost unlimited authority over life and property was granted to the President. He controlled industry, agriculture, wages, prices, use of plant facilities, the erection of new plants costing billions of dollars, and the rationing of supplies for civilians. The President of the richest and most productive country in the world led the non-Axis nations from a wheel-chair through the greatest crisis of modern times.

It is true that Roosevelt had excellent generals and admirals; but it was he who had to make the decisions. It was he, for example, who staked two billion dollars on the development of the atom bomb. In fighting the depression and World War II, Roosevelt spent much more money than all previous administrations together. In the first year of the war, Congress authorized expenditures amounting to two hundred and forty billion dollars.

When 1944 came, the tradition that forbade "swapping" horses in the middle of the stream outweighed custom, and Roosevelt was nominated for a *fourth* time. There were plenty of high school boys and girls who had never known any other President. It was, however, well understood that he might not serve out his full term. Great care was used in selecting a running mate, and the party convention's choice was Senator Harry S. Truman, of Missouri.

On November 7, 1944, Roosevelt won again. Some five months later, on April 12, the President died in Warm Springs, Georgia, of a cerebral hemorrhage. He was sixty-three years old.

F.D.R. was buried at Hyde Park, N.Y., and thousands of Americans make the pilgrimage each week to his grave, high on the banks of the Hudson. He still lives in the memory of those who were his devoted followers—and those who differed with him. Even the latter recognize the far-flung length of his shadow against the history of our time.

HARRY S. TRUMAN

The Man from Missouri

IT was getting close to graduation time for the senior class at Independence High School. The boys and girls chattered eagerly about what they were going to do after commencement day, and no one was more excited than seventeen-year-old Harry Truman. "I'm going to West Point," he said proudly. In 1901 Independence was a neighborly little town, where everybody knew everybody else, so the news spread quickly. Bess Wallace, in particular, was pleased; she and Harry had known each other since they were six years old. They went to Sunday school, grammar school, and high school together, and were graduated in the same class. In Volume I of his *Memoirs,* the thirty-second President of the United States pays her, more than half a century later, this tribute: "For me she still has the blue eyes and golden hair of yesteryear."

A few weeks after their graduation the news came that Harry had passed his written examination. Later, in his physical tests, he was not so fortunate. Years before, an oculist had fitted him with glasses, and they had always been a handicap in baseball and other games. No one thought the need for glasses would bar him from the Military Academy, yet that was what happened. When the report came, Harry read it quietly, then read it again. There was no mistake: West Point would not accept him as a cadet because of defective eyesight.

The news stunned the boy. All his bright dreams of the future seemed shattered. Now he must find a job, for the Trumans were not wealthy. The head of the family, John Anderson Truman, did well at some times and badly at others, trading horses and mules. In England, the Trumans' name was an old one. In America, they had been pioneers, following the frontier from Maryland and Virginia to Kentucky, then on into Missouri. John Anderson Truman grew up in Jackson County; and so did Martha Ellen Young. The two were married on December 28, 1881; and Harry, their first child, was born May 8, 1884, at Lamar, Missouri. The youngster was about a year old when the family migrated to Cass County, where his father ran a farm. When the boy was three, they moved to the farm of Solomon Young, Mrs. Truman's father, near Grandview, Jackson County.

There Harry, his younger brother Vivian, and their sister grew up. Some of his happiest recollections, says the ex-President, are of the years they spent on the Solomon Young farm. His grandfather took him to the Belton Fair in a high-wheeled cart, and he sat in the judges' stand, watching the races and eating striped candy and peanuts. He looked forward to hog-killing time in the fall, with the outdoor fires for rendering the lard, and the "cracklings" with bits of lean meat adhering to them.

His father bought him a beautiful black Shetland pony and a saddle with all the trappings, and Harry's Shetland trotted beside his father's big horse from one part of the farm to another. There were cattle and mules, hogs and sheep on the six-hundred-acre tract. His father and Grandpa Young were partners. In the evening he listened to them discuss farm problems; and in the various seasons he watched the harvesting and threshing of the wheat, the planting and shucking of the corn, and mowing and stacking of the hay.

Later, his father took the family to Independence and installed them in a big house with a barn and several acres of land. This soon became the gathering place of the boys and girls of the neighborhood, and at Sunday school Harry met the girl with the beautiful blue eyes.

By the time he was thirteen or fourteen, he had read all the books in the Independence library—and the family Bible. Then his father bought a house in another section of Independence, and Harry found there were boys and girls all around them. He was old enough to help with the chores. He split wood and filled the kitchen woodbox, weeded the garden and mowed the lawn, yet he and Vivian seemed to have time to enjoy the visits of their friends.

As Harry grew older, his interest in government became greater. He began reading history as a boy, and kept it up ever afterward. In his *Memoirs* he says: "I know of no better way to get a solid foundation in political science and public administration than to study the histories of past administrations of the world's most successful system of government."

His first paying job was opening up an Independence drugstore at six-thirty each morning, mopping the floors, sweeping the sidewalk, and having everything shipshape when the proprietor came in. When the work schedule became too heavy and interfered with his regular high school studies, his father quietly remarked that it might be better to quit the job and devote more time to his books. So, in addition to his regular daytime classes, he took up the study of Latin and algebra two nights a week at the home of his Aunt Ella Noland. The other three pupils were his two cousins and Bess Wallace. On two other evenings, Harry and a high school classmate foregathered at the home of a teacher, where they took extra courses in history and geography. They hoped to obtain appointments to West Point or Annapolis.

That fall (1901) after graduation from high school, Harry obtained a job as timekeeper on the Santa Fe Railroad, working for a contractor. The salary was $35 a month and board. When the contract was finished (a matter of months) Harry took a job in the mailing room of the Kansas City *Star* at $7.00 a week.

Harry's father had bought and sold two houses in Independence; now he purchased a home in Kansas City. The two Truman boys got jobs in the National Bank of Commerce. When the Kansas City house was swapped for a farm and the parents moved to Clinton, Harry and his brother stayed on and lived at a boarding house. H.S.T. was then earning sixty dollars a month. He spent the weekends with his grandmother and his Uncle Harrison Young at Grandview. In 1904, he and Vivian settled down there and later their parents joined them. The two young men ran the farm for the next ten or twelve years. Harry hoped Bess Wallace would wait for him, for he was not yet in a position to marry.

At the age of twenty-four, Harry Truman joined the National Guard at Kansas City. At the farm, in the evenings, he read military books or sat down at the old piano and played familiar tunes. On Sundays he drove over to Independence to go to church with Bess. He was twenty-nine before he was able to buy his first automobile. By the time he was thirty-three the farm was in good shape, his brother had married, death had claimed his father, and his mother and sister were left in Harry's care.

There was a great deal of prospecting for oil in the midcontinent fields at this time. Harry acquired a third interest in a new company, and was made Treasurer. They actually were drilling for oil when the entry of the United States into World War I put an end to his dream. Quickly they disposed of all leases. (Later in 1917, the operators who bought Truman's interest struck one of the largest oil pools ever opened in the state of Kansas.) Harry reported to the National Guard, and in September his unit entrained for one of the camps at Fort Sill, Oklahoma. He took with him Bess Wallace's promise to marry him when he got back. He was made regimental canteen officer, and with the aid of Sergeant Jacobson, of Kansas City, operated the canteen for six months on borrowed capital, earned $15,000 in dividends, and repaid the loan.

In the process of integration and expansion, Battery F was formed, and Truman was elected first lieutenant. Later the unit became the 129th Field Artillery of the 35th Division. In March, 1918, the unit sailed for France, where Lieutenant Truman spent five weeks in a field artillery school, rejoined the regiment, and in July was put in command of Battery D of the 129th. In September, they participated in the Battle of St. Mihiel, then joined the Meuse-Argonne drive. On the night before the fighting in the Argonne Forest began, the man from Missouri slept at the edge of a wood. He got up early the next day—otherwise this might not have been written, for the enemy laid down an early-morning barrage on the exact spot where he had been sleeping!

He had been a captain for some time, but the commission did not catch up with him until October. The end of the war, November 11, 1918, found the unit in front of Verdun. By April they were back in the United States, and the following month were discharged. Captain Truman was then thirty-five years old. Within two months, he and Bess Wallace were married in the Trinity Episcopal Church at Independence. After a wedding trip to Chicago and Port

Huron, Michigan, they settled down at Independence.

Captain Truman and Sergeant Jacobson, who had done so well with the regimental canteen, pooled their savings, borrowed some capital, and established a men's furnishings store in Kansas City. By fall they were open for business.

This was a period of general prosperity, but in 1921 farm prices dropped and interest rates were increased. By January 1, 1922, their creditors and the banks that had loaned them money began to press them. Later in the year, when they closed out the stock, they were hopelessly in debt. Their attorney advised a settlement with the creditors, and eventually the accounts were paid in full. Neither wished to go into bankruptcy, but in 1925 Jacobson was forced to file a petition.

At the age of thirty-eight, then, a business failure was chalked up against the record of Harry S. Truman. But he had friends. One of these was Jim, son of Mike Pendergast, who, with his brother Tom, wielded considerable political influence in that part of Missouri. Jim had been a lieutenant in Captain Truman's battery. The Pendergasts supported Truman as a candidate for county judge, and he won in both the primary and the election. In 1924 he ran for re-election, and was defeated. But in 1926, again with the active support of the Pendergasts, he was elected presiding judge. At night he studied law. He was glad to have a job, for about that time a little girl was born in the old house at Independence. They named her Mary Margaret.

Judge Truman was not a judge in the usual sense, for the county court was an administrative body. It levied taxes and spent money for roads, public buildings, homes for the aged, schools for delinquent boys and girls, and so forth. His first task as presiding judge was to set up a system of roads for Jackson County, construct new public buildings, and get the interest rate on borrowed money reduced from 6 per cent to 4 per cent. While he was in office, he was responsible for the spending of sixty million dollars of tax money and bond issues. Moreover, he says in *Memoirs,* Vol. I: "A new court house for Kansas City and other projects were successfully carried out, during my eight years as presiding judge, without one breath of scandal. . . . When I left the county, its finances were in first-rate shape."

Harry S. Truman was then fifty years old. He hoped that, after compiling such a record, he might represent his people in Washington as a Congressman; instead, he was elected U. S. Senator, and took his seat on January 3, 1935. It was hard work, but the next decade, according to Mr. Truman, was the happiest of his life.

In his first year as Senator he voted for a number of history-making bills. One of these was the Wagner Labor Relations Act of 1935. He gave the Tennessee Valley Authority, then an experiment, his whole-hearted support; likewise the Social Security Act of 1935.

Senator Truman's first real job was an investigation of the country's railroads. Being thorough and meticulous by nature, he was able to bring to light an enormous racket in receiverships. His report, in which he pulled no punches, resulted in the passage of a national transportation act. The man from Missouri was beginning to stand out in the Senate.

Later, he became chairman of the Committee to Investigate the National Defense Program. World War II was being waged in Europe, and the United States had passed the Lend-Lease Act, promising materials and services to Great Britain and France. Without any advance notices, Senator Truman started off on a trip to see what was going on.

When he returned with the facts, showing that at many plants and construction camps there was graft, waste, and bad management, the so-called Truman Committee was set up to correct the situation. He reckons that the recommendations of his investigating committee into the defense program resulted in the saving of fifteen billion dollars.

Many of the Senator's friends in Missouri advised him not to run for re-election in 1940. As he explains in his *Memoirs:*

> In the first place, Tom Pendergast had been sent to prison in connection with an income-tax-fraud investigation; and the Jackson County organization, which had supported me in the 1934 campaign, had fallen into discredit as a result. I realized that attempts would be made to link my name with the misdeeds and misfortunes of Pendergast and to make it appear that I was the product of a corrupt political machine. . . .

However, he did make the race, and when the votes were counted in November, he was still the U. S. Senator from Missouri.

Senator Truman went to the Democratic Convention in 1944 to make the speech nominating his friend Byrnes for Vice President. But the party—and President Roosevelt—had other ideas; the delegates nominated Truman.

Inauguration Day, January 20, 1945, found H.S.T. taking the oath as Vice President. His chief, F.D.R., was going into office for a fourth term. President Roosevelt left for the conference at Yalta two days later, tired and careworn. He returned in a few weeks, and died on April 12 while resting at Warm Springs, Georgia. Vice President Truman, first in the line of succession, was called hurriedly to the White House and sworn in as President.

The United States and her allies were then in the final days of the greatest war in history, and were close to victory. The presidency had been a highly complicated and exacting job for more than forty years; but to this already heavy burden the crushing responsibilities incident to World War II were added. Certainly no Chief Executive ever fell heir to such a tremendous burden on such short notice as Truman. But before he had been in office a month, he was able to proclaim from the White House, over a radio hookup, the unconditional surrender of the German forces and the end of the war in Europe.

Japan, too, was nearer than the Emperor realized to the day when that country would be called upon to surrender unconditionally. At the rate the B-29's were dropping jellied gasoline bombs on Japanese cities, the enemy in the Pacific could not hold out much longer. What the Emperor did not know was this: in the previous two and one half years a group of scientists, working secretly and at top speed in the United States, had virtually perfected an atomic bomb of such great power that it was sure to bring about revolutionary changes in warfare, and quite possibly in the course of history and civilization too. Within a month or two, Harry S. Truman would have to make a decision of the greatest importance to the entire world: should the new top-secret weapon be used to bring about the surrender of Japan and the end of World War II? The President's military advisers were in favor of this; so was the President. But only the President could make the decision.

President Truman did not hesitate an instant. He sent Japan an ultimatum and, when no reply was received, ordered the first bomb to be dropped on Hiroshima. Three days later, a second bomb was dropped on Nagasaki. Five days after that, Japan surrendered. As the victor, we asked for no reparations; no territory. Nor had we done so in Europe. No nation in history had ever been so magnanimous in such circumstances; none with the military power of the United States was ever so generous to its enemies.

Our position of world leadership brought with it new responsibilities and staggering obligations. How could the United States run the gauntlet of inflation, and at the same time switch from an economy based on military require-ments to a civilian economy without "cracking"? There was also a devastated Europe to be reckoned with. Among the world's many urgent needs was that for food. A great many countries in Europe, including England and Belgium, had lost a large portion of their shipping during the war. Much of their agricultural production had been destroyed or made idle. In the year immediately following the war, more people faced starvation, according to President Truman, than during all the war years combined. There was a serious world shortage of wheat and rice. Famine, the aftermath of war, was on the march. The Chief Executive felt that unless the economic life of the beaten countries could be restored, along with that of the victors, it would be impossible to re-establish peace in the world.

The President called upon a former occupant of the White House, Herbert Hoover, for help. Former President Hoover undertook a fact-finding survey that carried him on a trip of 35,000 miles around the world. He brought back a con-cise report on the food needs of twenty-two famine-ridden countries. Within six months, the United States shipped six million *tons* of bread grains to help feed the hungry of other lands. In the first two years that followed the surrender of Germany and Japan, this nation provided more than fifteen billion dollars in loans and grants for the relief of the victims of war. It was General George C. Marshall, then Secretary of State, who outlined a course of action for the nation to follow. This program, designed to place Europe on its feet economically, became known as the Marshall Plan. Over a period of four years, the cost, it was estimated, would be seventeen billion dollars.

The Truman administration was aware that the Soviet government, in its campaign to spread communism over the world, would press wherever weakness showed. It was also aware that this country was the only nation able to meet that pressure in a manner that the Russians—and the world—would understand. Already Turkey and Greece had been subjected to undue influence by the Soviet; they were badly in need of aid—quickly, and in substantial amounts. The alternative would be disaster to our security and to the security of free nations everywhere.

A meeting of the Cabinet followed. Congress began work on legislation to put an aid program for the two countries into effect—before the "iron curtain" could be extended across the Eastern Mediterranean and Greece might disappear into the Russian orbit. The President's request for aid was granted after considerable debate. American personnel and funds were furnished to assist in such fields as industry, agriculture, public finance, foreign trade, public administration, shipping, and labor. Projects for the development, rehabilitation, or construction of roads, bridges, railroads, airfields, industries, fisheries, food processing plants, and public health were initiated.

The Point Four idea originated at about the same time as

the Marshall Plan concept. This was a world-wide, continuing program of helping underdeveloped nations to help themselves through the sharing of information already tested and proved in the United States. By the end of 1951, Point Four had been extended to thirty-three countries. The budget to carry out the program had been expanded from $34,000,000 to $147,000,000 (in round figures); and for the fiscal year 1953 to $155,000,000. Point Four was not a lending program or a give-away plan. It was not against communism or anything else. It was a positive plan for self-help. It recognized the historic fact that colonialism had run its course. In its immediate and long-range effects, however, Point Four provided the strongest deterrent to communism then known. Thus the Point Four program became firmly identified with the Truman administration. Doctors, nurses, farm experts, educators, home economists, and other specialists spent years—and hundreds of millions of dollars—in building up this effective backfire against Soviet propaganda.

Under the circumstances, President Truman might have taken a well-deserved rest at the end of his term. Instead, he ran for re-election in 1948—and won, despite the almost universal prediction of public-opinion polls that he would be defeated. Learning from the pollsters that his popularity with the voters had hit an all-time low, Truman decided to go directly to the people with his campaign message. He traveled to the Pacific coast and back to Washington, making speeches in cities and towns and even villages. The final figures showed that he had received a popular vote of 24,105,695 and carried 28 states. Governor Dewey, of New York, his Republican opponent, had received 21,969,170 votes and carried 16 states.

The years of Harry Truman's second administration were

filled with turmoil. First came the blockade of Berlin by the Soviet military government. Russia controlled the country surrounding Berlin, and thus was able to prohibit American and British supply trains from passing through the Russian zone. The blockade began on April 1, 1948. It effectively barred all river, rail, and highway traffic into and out of Berlin. There was no way out for the Americans and British except through the air, and in the interval between the beginning of the blockade and the date it was lifted (September 30, 1949), American and British planes had transported by air 2,343,315 tons of food and coal into West Berlin.

In 1950, in accordance with the policy of the United Nations to resist aggression, President Truman ordered United States forces to support the Korean republic against Communist invasion, and to protect Formosa. Once again our nation was at war, this time under the banner of the United Nations.

There were other problems which concerned the President, but none so fantastic and hard to solve as the Berlin blockade. An attempt upon the President's life also was made during his second term, while he was living at government-owned Blair House. It did not succeed.

The stay of the Truman family at Blair House was occasioned by the complete renovation of the White House. Work on the reconstruction project was begun in December, 1949; the job was completed and the Trumans were able to return to the Executive Mansion in March, 1952. Less than a year later, President Eisenhower and his family moved in, and the Trumans went back to their home in Independence, Missouri.

DWIGHT D. EISENHOWER

A Five-Star General in the White House

D WIGHT D. EISENHOWER, thirty-fourth President of the United States, grew up in Abilene, Kansas, a former cow town fragrant with gun smoke, cattle pens, and dust. But he was born on October 14, 1890, in a frame house near a noisy railroad yard at Denison, Texas. He was the third son of David J. Eisenhower and Ida Stover Eisenhower.

David's father, the Reverend Jacob Eisenhower, whose ancestors had come to America from Germany and Holland in 1741 and settled in eastern Pennsylvania, was a member of the sect known as the River Brethren. The Brethren were not unlike the Quakers in their beliefs; they were hard-working and devoutly religious, and they hated war and slavery. In 1878, the Reverend Jacob sold his hundred-acre farm, with its brick house, and joined a mass migration of the sect to the rich farm lands of Kansas; Pennsylvania was becoming too worldly.

It was the custom of the Reverend Jacob, upon the marriage of a son, to present the couple with two thousand dollars and a farm of 160 acres. David, however, was not interested in farming; he wanted above all things to study engineering. At Lane University he met Ida Elizabeth Stover, and the two fell in love. They were married in 1885, and David used the money he received as a wedding present to set up a store in Hope, near Abilene.

Unfortunate in the selection of a business partner and lacking experience, David failed in business. This was so humiliating to the moody and sensitive young man that he left Abilene and obtained a job with the railroad at Denison.

Ida, thrifty and courageous, joined her husband there. And it was there Dwight was born. A year later, David brought his family back to Abilene. When Dwight was old enough to help his brothers, he worked in the local creamery and sold garden truck from door to door. The boy had sandy hair, bright blue eyes, and a lopsided grin.

The railroad that bisected Abilene formed a natural barrier between the sections, and the Eisenhowers lived on "the wrong side of the tracks." But the brothers did not let that bother them. Their father probably never earned more than a hundred dollars a month at the creamery, but he and Ida managed to bring up six healthy boys, each of whom succeeded—in banking, education, the law, the Army, and other vocations. Their father had a team of horses, pigs, and a cow; their mother kept ducks and chickens; and the boys themselves raised Belgian hares. There was a baseball diamond on a nearby vacant lot; the clear, cool waters of the Smoky River for swimming in summer; a workshop in the cellar for rainy days; and plenty of ice for skating in winter. The boys all had their chores to do; they took turns at getting out of a warm bed at five in the morning and building the kitchen fire.

Even in those early years, Dwight Eisenhower's outstanding characteristic was a remarkable capacity for making friends. His mind was quick and retentive. His brothers recall that he was stimulated by ideas; that he had a passion to *know*. At sixteen he developed an interest in history that has never flagged. He played a good game of football and baseball. He had integrity, courage and physical toughness. And he never held a grudge. While still in high school he worked on alternate evenings in the engine room of the creamery, shoveling coal into the firebox once an hour and doing his homework in between. Sometimes his school chums dropped in at the engine room for a game of cards. "Ike" liked the girls and they liked him, but there does not seem to have been any lasting attachment.

After a couple of years of riding the range, harvesting wheat, working at the creamery, and playing professional baseball following his graduation from high school, young Eisenhower was persuaded by a friend to take the preliminary examination for entrance into the United States Naval Academy at Annapolis. He asked for—and received—advice and letters of recommendation from professional and business men of Abilene and obtained the cooperation of the local newspaper editor and one of the U. S. Senators from his state. In addition to the Navy examination, Dwight took that for the U. S. Military Academy at West Point. His rating was second among the eight candidates from Kansas; and when the Number One candidate dropped out of the contest, young Eisenhower automatically became eligible for West Point. He entered on June 14, 1911.

It may be said, therefore, that the future President's character was shaped by a Middle Western farm-town environment and rounded out by the ideals and disciplines of the Military Academy. He made the West Point football team, but later suffered a knee injury that ended his football career.

Eisenhower was graduated in 1915, commissioned a second lieutenant, and stationed at Fort Sam Houston, Texas, not far from San Antonio. He was then almost twenty-five years old, tall, and happy in the choice of his profession.

Lieutenant Eisenhower was only a "shavetail," but he had

a strong character, a sunny disposition, and charming West Point manners. He found a new interest in life when he met Mamie Geneva Doud, a Denver girl who was spending the winter with her parents in San Antonio. Miss Doud had dark brown hair and deep blue eyes. She was small and slender, and loved gaiety. She was the daughter of a prosperous retired grain and cattle merchant. But Lieutenant Eisenhower was in no way abashed by the difference in economic and social status between the Douds and the Eisenhowers. He suddenly discovered he was in love. He had never felt this way toward any other girl. On July 1, 1916, the day on which he received his promotion to the rank of first lieutenant, he and Mamie were married at Denver.

The Eisenhowers lost their first child, a boy, through scarlet fever; their second son, John, grew up to become a cadet at West Point and was graduated from the Military Academy on June 6, 1944. On that day, incidentally, his father was "sweating out" the Normandy invasion. John, now a major, is married to Barbara Jean Thompson, and they have four children.

When the United States declared war against Germany and her allies in April, 1917, the future President was not sent overseas; he was too good at training men. He was by 1918 a lieutenant colonel. But reductions in rank always follow a war, and Eisenhower reverted to the rank of captain. In the ten years immediately following World War I he was graduated from the Infantry Tank School, the Command and General Staff School and the Army War College. Later he completed the course at the Army Industrial College.

For four years he was executive assistant to the Chief of

Staff at Washington, General Douglas MacArthur. Mac-Arthur then was sent out to the Philippines as military adviser to the Commonwealth, and he chose Eisenhower as his senior military assistant. There Eisenhower learned to fly an Army plane. When "Ike" returned to the United States five years later, Germany had started World War II. The big questions in Eisenhower's mind were: Would the United States enter the conflict; and would he be allowed to go overseas?

Meanwhile, some important Army maneuvers were being carried on in the United States, and Eisenhower became Chief of Staff of the Third Army. In this job he was able to put to use some of the things he had learned at the Command and General Staff School, where he had stood first in his class. He was promoted from major to lieutenant colonel, then to colonel. In 1941 he became a brigadier general and Chief of the War Plans Division of the General Staff; then Assistant Chief of Staff, Operations Division, with the rank of lieutenant general. He was made a full general in February, 1943, and designated Commander-in-Chief of Allied Forces in North Africa. When the time came for General George C. Marshall, Chief of Staff, to name a Supreme Commander of the Allied Expeditionary Forces, he selected Eisenhower. In December, 1944, President Roosevelt sent to the Senate the nomination of Eisenhower as a General of the Army, with its five stars. The nomination was approved; in 1946 the rank was made permanent.

In Dwight Eisenhower's last year at high school, the class prophecy said he would wind up as a professor of history at Yale University. Instead he made history, for he was at one time in sole command of the greatest combination of land, sea, and air forces that had ever been known.

The General's greatest contribution to victory was not the invasion of Normandy, the liberation of France, and the crushing of Hitler's army in the West. Other generals— French, British, American—might have accomplished these things under favorable circumstances. But General Eisenhower had the great quality of being able to inspire others to do their best. He brought men of different and antagonistic nationalities together. French, British, Arabs, and Americans alike had faith in his fairness and in his military judgment. That the General succeeded in transforming his various commanders into a smoothly working machine is perhaps his first claim to greatness.

It should be remembered that this officer was the grandson of a minister whose ancestors fled from the German Rhineland to avoid religious persecution and the ravages of civil war. He grew up among Quakers. As a youth, Dwight Eisenhower was easygoing, tolerant, and free from any great personal ambition. Until he went to West Point, his whole training was opposed to the idea of war. Yet when he was given a task by the President of the United States, he put everything aside and concentrated on that task.

After receiving the surrender of the German armies in Rheims on May 7, 1945, General Eisenhower served for a short time as commander of the U. S. Occupation Forces in Germany, then returned to Washington to serve as Army Chief of Staff for more than two years.

At the end of this term, with retirement from the Army in the offing, the General began to receive offers to head one corporation or another. Then the trustees of Columbia University, with large numbers of war veterans among the students, asked him to take the chair vacated by the death of President Butler. Because his rank of General of the Army had been made permanent, his salary and allowances from the Army continued. These moneys, plus the sum received for the outright sale of his book, *Crusade in Europe,* enabled him to serve Columbia for a year and a half without salary. Then President Truman asked him to head the North Atlantic Treaty Organization, a treaty group which had been entered into by the United States, Great Britain, France, Canada, Iceland, and seven European nations for mutual security.

Meanwhile, President Truman's amazing victory in 1948 over Governor Dewey, the Republican candidate for President, had dumbfounded Dewey's followers. The Republicans began to look around for an outstanding leader to head the 1952 presidential ticket. Eisenhower, then president of Columbia, on leave with NATO, was their choice. There was general dissatisfaction in the United States because the war in Korea dragged on and on, and the Republicans believed Eisenhower, with his World War II experience and his flair for conciliation, could bring the conflict to an end. There was also resentment over the disclosure of corruption in Washington, criticism of taxation in general and of the high cost of living. New faces were needed in Washington, declared the General's advisers: Republican faces.

In 1952, General Eisenhower gave up his NATO job and asked to be placed on the Army's retired list. This left him free to engage in political activities. He had not declared a preference for either the Republican or Democratic party prior to that time, because of his conviction that Army officers should not be actively engaged in politics.

The movement to make him President spread like a prairie fire. One poll showed that, of voters who favored General Eisenhower, 58 per cent did not know (and presumably did not care) whether he was a Republican or a Democrat. They believed that "Ike" possessed, in a high degree, the moral qualities that unite men and encourage them to cling to their freedom and uphold the free-enterprise system.

General Eisenhower was nominated at the Republican convention in Chicago by 845 votes out of 1,206. On November 4, 1952, he was elected over Adlai E. Stevenson, governor of Illinois, the Democratic candidate, by 442 to 89 electoral votes. At the end of the campaign, Eisenhower received the biggest popular vote of any presidential candidate in history—33,936,252. He "cracked" the Democratic South, and carried eighteen states that for twenty years had been Democratic under Presidents Roosevelt and Truman. Yet the Republican party itself, as represented in Congress, came through with the narrowest of margins in the Senate and only a slender majority in the House of Representatives.

The new President came to power at a time as critical as any in American history. Important matters in Europe and Asia and at home had to be acted upon quickly and decisively. The rich oil resources of the Middle East were one of the prime objectives of Soviet Russia, for without oil no extensive war could be fought. Control of East Germany by Soviet Russia, and the inability of France and West Germany to work together, created problems for the United States. Furthermore, a "cold war" had existed virtually since the end of World War II, and was seriously disturbing the relations, friendly during the war, between the United States and the Soviet Union. Finally, there was indisputable evidence that this country no longer held a monopoly of the atomic bomb; the Russians had managed, with the help of German physicists, to evolve a bomb of their own. Like us, Russia had the long-range planes and submarines to deliver this devastating weapon to any part of the world. This fact added immeasurably to the hazard of the "cold war" between the free world, as represented by the United States, and the Communist world.

It was under such circumstances that Dwight D. Eisenhower was inaugurated on January 20, 1953, with the Chief Justice of the nation administering the oath. After the ceremonies, President Eisenhower was welcomed into office by a parade that lasted five hours.

In the first year of his administration, the President asked for a survey of the nation's overseas commitments, and decided to reduce the enormous cost of the military establishment by relying more on a bolder diplomacy, cutting down the overseas forces, and depending more for security on long-range planes. He also reduced the activities of the government and removed some 183,000 persons from the payroll. All wage and price controls were removed.

Even before the President-elect was inaugurated, he redeemed one of his campaign promises by making the trip to Korea in an effort to bring an end to the fighting there. The armistice did not immediately follow, but when it came, six months later, President Eisenhower was generally credited with bringing it about. He also fulfilled another campaign promise when he signed a bill giving the states title to submerged coastal lands within their historic boundaries.

It was during the first year of the Eisenhower Administration that the Atomic Energy Commission disclosed a program for the construction of a multimillion-dollar atomic energy plant for peacetime use. The new regime also created an additional Cabinet post—Secretary of the Department of Health, Education, and Welfare—and Mrs. Oveta Culp Hobby, of Texas, was appointed Secretary.

President Eisenhower made two appointments to the Supreme Court which met with general approval—Chief Justice Earl Warren and Associate Justice John Marshall Harlan. In July, 1956, the President signed a bill providing ways and means for carrying out a 41,000-mile superhighway program, in which the government would allocate to the states twenty-five billion dollars as its 90-per-cent share of the cost, and an additional two and one-half billion—to be matched, dollar for dollar, by the states—for primary, secondary and rural roads.

In its first four years the Eisenhower Administration created a climate under which the nation achieved almost full employment: 64,000,000 employed workers, 2,500,000 unemployed. Personal income reached a record annual rate of $315,000,000,000 in March, 1956. In the meantime, the value of the dollar showed remarkable stability, with the cost of living going up at the rate of 1 per cent a year. Stabilizing the dollar meant that people living on relatively fixed incomes, insurance annuities, pensions, and interest on past savings, with a little economy here and there, were able to maintain their purchasing power and their standards of living. But inflation (described as an increase in the amount of money without an adequate increase in the amount of things to spend it on) is still the country's Number One economic problem, according to the government's advisers.

During one period in the Administration, there was hardly a day when Congress wasn't investigating something or somebody. Naturally, this constant turmoil did not speed up the President's legislative program. Nor was he able to get from Congress everything that he requested, such as health reinsurance, federal aid for school construction, changes in the Taft-Hartley Labor-Management Law, home rule for the District of Columbia, postal rate increases, and a Niagara power bill, among other things. Nor was the Eisenhower Administration able to solve the farm-surplus problem, an inheritance from previous administrations.

In dealing with the Eighty-third Congress, which convened on January 3, 1953, the President steered close enough to the middle of the road to win some Democratic support in many instances. Thus he was able to bring about the first general tax reform in fifty years: Taxes were reduced in 1954 by a total of more than seven billion dollars. Revision of the Atomic Energy Act opened the door for development of a private atomic power industry within the United States. Another Eisenhower achievement was a partnership arrangement with the government of Canada in St. Lawrence Seaway construction. This would make it possible to load American and Canadian ships with grain as far inland as Duluth and Port Arthur, and transport it to Europe by way of the Great Lakes and the St. Lawrence River. President Eisenhower's recent White House predecessors were unable to make any headway with similar legislation.

The bill to extend the Social Security program, and increase both benefits and payments, also extends coverage of the system to approximately ten million additional persons. Both Republicans and Democrats voted for this bill. Much of President Eisenhower's influence over Congress comes from his very modesty; he asks, but does not attempt to dictate.

General Walter Bedell Smith, Chief of Staff in Europe, credits General Eisenhower with six historic decisions during the war which, if they had not been right, could have resulted in disaster. Years later, as President, he had other decisions to make. Perhaps one of the most important was his now-famous "open skies" disarmament plan presented at the Geneva Conference. Equally important was his offer to share with the other nations of the world the peaceful fruits of atomic fission. Under all the stress and strain which a Chief Executive must experience, President Eisenhower held up well until September 24, 1955. Early that morning he suffered a moderately severe coronary thrombosis, with a possibility that the heart tissue itself had been injured by a blood clot. He was visiting Denver at the time, and was taken to Fitzsimmons Army Hospital, with the White House physician in attendance. Specialists were called in from Washington and Boston, and President Eisenhower spent the next seven weeks recuperating from his heart attack. He was then flown to Washington, and from there to his Gettysburg farm, where he spent another rest period of six weeks. In Washington, routine administrative affairs were handled by the staff, and Cabinet meetings moved smoothly, with Vice President Nixon in the chair.

For a time it seemed that the President might be compelled to forego politics; that he might not be well enough

PRESIDENTS OF THE UNITED STATES

to run for a second term. But the Boston specialist who had had his case in charge came forward with an announcement that the President's recovery had been thoroughly satisfactory, and that he could look forward to five or ten years more of normal activity. This opened the door for the President's statement, in February, 1956, that he would run again.

In June, however, the President experienced his second serious illness in less than a year. After an operation to remove an obstruction in the small intestine, the Army medical men at Walter Reed Hospital, Washington, pronounced their patient "better than ever." They had relieved by surgery an ailment of long standing. Back to the farm went the President for another period of convalescence—and another announcement: he would go ahead with his campaign and leave the decision not to the doctors, but to the voters.

On November 6, 1956, the American people gave an overwhelming vote of confidence to the Republican candidates, Eisenhower and Nixon. The President piled up 35,582,236 popular votes to 26,028,887 for his Democratic opponent, Governor Stevenson; minor parties accounted for 507,813 votes. President Eisenhower carried forty-one states and Stevenson seven.

Despite the proportions of his victory, however, Eisenhower remained the first President since 1848 who did not carry into office with him a majority in at least one branch of Congress. The Democrats again controlled the House of Representatives and the Senate. He was also the first Chief Executive to be affected by the Twenty-Second Amendment to the Constitution, which provides that a President may serve only two terms. As early as the first year of President

Eisenhower's second administration both Republicans and Democrats were beginning to think about possible new candidates, which in itself put limitations on the influence of the President, and increased his problems.

In September, 1957, he was faced with the most serious domestic challenge in his entire tenure of office, when he sent Federal troops to Little Rock, Arkansas, to enforce the Supreme Court order desegregating our schools. President Eisenhower's action caused a loud clamor in the South, which seethed with anger against the President who had always stood for states' rights. But integration of schools, which already had been effected in our nation's capital and in many other parts of the country, continued slowly and steadily in southern as well as northern states.

Meanwhile, scientists of many nations including our own were engrossed in efforts to explore and conquer outer space. The United Nations had set up the International Atomic Energy Agency; and the United States opened the first large-scale nuclear reactor in this country to produce electric power for civilian use.

In October, 1957, Soviet Russia startled the world by launching the first man-made moon, an artificial satellite called Sputnik I. On the following January 31st, the United States sent its first satellite, Explorer I, into orbit and others followed.

For the third time since he had entered the White House, the President on November 25th, 1957, suffered a serious illness—a mild stroke. The NATO meeting was to be held in Paris in December, and Eisenhower was determined to be there. He did attend, meeting privately for four days with one head of state after another. Out of the conferences came an agreement to explore the possibilities of negotiations which might eventually lead to another summit conference.

Two new stars were added to our flag in 1959, with the admission of Alaska and Hawaii into the Union. During most of that year and the year 1960, President Eisenhower kept traveling—to Europe, to Asia, to Africa, to Latin America. (He traveled more than three hundred thousand miles during his eight years in office.) And everywhere he went, preaching his message of peace and freedom, millions of people greeted him with cheers and applause.

When in May of 1960, the President flew to Paris for the summit meeting, he had higher hopes than were justified by the Geneva Conference in 1955, which had disappointed him. He felt this time that his "open skies" proposal and his "atoms for peace" program might meet with some success and at last the big powers might make some progress in settling their differences. Premier Khrushchev had paid an unprecedented visit to the United States the previous September. He made a transcontinental tour of our country and conferred with the President at Camp David, Maryland, and in turn invited the President to visit Soviet Russia. This the President planned to do after the summit meeting was concluded.

President Eisenhower's optimism, however, was doomed to go down in disappointment and defeat. On May 5th, Khrushchev announced that an American plane had been shot down over Russia. The United States responded that it was a weather observation plane which had been on a flight over Turkey and had gone astray. A few days later the Soviet Premier reported that the American pilot had been captured. The Soviet Premier made a bitter verbal attack on the United States and refused to meet with President Eisenhower at the summit conference, unless he apologized publicly and met other Soviet demands. The Russian leader also withdrew his invitation to the President to visit Moscow.

Ostensibly, Khrushchev's reason was outrage over the affair of the U-2 plane, but by his own admission Moscow had known about such flights for years, just as the United States for years had known of the presence of Russian intelligence agents in this country. There was much speculation as to Khrushchev's real reason for wrecking the summit meeting in Paris before negotiations began. Some believed it was a maneuver to divide the American people; others thought he did not want a showdown on the Berlin situation; while many were convinced that the Russian Premier's sole reason for withdrawing the invitation to visit Moscow was his fear that millions of Russians would pour into the streets in an overwhelming demonstration of friendship for President Eisenhower.

Thus, in 1960, as in previous postwar years, the struggle between the Western and Communist worlds dominated the international scene and spread into new arenas.

The trouble spot closest to home for our country was the pro-Communist regime of President Fidel Castro in Cuba. On January 3rd, 1961, after two years of harassment by Castro, President Eisenhower ordered the State Department to break off diplomatic relations with Cuba. Months before Castro had confiscated one billion dollars' worth of American-owned property in Cuba; and on the eve of the New Year came Castro's drastic edict that within forty-eight hours the United States must reduce its embassy and consulate staffs to a total of eleven Americans. This included secretaries, clerks, and other assistants. President Eisenhower called an emergency meeting with his top advisers, before the final decision was made to sever diplomatic relations.

"There is a limit to what the United States in self-respect can endure," said the President. "That limit has now been reached."

Before the United States broke relations with Cuba, six Latin American nations had already done so: Peru, Paraguay, Guatemala, Haiti, Nicaragua, and the Dominican Republic.

On September 19, 1960, Khrushchev again arrived in the United States to attend a special session of the UN Assembly. President Eisenhower also attended and in his speech before the UN he reiterated his pleas for peace. At this meeting thirteen new nations of Africa were represented at the UN for the first time. The President's major theme, however, was not Africa but the world community it had joined.

"We must," he said, "build a world of justice under law and we must overcome poverty, illiteracy, and disease." To this end he proposed that we direct our farm surpluses to the hungry in a "food for peace" plan through the UN; use United States air- and sea-lift capacity as a permanent stand-by force at the UN's disposal for future emergencies; demilitarize outer space; reduce nuclear stockpiles and transfer fissionable material to peaceful purposes, provided Russia would follow suit; and reduce the danger of "war by miscalculation" through a UN surveillance body.

"The United States," said Mr. Eisenhower, "wants the Soviet Union and all the nations of the world to know enough about United States defense preparations to be assured that United States forces exist only for deterrence and defense—not for surprise attack. I hope the Soviet Union will similarly wish to assure the United States and other nations."

As his administration drew to a close, the President in his final State of the Union message to Congress on January 12, 1961, seemed proudest of the fact that he had ended the war in Korea when he first took office, and Americans since then "have lived in peace in highly troubled times."

It may well be that the most important and enduring heritage President Eisenhower has bequeathed to posterity is the affection, admiration, and good will he has engendered in the hearts of millions of plain people all over the world. Both as a general and a President he has won the respect and loyalty of those at home and abroad for his courage, humility, and honesty.

His unceasing efforts to promote peace and freedom for all mankind will be long remembered. These efforts General Eisenhower plans to continue in his role of private citizen as long as he lives.

JOHN FITZGERALD KENNEDY

"New Frontier" President

ALL night long the snow fell, the winds rose almost to gale fury, and the temperature dropped way below freezing. With the coming of daylight the storm abated and as the sun climbed higher our nation's capital glittered brilliantly in its deep blanket of white. The wind was still bitingly cold and breath was like smoke on the frosty air, but the sky was blue and cloudless.

Many people had been anxiously watching the weather, for it was Inauguration Day, January 20, 1961. Three thousand men using plows and trucks had been working around the clock to remove almost eight inches of snow from Washington's main streets for the big parade and the tens of thousands of citizens who had come from all over the United States to see the new President, John F. Kennedy, and his Vice President, Lyndon B. Johnson, take the oath of office.

President Eisenhower had invited the President-elect and his wife to have coffee in the family dining room at the White House, before braving the elements and proceeding to the Capitol. It was an informal and happy gathering. The old and the new chief executives with their wives and other members of their party exchanged many pleasantries about the top hats and tails the men were wearing for the occasion. It was the first time such a friendly and informal get-together had marked an Inaugural Day.

The election of John Kennedy established many precedents and shattered many traditions. He was the youngest man and the first Roman Catholic ever elected President. He was the only man to become the father of a son after his election,

336

but before his inauguration. (John F. Kennedy, Jr., was born on Thanksgiving Day, November 24, 1960.) He was the first President to appoint his brother a member of his Cabinet. Inauguration Day 1961 also marked the first time both the mother and the father of an incoming President were on hand to witness the impressive ceremony of his oath-taking.

The hearts of Joseph and Rose Kennedy must have been full as they watched their son raise his right hand and repeat in clear, resolute tones the oath which made him thirty-fifth President of the United States. Their thoughts, in that moment, must have raced back over the years to a little blue-eyed boy with a flashing smile, who played happily in the yard of an old frame house in Brookline, and who now was receiving the highest honor this country can offer any man.

John Fitzgerald Kennedy was born in that house in Brookline on May 29, 1917. The family lived there for several years. It was a quiet middle-class section of the Boston suburb, and it was there Jack spent his early childhood.

Both his grandfathers had been powerful political figures in Boston. Joseph Kennedy, Jack's father, was a shrewd, ambitious businessman. He vowed to make a million dollars by the time he was thirty-five, and he did—probably several times over. Following his graduation from Harvard, he got a job as bank examiner and was elected president of the bank at the age of twenty-five. In 1914 he married Rose Fitzgerald, the Mayor's daughter. Children came rapidly; Joe, Jr., followed by John F., then five girls, then Robert, and lastly Edward.

As the Kennedys became more and more prosperous, there were moves to bigger houses and better neighborhoods. Jack attended grade school at Dexter, a private academy.

There were pleasant days of going to baseball games with his grandfather and visiting Concord Bridge, Bunker Hill, and other historic spots with his mother. Then Joseph Kennedy moved his large family to the New York City area, where they lived first in Riverdale and later in Bronxville. Jack then went to the Riverdale School. According to his teachers he was a tall, rather slight lad, polite, industrious, and likable, with a special interest in history—and a hot temper.

Looking back, President Kennedy could not remember any hardships during his childhood. It was a happy and prosperous life with the companionship of many sisters and brothers. The family was a closely-knit one, presenting a united front against the outside world. This devotion of the Kennedys to one another exists to this day, and was of considerable help to John Kennedy during his presidential campaign.

In school he tried for football, baseball, and other sports with moderate success. He became an excellent swimmer, which during World War Two was to save his life and the lives of some of his shipmates.

For a year he went to Canterbury School in New Milford, Connecticut. The following fall he shifted to Choate where he was graduated. As his father's fortune continued to grow during the nineteen-twenties, Jack spent many winter vacations at the family's home in Palm Beach, and summers in Hyannisport on Cape Cod. He was especially fond of Hyannisport.

Jack's father sent him to England when he was eighteen to take a summer course at the London School of Economics. His career at Princeton was brief. It was cut short by illness, and he later entered Harvard. When he was in his sophomore year at the end of 1937, President Franklin D. Roosevelt appointed Joseph Kennedy Ambassador to Britain. Jack and his older brother, Joe, visited their parents at the Embassy as often as they could. Jack watched restlessly as Europe girded for World War Two. Eager to see things at first hand, he crossed the Atlantic late in the winter of 1939, visiting France, Poland, Riga, Russia, Turkey, Palestine, the Balkans, and Berlin. He talked with representatives of all parties, rich and poor, to get a balanced view of what was going on, and from each capital he sent detailed reports to his father in London.

In June, 1940, Jack Kennedy was graduated from Harvard with honors both in political science and for his thesis, *Appeasement at Munich.* Later, under the title of *Why England Slept,* this was published in book form and reached the bestseller lists in both England and the United States.

After his graduation, Jack Kennedy at first planned to go to Yale Law School, then changed his mind and took up a business school course for six months. He made a long tour of South America in 1941. Since it seemed more and more likely that the United States would get into war, Kennedy tried to enlist in the Army. The Army, however, rejected him because of a back condition that had troubled him for years.

Kennedy was disappointed but not defeated. After five months of rigorous physical exercises, he passed a Navy test in September. When the Japanese attacked Pearl Harbor he persuaded his father to use his influence to get him active sea duty. Jack was twenty-five when in 1942 he was assigned to a Torpedo Boat Squadron in the South Pacific. By March of the following year he was commanding his own PT boat in the Solomon Islands. Five months later he was part of a big air-sea-ground attack against the Japanese around New Georgia.

Shortly after midnight on August 2, 1943, a Japanese destroyer, bearing down on the small PT boat, smashed into her amidships and cut her in two, then slid away into the darkness. Two men were killed outright. John Kennedy was thrown on his back to the deck. Half of the PT boat was still afloat and he and eleven others clung to it. What happened next makes a dramatic story. Jack Kennedy swam five hours, holding the end of a belt between his teeth towing a badly burned shipmate to safety on a small island three miles away. They thought they might get help there, but the island was uninhabited. The men were cold, hungry, thirsty, sick, and hurt. Jack's back was badly injured but later he swam many more miles from island to island, and finally met some friendly natives with a canoe. They agreed to carry word to his base, and with his penknife he scratched the message on a coconut shell, reporting their position and their need for help.

As was customary, the rescued were ordered to return for duty to the United States. Kennedy refused. He succeeded in hiding the extent of his spinal injury from his command-ing officers, took another boat, and went back into combat. Later Lieutenant John F. Kennedy was decorated with the Navy–Marine Corps Medal for Heroism, and the Purple Heart.

The first tragic event in the Kennedy family came when Jack's older brother, Joe, was killed in action. His plane ex-ploded in mid-air and disintegrated. His body was never recovered. When the Kennedys received the news, Jack was in a Navy hospital in Chelsea, following an operation on his spine. It was there that he began work on *As We Remember Joe,* a privately published book written by the grief-stricken family and friends. Joe had always been Jack's idol. Joe had had lofty ambitions. He ruled his younger brothers and sisters with a sometimes iron hand, but remained their hero. Joe had said he would some day be President of the United States. They believed him and after his death it seemed only right and natural for Jack to take Joe's place and turn to politics.

In 1946, 1948, and 1950 he bested his opponents for a seat in the House of Representatives. He was only twenty-nine when he first took his seat in Congress and he looked much younger with his shock of unruly hair and his radiant boyish smile. But Congressmen soon realized he was equal to his job.

In January, 1953, after a hard-fought campaign in which his entire family helped, Kennedy moved into the Senate. He had run against Henry Cabot Lodge and had won. Soon the energetic young millionaire Senator from Massachusetts was regarded as an increasingly important political figure.

On September 12, 1953, a few weeks after Congress adjourned, Jack Kennedy and Jacqueline Bouvier were married in St. Mary's Church in Newport, Rhode Island. Jackie's family was wealthy, prominent, and cultivated. She grew up in New York and Washington and attended Vassar and the Sorbonne, before becoming a student at George Washington University. A Catholic of wealthy background, widely traveled, good-looking, young (twelve years younger than her husband), and highly intelligent, Jacqueline Lee Bouvier came from somewhat the same social environment as Jack Kennedy.

A year after their marriage surgeons performed a delicate operation in an effort to cure the spinal trouble which had plagued Jack Kennedy for years. For six months he lay on a hospital bed, but this time the operation was a success. It was during his long convalescence that he wrote the best seller, *Profiles in Courage.*

Profiles in Courage drew high praise from most critics and was translated into seven languages. More than a year after its publication it was awarded the Pulitzer prize for biography. (Kennedy turned the $500 prize over to the United Negro College Fund.)

Caroline Kennedy, first child of Jacqueline and John Kennedy, was born in Georgetown in November, 1957. At the time of Caroline's birth, her father was still a Senator, but political circles already regarded him as an important contender for the Presidential nomination for the Democratic party. During the summer of 1960, he won that nomination, and the following November he also won the election, but by a very narrow margin over his Republican opponent, Vice President Richard Nixon.

Whether John Kennedy was helped or hurt by the religious issue will be a matter of debate for years to come. Many people were violently opposed to having a Roman Catholic in the White House. Yet Kennedy said repeatedly, in response to questions:

"As a public official sworn to uphold the Constitution, I have no obligation to any private institution, religious or otherwise. My obligation is to the good of all. . . . For the office-holder, nothing takes precedence over his oath to up-

hold the Constitution and all its parts. I believe . . . that
the separation of church and state is fundamental to our
American concept and heritage and should remain so."

President Kennedy's advent into the White House her-
alded the beginning of an administration called the New
Frontier. In his inaugural speech the President said:

> The torch [of freedom] has been passed to a new
> generation of Americans, born in this century, tem-
> pered by war, disciplined by a hard and bitter peace,
> proud of our ancient heritage—and unwilling to
> witness or permit the slow undoing of those human
> rights to which this nation has always been com-
> mitted, and to which we are committed today at
> home and around the world.

President Kennedy's Cabinet was the youngest in the history of the United States, with an average age of forty-seven.
Thus the passage of power was from one generation to another—from men who directed World War Two to men
who fought that war.

President Kennedy's inaugural speech was one of the
shortest on record. In it, he pointed out:

> In the long history of the world, only a few genera-
> tions have been granted the role of defending free-
> dom in its hour of maximum danger. I do not
> shrink from this responsibility—I welcome it.

In other vital passages of his speech he also said:

> Let every nation know, whether it wish us well or
> ill, that we shall pay any price, bear any burden,
> meet any hardship, support any friend or oppose

any foe in order to assure the survival and success of liberty.

Let us never negotiate out of fear. But let us never fear to negotiate.

My fellow Americans, ask not what your country will do for you. Ask what you can do for your country. My fellow citizens of the world, ask not what America will do for you, but what together we can do for the freedom of man.

Even on his gala Inauguration Day John Fitzgerald Kennedy had no illusions about the many grave responsibilities he faced. He believed, and so expressed himself, that the nature of our times would have a tremendous impact upon the presidency. "The age of consolidation is over," he said, "and the age of change and challenge has arrived. The next year and the next decade—in all likelihood the next generation—will require more bravery and wisdom on our part than any period in our history. We will come face to face every day, in every part of our lives and times, with the real issue of our age—the issue of survival."

As soon as he assumed his duties, the new President surrounded himself with the ablest men he could find to help him work for the freedom and brotherhood of man and for peace in the world. He chose young, intellectual, scholarly men whom he knew and admired and who were completely devoted to his cause. To the final hour of his all too short service to our nation, President Kennedy never abandoned his ideals. He struggled for an America in which every man would have a job and every child would have a good education, with equal opportunities for all.

Jack Kennedy realized early in his administration that his dream of a "New Frontier" would not easily be won. The Eighty-seventh Congress did not see entirely eye to eye with him. The first major fight was over Kennedy's all-out effort to liberalize the House Rules Committee. That resolution was carried by a scant five votes. During the year, in sixty-six messages sent to Capitol Hill, the President made 355 specific legislative requests. Of those, Congress approved 172. They generally gave him everything he asked for in the field of national security. They approved the Kennedy administration's requests for the biggest housing bill in history, an increased minimum wage, and new federal highway financing. But aid to education and medical care for the elderly (two pet projects of President Kennedy) never even came to House votes. And for foreign aid he got only half of what he asked.

But through all his troubles, President Kennedy never lost his frankness, his wit, and his sense of humor. Once during the campaign, when Harry Truman had said that so far as he was concerned, the Republicans could go to hell, Mr. Kennedy sent him a telegram: "Dear Mr. President, I have noted with interest your suggestion as to where those who vote for my opponent should go. While I understand and sympathize with your deep motivation, I think it is important that our side try to refrain from raising the religious issue." Some time later, when the Kennedys were established in the White House, Press Secretary Pierre Salinger told the President that hundreds of letters were coming in asking why he always walked a few steps ahead of Jacqueline Kennedy. He chuckled over this and said: "Jackie will just have to walk a little faster." Actually it is prescribed by protocol that when the President is in the White House, he is to precede others; but this President and his wife, in carrying out their official duties, were gracious, informal, and charming. Both had been reared in the social graces; both had traveled extensively at home and abroad. They had been entertained and had entertained in the highest circles; both were equally at ease on a campaign platform among the voters or in the presence of royalty. Together President and Mrs. Kennedy erased the idea that, compared with other world capitals, Washington was "a hick town." It had, residents said, few cultural advantages beyond its museums and occasional concerts. The Kennedys soon changed all that. They brought new style and flair to the nation's capital. Notables in music, ballet, art, literature, and poetry were invited to Washington and especially to the White House. Some people thought what they termed "the arty atmosphere" might hurt the President politically, but apparently it served to enhance his popularity.

In the spring of 1961, the President and his wife traveled to Europe, and together the handsome smiling young couple captured the imagination of the populace everywhere they appeared. Queen Elizabeth and Prince Philip, along with other Britons, welcomed them enthusiastically. The same was true of President de Gaulle, when they visited France. Later, when they were in Vienna, Premier Khrushchev greeted them cordially.

At home in Washington, President Kennedy worked long hours every day, and it was usually only in the evening that he had leisure to see and play with his little daughter, Caroline, and his small son, John, Jr., whom the President called John-John.

Rocking chairs, similar to those old wicker rockers which used to be plentiful on the wide verandas of an earlier era, became a familiar sight in the White House. Probably few people realized the pain President Kennedy suffered almost constantly, due to many years of trouble with his back. His doctor, however, was well aware of his condition, and prescribed a specially built rocking chair with broad arms. This was fine for the President. It was fine for the furniture business, for people all over the country hastened to buy the old-fashioned, almost forgotten rocker. It was fine, too, for active young John-John. He would climb into one of the chairs and sway perilously back and forth, saying: "Look at me; I'm rocking—I'm rocking too fast!" Then he would grin happily when someone came to his rescue. It was a good way, he thought, to get some attention in such a busy household.

In April, 1961, José Miró Cardona, president of the Cuban National Revolutionary Council, called on Cubans to unite and overthrow the Castro regime. On April 17, some 1400 Cuban patriots, who had trained in the United States and Guatemala, landed at the Bay of Pigs on Cuba's southern coast. They were defeated by Castro forces and killed or imprisoned. The attempt caused severe criticism in Congress of the activities of the U.S. Central Intelligence Agency. President Kennedy had previously declared to the American people that, while we were aiding and instructing the Cuban National Revolutionary Council in every way possible, there would be no intervention by the United States, and no Americans would engage in fighting on Cuban soil. The defeat of the Cuban National Revolutionary Council was an overwhelming blow to our country. Castro was now more firmly entrenched than ever. President Kennedy went on television in an impromptu meeting with the press, in which he took the entire blame for the fiasco on his shoulders. This is a subject which will still be under discussion many years hence, but some of the articles and books on the Bay of Pigs disaster point out that President Kennedy had been assured by the C.I.A. that all would go smoothly. That matter was not brought out in the press conference. Kennedy fared badly in that hour of defeat; but he was magnificent in the fall of 1962. United States reconnaissance planes flying over Cuba had taken thousands of pictures, showing that Russia was cramming the 750-mile-long island with jet bombers and missiles, pointing directly at America's heartland. Our country could do one of three things: Make war on Cuba; do nothing; or insist that the Russians remove all the Cuban installations. President Kennedy made his decision. "Operation X" was set up, ready to rip out the missiles, should we be forced to invade Cuba. Meanwhile, we set up a quarantine on all military equipment shipped to Cuba. By this means, Kennedy forced Russia to halt the shipment of arms, and also to remove the missiles and other equipment from Cuba. This was perhaps the most important decision that President Kennedy had to make. By many people throughout the nation and across the world, it was called his finest hour. But he made other important decisions also.

He defied Soviet attempts to force the Allies out of Berlin. He made the steel industry rescind its price rise. He backed civil rights, a mental health program, arbitration of railroad disputes, and more medical care for the aged. Astronaut flights and satellite orbiting were greatly developed during his tenure—and later, Cape Canaveral was renamed Cape Kennedy.

A definite step in the direction of lasting peace was taken by the President in 1963, when the United States and Soviet

Russia signed a treaty agreeing to ban the testing of nuclear weapons in the atmosphere.

President Kennedy also introduced a Trade Expansion Act to remove impediments to world trade by reducing tariffs. He established the Peace Corps, sending men and women of every age and in every field all over the world to promote amity, aid, education, and health, and to relieve poverty and ignorance.

Many grave problems of state, however, still faced the President. He remained firm in his efforts to assist people in various parts of the world to resist Communist regimes. In our own country he was struggling with the rising tide of unrest and dissension over civil rights. He believed that every citizen of the United States, regardless of race, color, or creed, should have equal rights for work, for decent places in which to live, and equal voting rights and other opportunities.

Whenever they could, the Kennedys left the summer heat of Washington and returned to the freedom, the good salt air and sea at Hyannisport. There, with his wife and children, the President went swimming, fishing, and sailing in his beloved Nantucket Sound, and spent many carefree hours on the beaches and waters surrounding Cape Cod.

Grief marked the happy personal lives of President Kennedy and his Jacqueline during the summer of 1963. On August 7, Mrs. Kennedy bore a baby son, who was christened Patrick Bouvier Kennedy. But within two days the little boy died of a respiratory illness.

In the fall of 1963, President Kennedy made a tour of various Texas cities. Dallas was to be the last stop, and on Friday, November 22, he and his wife were riding in an open car through the crowded streets of downtown Dallas. With them, in the jump seats, were Governor and Mrs. Connally of Texas.

It was a glorious sunny day, and the crowds were out in full force to cheer their President and his First Lady. President Kennedy was hatless, as usual, and he and his wife were responding gaily to the applause of the crowds on both sides of the streets, when suddenly three shots rang out in rapid succession. They were from the gun of an assassin, whose distorted mind had planned every step of the murder of the young President who rode so fearlessly among his fellow citizens.

At first the crowds thought the sounds must be from a backfire or a burst of firecrackers. But the bullets were real. Fired from an upper floor of a building along the line of march, the bullets struck both Governor Connally and President Kennedy, who, fatally wounded, slumped into the arms of his wife. At Parkland Memorial Hospital, where the President and the Governor were taken, finally the dreaded announcement came. Governor Connally was wounded. The President was dead. By telephone, radio, and television the word sped, and plunged millions into grief and uncertainty. It seemed impossible that this man with the sunny personality, and the vigor and intellectual grasp of the many problems which faced him, was suddenly gone. Men and women cried openly in the streets; the faithful went to their churches to pray.

The assassination was the first of a chain of almost incredible events. As Lyndon B. Johnson was taking the oath of office of President of the United States in the plane at the Dallas airport, Lee Oswald, the accused assassin, was being arrested by Dallas police. Before the suspect was captured, he shot and killed police officer J. D. Tippit who had tried to arrest him for questioning. Two days later Oswald himself was shot to death by Jack Ruby, a Dallas nightclub operator, while being transferred from the city to the county jail. Ruby was immediately taken into custody.

On Monday morning, November 25, 1964, the day of the Kennedy funeral, all was ready for an impressive and solemn occasion. Some two hundred dignitaries, including Prince Philip, President Charles de Gaulle, President de Valera of Ireland, and Premier Hayoto Ikeda were present both at St. Matthew's Cathedral and at the graveside. With courage and dignity, Mrs. Kennedy (helped by her brothers-in-law, Robert and Edward) had arranged every detail for a fitting funeral. Burial was in Arlington National Cemetery, and at the grave, as the service was completed, Jacqueline Kennedy, with Robert and Edward to help her, lighted an eternal flame. Thus, the final act of the tragic drama which had gripped the nation and the world for four terrible days, came to an end.

Many memorials have been set up for President Kennedy since then, but the one Mrs. Kennedy thinks and hopes would have been nearest to his heart is the John Fitzgerald Kennedy Library in Cambridge. This is to be built on a two-acre site he had selected only two months before his assassination, from several plots offered by Harvard University.

The President had his future carefully organized. He expected to be reelected in November, 1964, and finish the business of his administration. Then, too young to retire, he planned to return to his native Massachusetts and devote himself to a life of teaching and writing. He was going to use the library as his office. He wanted to talk with young people at Harvard, where he had gone to school, and also at a half-dozen other nearby colleges. At the same time he planned to write his memoirs. President Kennedy, alas, was not destined to move into the office in the ten-million-dollar presidential library, which is expected to open late in 1966. But visitors to the library for generations to come will learn a lot about an American President. Everything about John Fitzgerald Kennedy that has any conceivable interest has been carefully preserved. Even his rocking chair will have a place in the library, along with his desk ornaments and other memorabilia. There are tape recordings of important speeches, motion pictures, television footage, and thousands of photographs from all parts of the world. Never in history has there been such a campaign to preserve for future generations every scrap of information for a presidential library.

Jacqueline Kennedy, all the other members of the Kennedy family, the President's secretary, Mrs. Evelyn N. Lincoln, and many of Kennedy's closest associates, have thrown themselves wholeheartedly into every phase of planning for the library.

But the genial smile of John Fitzgerald Kennedy will be missing, and for his wife, his children, and many of the rest of us, things will never again be quite the same.

LYNDON BAINES JOHNSON

"Great Society" President

LYNDON BAINES JOHNSON was thrust into the office of the presidency of the United States more suddenly than any other Chief Executive in history. He took the oath of office minutes after President John Fitzgerald Kennedy was pronounced dead. On the afternoon of November 22, 1963, Federal Judge Sarah Hughes swore in her fellow Texan, Lyndon Johnson, in the plane at Dallas Airport which was to carry Kennedy's body to Washington.

It is sadly true that in the history of the United States three other Presidents had previously been assassinated. But these tragedies occurred in slower motion than the shooting of President Kennedy. There was Abraham Lincoln, whose memorable words, "With malice toward none; with charity for all . . ." were disregarded by John Wilkes Booth, who put a pistol to Lincoln's head and fired, as he sat in the box of a Washington theater with his wife. Lincoln lingered on for several hours, but died the next morning.

President Garfield, less than four months after his Inauguration, was shot down by Charles J. Guiteau, a disappointed office seeker, in the railroad station at Washington. Garfield put up a desperate fight for his life, and survived for several months.

President William McKinley was another victim of an assassin's gun. On September 6, 1901, he was shot by Leon Czolgosz, an anarchist, while making a welcoming speech to crowds at the Pan-American Exposition in Buffalo, New York. McKinley lived for eight days before death claimed him.

For Lyndon Johnson there was no reprieve—no months, weeks, days, or even hours in which to brace himself for the tremendous responsibility that so suddenly had been placed upon his shoulders. Inexpressibly shocked and saddened as he was by the swift, tragic turn of events, the new President took up his duties with energy and dignity, showing to the people of the United States and the world the smoothness with which our democracy works. President Kennedy was gone and there was grief throughout the land, but it was not without a leader. An assassin had killed a President, but he could not destroy the government of the United States of America. The smoothness of the transition and the speed with which it was accomplished were a credit to our nation.

When Lyndon Baines Johnson became President, few men before him had reached that office so capable of carrying out the aspirations of their predecessor. With his years of experience in the Senate and in his role as Vice President, President Johnson has been called the best-prepared Chief Executive ever to enter the White House. Many people had regarded him as a compromiser and a politician, but when he addressed Congress five days after taking the oath of office, it was clear that if an ineffectual Johnson ever existed he was not the thirty-sixth President who spoke so forcefully concerning the problems facing our nation and his determination to do his best to cope with them. Just as President Kennedy had said, "Let us begin," President Johnson, pledging himself to continue his predecessor's policies, said earnestly, "Let us continue."

The story of Lyndon Johnson's early years is one more example in the great American tradition of "poor boy makes good." He was born in a modest frame house beside the Pedernales River, the son of a sharecropper father, Sam Ealy Johnson, Jr. His Johnson ancestry was English and Scottish, with tinctures of German and Irish. The family's beginnings in the United States date back to John Johnson, of Oglethorpe, Georgia, who after serving in the Revolutionary War, married a girl named Ann Ealy. That was in 1787.

The Johnsons migrated to Texas after one of John Johnson's sons, Jesse, went there by wagon train in 1846, taking with him his wife, his ten children, his slaves and cattle. President Johnson has often referred to himself as a man of the West, rather than the South, because Jesse's son Sam Ealy Johnson, with two of his brothers, carried on one of the West's first trail-driving operations, herding cattle up to the railheads of Abilene, Dodge City, and even into Montana.

Sam Ealy Johnson was destined to become the grandfather of Lyndon Baines Johnson. Sam Ealy Johnson, Jr., married to Rebeckah Baines, was Lyndon's father. Lyndon's mother's father had been an active politician who served as Secretary of State for Texas from 1883 to 1887. Lyndon's own father was elected to the Texas legislature in 1904, but during much of his adult life he followed such occupations as schoolteacher, real-estate dealer, road commissioner, and inspector of road-building for the state railway. He was one of the first owners of a Model-T Ford car, but seldom had much money and was often in debt for small sums.

Against this background Lyndon Baines Johnson was born on August 27, 1908, in the small shack near Stonewall, Texas, about fifteen miles from Johnson City. After Lyndon came four more young Johnsons.

When Lyndon was in his fifth year, the family moved to Johnson City, where the boy went to school. According to his various teachers, he was a mischievous lad, eager for learning, but full of pranks and hard to control. By the time he

356

was graduated from high school at the age of fifteen, Lyndon felt he must get to work to help with the family expenses. He earned money by peddling magazines, shining shoes, delivering groceries, and doing other odd jobs.

Lyndon's mother, a graduate of Baylor University and later a teacher, urged her son to go to college, but he was eager for adventure. With three other boys he started for California in a battered old car, loaded down with blankets, pots and pans, molasses, cornbread, and bacon. But luck was not with them. They managed to live through a few wretched months picking fruit, washing cars, doing dishes in cheap lunch-rooms, and taking other jobs where they might pick up a dollar or two. After that, they were glad to go back home to Texas.

Lyndon then got a job as a laborer on a road gang, and there he stayed until 1927. Finally, because of his mother's insistent urging, he agreed to go to college. He was eighteen then, and after some hard examinations, he was admitted to Southwest State Teachers College. There he worked his way through as gardener, waiter, janitor, silk-sock salesman, and at other chores. When he was graduated he had two hundred dollars in the bank.

In 1931, while Lyndon was teaching school, he campaigned for Richard M. Kleberg of Texas who won an election to Congress, and when Kleberg went to Washington, Lyndon was taken along as his secretary. Lyndon was twenty-three at the time, and he speedily became engrossed in the science of politics. He learned much under the guidance of Sam Rayburn and John Nance Gardner, and when Franklin Delano Roosevelt was made President, Lyndon found his hero in the New Deal's Chief Executive. In 1935 Roosevelt appointed Lyndon Johnson administrator of the National Youth Administration in Texas. He was twenty-seven years old then, the youngest NYA chief in the country.

In September, 1934, Johnson had met a girl named Claudia Alta Taylor, who was nicknamed "Lady Bird." After a whirlwind courtship they were married in San Antonio that November.

Lyndon Johnson was becoming better and better known as a bright young politician, and in 1937, when Representative James Buchanan of Texas died with a year of his term unserved, Lyndon with the backing of President Roosevelt and others was elected to the office of Congressman.

Johnson's career in Congress, covering a period of some two decades, was highly successful. His work was well known, and he now had many potential backers. Over the years Johnson also found time to devote attention to his own financial independence. Today, he is said to be worth approximately fourteen million dollars.

In 1961 Johnson had aspirations of being nominated for the presidency, but with young John F. Kennedy also in the running, he didn't have a chance, and was content to accept Kennedy's suggestion that he run with him on the Democratic ticket as Vice President.

Probably at that time Lyndon Johnson had no remotest thought of ever becoming President, but destiny has a strange way of manipulating men's lives. When the tragedy of Kennedy's death shocked the nation and the world, Lyndon Johnson stepped in as Chief Executive.

From the very moment President Johnson took over the reins, it was clear he planned to carry out everything possible that had been close to the heart of his predecessor.

President Johnson worked from twelve to fifteen hours each day. Many feared for his health and worried lest he have another heart attack similar to one he had had in previous years. But he seemed to thrive under the work, and he was determined to get action. At his urging, the Civil Rights Bill, forbidding illegal discrimination in places of public accommodation, was passed into law, providing new weapons against discrimination in voting, schools, and employment.

The tax-cut bill, providing an $11,545,000,000 reduction to encourage economic expansion, was passed, despite a continuing federal budget deficit.

Other bills that were passed were one for a wilderness preservation system; the allotment of nearly $1,000,000,000 for an attack on poverty; a Mass Transportation Act providing $375,000,000 for direct aid to improve the nation's transportation facilities. Pay raises amounting to $556,000,000 for federal employees from postmen to judges were declared, and another bill raised military salaries. Housing received a billion dollars in aid for slum rehabilitation, urban renewal, etc. President Johnson called the Eighty-eighth Congress "the most constructive of the twentieth century," and was proud of the record.

In November 1964, Johnson was elected in his own right, and in January 1965, he spelled out to the nation his own aspirations for what he called "the Great Society." He had worked closely for many years and attended many meetings with Presidents Roosevelt, Truman, Eisenhower, and lastly President Kennedy, and he had learned much during those years.

"The Great Society" which President Johnson hopes to

introduce requires an ambitious program. It calls for better education, better schools, and better teachers; a massive attack on disease, and better medical care for the aged. It plans to improve and preserve the natural beauty of the United States, to eradicate air and water pollution; it declares war on poverty and the development of regions in our country now suffering from lack of employment. It promises the carrying out of civil rights, with better homes and job opportunities for all; the increasing of social security; reduction of taxes; and continuance of assistance to countries all over the world to gain freedom from oppression.

At present, the President with his dreams of "the Great Society" is struggling with the precarious situation in Vietnam, the unrest in our country in trying to establish peaceful integration; the appalling increase in crime in the United States; and many other pressing problems.

At this writing, the civil rights situation in Alabama has reached a state of crisis, and President Johnson has presented to Congress a bill to ensure equal voting rights in city, state, and federal elections for all Negroes of voting age in the United States.

The situation in Vietnam has become steadily worse, and the President, true to his promise of help to the South Vietnamese, is sending troops, arms, and supplies to them. At present we are pouring more than a million dollars per day into South Vietnam. However this is but a small portion of the millions we are giving in aid to other countries around the world. As United States Senator Frank Church, a Democrat from Idaho and a member of the Senate Foreign Relations Committee, stated in an article in *The New York Times,* of February 14, 1965:

360

Since the days of the Marshall Plan, the United
States has constantly expanded the scope of its commitments to foreign governments. From Western
Europe we have moved into Africa, the Middle East,
and the Far East. . . . Our troops are now stationed
in no fewer than 30 countries; we are pledged to
defend 42; and we are extending aid, in one form
or another, to nearly 100 nations.

Certainly, with modern transportation and communication, and with changing ideologies, we have come a long way
from the early years of America's beginnings and the once-
famous Monroe Doctrine of our fifth President, James
Monroe.

Only future historians will be able to chronicle how and
when we will attain "the Great Society" which President
Lyndon Johnson envisions. In his book *My Hope for America,* the President writes of his plans and dreams:

And man shall say to man: 'There on this earth
as in the eyes of God, walks my brother!'

This is my dream. It is not the grand vision of a
powerful and feared nation. It concerns the simple
wants of people. But this is what America is all
about. . . . Reality rarely matches dreams. But only
dreams give nobility to purpose. This is the star I
hope to follow.

BIBLIOGRAPHY

JOHN C. ABBOTT, *Lives of the Presidents,* B. B. Russel & Co., Boston, 1867.

JAMES TRUSLOW ADAMS, *The Adams Family,* Little, Brown & Company, Boston, 1930.

JOHN QUINCY ADAMS, *Lives of James Madison and James Monroe,* George H. Derby & Co., 1850.

SAMUEL HOPKINS ADAMS, *Incredible Era, the Life and Times of Warren Gamaliel Harding,* Houghton Mifflin Company, Boston, 1939.

HERBERT AGAR, *The People's Choice,* Houghton Mifflin Company, Boston, 1933.

FREDERICK LEWIS ALLEN, *Only Yesterday,* Harper & Brothers, New York, 1931.

CHARLES M. ANDREWS, *The Colonial Period of American History* (vol. IV), Yale University Press, New Haven, 1938.

PAUL M. ANGLE (editor), *The Lincoln Reader,* Rutgers University Press, New Brunswick, N.J., 1947.

WILLIAM RALSTON BALCH, *Life of President Garfield,* Edgewood Edition, Cottage Library Publishing House, Hubbard Bros., 1882.

CHARLES A. BEARD, *The Presidents of American History,* Julian Messner, Inc., New York, 1935.

CHARLES A. BEARD and MARY R. BEARD, *The Beards' Basic History of the United States,* Doubleday, Doran & Company, New York, 1944.

JACK BELL, *The Splendid Misery*, Doubleday & Company, Inc., New York, 1960.

STEPHEN VINCENT BENÉT, *Selected Works of Stephen Vincent Benét*, Farrar & Rinehart, New York, 1942.

CATHERINE DRINKER BOWEN, *John Adams and the American Revolution*, Little, Brown & Company, Boston, 1950.

EZRA BOWEN, *Social Economy*, Silver Burdett Company, New York, 1929.

CLAUDE BOWERS, *The Young Jefferson*, Houghton Mifflin Company, Boston, 1945.

IRVING BRANT, *James Madison*, Bobbs Merrill Company, New York, 1950.

DENIS W. BROGAN, *The Era of Franklin D. Roosevelt*, Yale University Press, New Haven, 1950.

VAN WYCK BROOKS, *The Flowering of New England*, E. P. Dutton & Company, New York, 1937.

JAMES MACGREGOR BURNS, *John Kennedy, A Political Profile*, Harcourt, Brace and Company, New York, 1959.

HARRY C. BUTCHER, *My Three Years with Eisenhower*, Simon and Schuster, New York, 1946.

MITCHELL V. CHARNLEY, *The Boys' Life of Herbert Hoover*, Harper & Brothers, New York, 1931.

MARQUIS CHILDS, *Eisenhower, Captive Hero*, Harcourt, Brace and Company, New York, 1958.

OLIVER PERRY CHITWOOD, *John Tyler, Champion of the Old South*, D. Appleton–Century Company, New York, 1939.

MARY FAIRMAN CLARK, *U.S. Presidents*, DeWolfe, Fisk & Co., Boston, 1898.

JOSEPHUS DANIELS, *The Life of Woodrow Wilson*, The John C. Winston Company, Philadelphia, 1924.

JOSEPH F. DINNEEN, *The Kennedy Family*, Little, Brown & Company, Boston, 1959.

ROBERT J. DONOVAN, *Eisenhower: the Inside Story*, Harper & Brothers, New York, 1960.

GEORGE WILLIAM DOUGLAS, *The American Book of Days,* The H. W. Wilson Company, New York, 1938.

H. J. ECKENRODE, *Rutherford B. Hayes, Statesman of Reunion,* Dodd, Mead & Company, New York, 1930.

DWIGHT D. EISENHOWER, *Crusade in Europe,* Doubleday & Company, Inc., New York, 1948.

DOUGLAS S. FREEMAN, *George Washington,* Charles Scribner's Sons, New York, 1948.

JOHN FROST, L.L.D., *Lives of the Presidents,* Phillips, Sampson & Co., Boston, 1865.

CLAUDE M. FUESS, *Calvin Coolidge, the Man from Vermont,* Little, Brown & Company, Boston, 1940.

HAMLIN GARLAND, *Ulysses S. Grant, His Life and Character,* The Macmillan Company, New York, 1920.

SIDNEY HOWARD GAY, *American Statesmen: James Madison,* Houghton Mifflin Company, Boston, 1886.

DOROTHY BURNS GOEBEL, PHD., *William Henry Harrison,* Indiana Historical Collections, vol. XIV, 1926.

FREDERICK E. GOODRICH, *Life and Public Services of Grover Cleveland,* privately printed, 1888.

ALBERTA POWELL GRAHAM, *32 Roads to the White House,* Thomas Nelson & Sons, New York, 1944.

SEYMOUR E. HARRIS, *Economics of the Kennedy years: And a Look Ahead,* Harper & Row, Inc., New York, 1964.

HAROLD HOWLAND, *Theodore Roosevelt and His Times,* Yale University Press, New Haven, 1921.

JESSE LYMAN HURLBUT (editor), *Lives of Our Presidents,* John C. Winston Company, Philadelphia, 1908.

HAYNES JOHNSON, *The Bay of Pigs,* W. W. Norton & Company, Inc., New York, 1964.

LYNDON BAINES JOHNSON, *My Hope for America,* Random House, Inc., New York, 1964.

JOHN F. KENNEDY, *Profiles in Courage,* Harper & Brothers, New York, 1956.

JOHN F. KENNEDY, *Why England Slept,* Wilfred Funk, New York, 1940.

GERALD W. JOHNSON, *Andrew Jackson, an Epic in Homespun,* Minton, Balch & Company, New York, 1927.

DELOS W. LOVELACE, *General "Ike" Eisenhower,* Thomas Y. Crowell Company, New York, 1944.

DENNIS TILDEN LYNCH, *An Epic and a Man, Martin Van Buren and His Times,* Horace Liveright, New York, 1929.

JOE McCARTHY, *The Remarkable Kennedys,* The Dial Press, New York, 1960.

SAMUEL McCOY, *This Man Adams,* Brentano's, New York, 1928.

DUMAS MALONE, *Jefferson, the Virginian,* Little, Brown & Company, Boston, 1948.

ENID LaMONTE MEADOWCROFT, *Abraham Lincoln,* Thomas Y. Crowell Company, New York, 1942.

JAMES MORGAN, *Our Presidents,* The Macmillan Company, New York, 1949.

JAMES MORGAN, *Theodore Roosevelt, the Boy and the Man,* The Macmillan Company, New York, 1919.

CHARLES MORRIS, *Heroes of Progress in America,* privately printed.

ALLAN NEVINS, *Grover Cleveland, a Study in Courage,* Dodd, Mead & Company, New York, 1947.

H. A. OGDEN, *G. Washington, a Book for Young People,* The Century Company, New York, 1932.

CHARLES S. OLCOTT, *The Life of William McKinley,* Houghton Mifflin Company, Boston, 1916.

HENRY FOWLES PRINGLE, *The Life and Times of William Howard Taft,* Farrar & Rinehart, New York, 1939.

EDITH GITTINGS REID, *Woodrow Wilson, the Caricature, the Myth, and the Man,* Oxford University Press, New York, 1934.

MARCUS ROSENBLUM, *The Story of Franklin D. Roosevelt,* Simon & Schuster, Inc., New York, 1934.

ELEANOR ROOSEVELT, *This I Remember,* Harper & Brothers, New York, 1949.

ELEANOR ROOSEVELT, *This Is My Story,* Harper & Brothers, New York, 1937.

FRANKLIN D. ROOSEVELT, *Looking Forward,* The John Day Company, Inc., New York, 1933.

EDWARD M. SHEPARD, *Martin Van Buren,* Houghton Mifflin Company, Boston, 1900.

WALTER BEDELL SMITH, *Eisenhower's Six Great Decisions: Europe 1944–1945,* Longmans, Green & Co., Inc., New York, 1956.

CORNELIA SPENCER, *Straight Furrow (The Biography of Harry S. Truman),* The John Day Company, Inc., New York, 1949.

W. O. STODDARD, *The Lives of the Presidents—Hayes, Garfield and Arthur,* Frederick A. Stokes Company, New York, 1889.

LLOYD PAUL STRYKER, *Andrew Johnson, a Study in Courage,* The Macmillan Company, New York, 1930.

ARTHUR STYRON, *The Last of the Cocked Hats,* University of Oklahoma Press, Norman, 1945.

WILLIAM ROSCOE THAYER, *Theodore Roosevelt,* Houghton Mifflin Company, Boston, 1919.

HARRY S. TRUMAN, *Memoirs,* Vol. I, *Year of Decisions* and Vol. II, *Years of Trial and Hope,* Doubleday and Company, New York, 1955 and 1956.

WILLIAM S. WHITE, *The Professional: Lyndon B. Johnson,* Houghton Mifflin Company, Boston, 1964.

OWEN WISTER, *The Seven Ages of Washington,* The Macmillan Company, New York, 1922.

HENRY A. ZEIGER, *Lyndon B. Johnson—Man and President,* Popular Library, New York, 1963.

INDEX

Hawaii:
annexation of, 215, 223, 224
statehood, 330
Hawthorne, Nathaniel, 112
Hayes, Rutherford B.:
ancestry, 170
boyhood, 171-72
early political life, 173
marriage, 172-73
presidency, 174
election, dispute over, 174
young manhood, 172-73
Civil War, officer in, 173
Health, Education, and Welfare
Department, 325
Henry, Patrick, 26, 36
Hermitage, the, 67, 68
Hiram College, 181
homesteading, 199
Hoover, Herbert C.:
boyhood, 280-81
early political life, 283
Secretary of Commerce, 283
marriage, 281
presidency, 284-86
London Naval Conference,
284
Reconstruction Finance Corporation, 284
stock market collapse, 284-86
world food survey, 311
young manhood, 280-81
"Hoover Doctrine," 284
House, Colonel Edward M., 253

Interstate Commerce Commission, 201

Jackson, Andrew:
boyhood, 60-62
early political life, 64, 67
marriage, 63
military career, 64-66

Jackson, Andrew (cont.)
expedition against Semi-
noles, 66
War of 1812, 64-66
presidency, 67-68
closing of the Bank of the
United States, 67
"spoils system," institution
of, 68
young manhood, 62-63
Jefferson, Thomas:
boyhood, 25-26
early political life, 27-30
Declaration of Independence,
author of, 28-29
Democratic-Republican
party, founder of, 30
governor of Virginia, 29, 45
minister to France, 30
Secretary of State, 30
Vice President, 30
marriage, 28
presidency, 31
Louisiana Purchase, 31
University of Virginia, founder
of, 31
young manhood, 26-27
Johnson, Andrew:
boyhood, 145
early political life, 146-50
governor of Tennessee,
146
military governor of Tennessee, 148
Vice President, 149
marriage, 146
presidency, 150-56
abolitionists, conflict with,
150-56
impeachment, 153-56
reconstruction proclamations,
150-51
Tenure of Office Law, 153,
155, 156

370

INDEX

INDEX

Johnson, Andrew (*cont.*)

INDEX

Johnson, Andrew (*cont.*)
Senator, first ex-President to serve as, 156
Johnson, Lyndon Baines:
ancestry, 455-56
boyhood, 356
civil rights, 360
early political life, 357-68
"Great Society, the," 360-61
Vice President, 358
Vietnam, 360-61

Kansas-Nebraska Bill, 114-15
Kennedy, Jacqueline, 345-46
Kennedy, John F.:
ancestry, 337
assassination, 350
children, 337, 343
marriage, 341-42
naval career, 339-40
political career, 341, 343
presidency, 336-37, 343-45
Cabinet, 343-44
inaugural address, 344-45
inauguration, 336-37
religious issue, 343
writings, 339, 341, 342-43
youth and education, 338-39
Khrushchev, Nikita, 330-31, 332
Korean War, 314, 333

League of Nations, 257-58
Lend-Lease Bill, 297
Lincoln, Abraham:
boyhood, 127-29
early political life, 132-35
debates with Stephen A. Douglas, 134-35
marriage, 133
presidency, 135-40
assassination, 140
Civil War, 136-39
Emancipation Proclamation, 137

Lincoln, Abraham (*cont.*)
first inaugural address, 136
Fort Sumter, attack on, 136
Gettysburg Address, 137-38
second inaugural address, 136
surrender of Confederate forces, 139
Lincoln, Tom, 127-28
London Naval Conference, 284
Louisiana Purchase, 31, 47-48

McKinley, William:
boyhood, 219
early political life, 220-22
governor of Ohio, 221
tin-plate industry, sponsor of, 221
marriage, 220
presidency, 222-26
annexation of Hawaii, 223, 224
annexation of the Philippines, 224
assassination, 226
gold standard, 225-26
Open Door policy, 225
Panama Canal, 225
Spanish-American War, 223-24
tariff bill, 223
McKinley high-tariff bill, 206
Madison, James:
boyhood, 34
early political life, 34
"Father of the Constitution," 36-37
Secretary of State, 38
marriage, 37
presidency, 39-40
first protective tariff, 40
War of 1812, 40
Marshall Plan, 312
Mexican revolution, 253-54

371

Mexican War, 99, 104, 113-14
Missouri Compromise, 49
Monroe, James:
 early political life, 45-48
  governor of Virginia, 47-48
  Louisiana Purchase, negotiator of, 47
  minister to Court of St. James's, 48
  minister to France, 47
  Secretary of State, 48
 marriage, 46
 presidency, 49
  boundary line between United States and Canada, establishment of, 49
  Missouri Compromise, 49
  Monroe Doctrine, 49
 young manhood, 44
  Revolutionary War, officer in, 45
Monroe Doctrine, 49, 57, 213-14
Monticello, 27
Mount Vernon, 5, 7, 11

Napoleon, 47-48
Nineteenth Amendment, 255
North Atlantic Treaty Organization, 322, 329-30

Open-Door policy, 225
"open skies" disarmament plan, 327
Oregon Territory, annexation of, 99
Ostend Manifesto, 116
Oswald, Lee, 350-51

Panama Canal, 225
Pan-American Congress, first, 207
panic of 1837, 75-76
panic of 1893, 211-12
Pendergast, Tom, 307, 309

Philippines, acquisition of, 224
Pierce, Franklin:
 boyhood, 112
 early political life, 113-14
 marriage, 113
 Mexican War, general in, 113-14
 presidency, 114-16
  Gadsden Purchase, 115
  Kansas-Nebraska Bill, 114-15
  Ostend Manifesto, 116
Point Four Program, 313
Polk, James Knox:
 boyhood, 96-97
 early political life, 97-98
  governor of Tennessee, 97
  speaker of the House, 97
 marriage, 97
 presidency, 98-100
  Mexican War, 99
  Oregon Territory, 99
Princeton University, 251
Pure Food Law, 235

reconstruction, period of the, 149-53, 164-65
Reconstruction Finance Corporation, 285
reconstruction proclamations, 150-51
Republican party, formation of, 116
Revolutionary War, 9, 45
Roosevelt, Eleanor, 289, 291
Roosevelt, Franklin D.:
 boyhood, 288-89
 early political life, 289-91
  Assistant Secretary of the Navy, 290
  governor of New York, 291
 marriage, 289
 presidency, 292-99
  depression of 1937, 296